DENYS HAY

Annalists and Historians

WESTERN HISTORIOGRAPHY FROM THE EIGHTH TO THE EIGHTEENTH CENTURIES

LONDON
METHUEN & CO LTD
11 NEW FETTER LANE EC4

First published in 1977
by Methuen & Co Ltd
11 New Fetter Lane, London EC4P 4EE
© 1977 by Denys Hay
Photoset by Red Lion Setters, Holborn, London
and printed by Richard Clay & Co, Bungay, Suffolk

ISBN 0 416 81180 9 (hardback)
      0 416 81190 9 (paperback)

Distributed in the USA by
HARPER & ROW PUBLISHERS, INC.
BARNES & NOBLE IMPORT DIVISION

Contents

Preface

I have contemplated writing a book on historiography for many years, perhaps almost since I first began working on the English history of Polydore Vergil in 1938. I have clear memories of reading translations of the main Greek and Latin historians during the often lengthy boredoms of the war. I find, too, that I have kept a letter dated October 1943 from my former tutor, V.H. Galbraith, professor of history at Edinburgh, in which he indicated in reply to a question I had put to him that there was indeed room for a history of historiography — though he wisely did not designate me as its author. In those days I envisaged some vast multi-volume treatment of the vast subject, which would have run from Babylon to Marc Bloch. What I attempt here is infinitely more modest.

Some such book is, I believe, desirable if not necessary. Even if what follows is not what I would have wished for, or what others may expect, the fact is that there is no comparable book in which a general survey of at any rate a long portion of the story is attempted, a portion, moreover, which seems to me to be critical. There are, of course, many admirable partial studies, although some are now out of date and they usually treat the writings of an historian, or of the historians of a period, mainly as source material, on a par with other materials available to later scholars. Such are the masterly volumes of W. Wattenbach and O. Lorenz for Germany, and of A. Molinier for France. There is nothing, even old-fashioned, to compare with these books for England.[1] Let us nevertheless honour the erudition of Sir Thomas Duffus Hardy (1804-78), and salute Mrs Antonia Gransden, who has begun to produce what will be undoubtedly a very complete discussion of English narrative sources in the Middle Ages.[2] What I am concerned with is the evolution of a *genre*, not the validation of authorities. Here we have only limited help from earlier books.

The intelligent, short but stimulating *Introduction to the History of History* by James T. Shotwell (1922) only goes to the brink of the Middle Ages. Other more ambitious books are scarcely worth reading, at any rate those that have come my way. The lengthy two-volume compilation by James Westfall Thompson, *A History of Historical Writing* (1942), is mainly scissors-and-paste; wherever one can check them, the facts are often wrong and the interpretation banal. The briefer work of Harry Elmer Barnes has the same title (1937) and is shorter, and that is about all one can say for it. Similar works of even less merit and sometimes of much greater tendentiousness exist in other languages; I was astonished at the fairly recent reprinting (1946) of G. Lefébure's inferior *cours de Sorbonne*. Recently there has fortunately been a new interest in historians as craftsmen, as men operating in a particular literary tradition. In particular, reference will be made in the following pages to several admirable works on one or two medieval chroniclers and Renaissance historians. But the only wide-ranging work which commands respect remains E. Fueter's *Geschichte der neueren Historiographie* (1911, and, despite claims of publishers, virtually not revised after the French translation of 1914: see below p.88 and p.196). Brilliant though the work of this Swiss journalist is, it is often over-schematic and some of his general ideas have to be treated with caution.

There are reasons enough why no one has produced the modern treatment which the subject needs. There is no history worth the name of Latin literature in the medieval and Renaissance periods. Histories of vernacular literatures normally ignore contemporary Latin works unless by authors who wrote in both a vulgar and a learned tongue; in English only C.S. Lewis's critical works earn added praise for the way they integrate discussion of English and Latin works in this way. Yet in most scholarly fields Latin writers were much more sophisticated and influential than vernacular writers, at any rate down to the seventeenth century. Most serious Latin prose in the Middle Ages was either exegetical, didactic or historical and there were legions of medieval historians. For half a century they have been somewhat neglected. The Rolls Series in England came to an end in 1897; the German *Monumenta* has only just survived the second world war; the 'new' Muratori seems to have died. Despite the efforts of a handful of individual editors, one gets the feeling that this kind of scholarship is becoming a thing of the past. Just as schoolchildren are no longer expected to be able to spell or express themselves grammatically, so young historians are no longer expected to read foreign languages and the texts written in them.

The chapters that follow must inevitably appear unbalanced. My own small competence draws me to Britain, Italy and France. If I drag in a word on Spain, Germany or the northern world, if I venture a remark on a Byzantine historian, it is because they have imposed themselves on my ignorance, so to speak. (I can hear the cynical reader exclaim 'not *that* old *topos* again'.) Even a partial discussion seemed worthwhile rather than no survey at all and I can assure the reader that in some form or other I have actually read a decent part of the writers whose names appear below. The book may seem uneven in another way, since it moves occasionally from large scale generalisations to passages of detailed analysis. Such detail tends to occur when I have not found the matter dealt with adequately by others or to illustrate a point from somewhat inaccessible material.

It must again be stressed that what follows does not pretend to cover thoroughly the 'narrative sources', as the methodologists call this type of record. Of these there are multitudes, including a number of impressive writers, who are not mentioned. Nor does the book deal directly with 'speculative' history, those larger schemes from Polybius down to Vico and Marx which have strangely little influence on the actual writing of history. I have not been able to disregard such ideological forces entirely. The Bible and Joachim are mentioned, although providential history was singularly marginal to the practices of the chronicler, despite what Croce and Collingwood say. Had either of them actually read a thirteenth-century chronicle?

Finally, why this period? I am convinced that we must knock down the flimsy fences which have been erected between 'medieval' and 'modern'. In the Italy of the Renaissance, when these divisions were slowly erected, men rethought the past and there gradually emerged two manners of writing about events in time. There was the recording of contemporary events, which is broadly speaking what ancient historians and medieval chroniclers had concerned themselves with, and which humanist historians continued albeit in a more stylish Latin. But with the Renaissance there was also born the notion of looking at the past as the past, and so emerged the antiquary. Thus the Renaissance witnessed the division of what we would call history into two types of activity: some historians became antiquarians and some became men of letters; and of course some were a bit of both. These distinctions were not much affected by the passionate propaganda of many humanist hacks or by the poisonous fumes of the Reformation and the Counter-Reformation, and by the seventeenth century the antiquarian researchers had attained an extraordinary standard of scholarship, even if 'history' for most readers still meant the contemporary and political narrative, void of significant analysis. And then, by the second half of the eighteenth century, the historian and the antiquary came together. With Robertson and Gibbon we have practically arrived at the mature historiography which was to be so dominant an intellectual interest in the nineteenth century. All this I first said, though as an aside, both in a lecture of 1950 (*Scottish Historical Review*, xxx, 1951) and in my *Polydore Vergil* (1952). The argument now appears in a more extended form. I had indeed intended to prop it up still further by appending substantial lists of scholarly works produced by the *érudits* of the sixteenth, seventeenth and early eighteenth centuries. But without a commentary I think this would have had little meaning and it would have turned an essay into a manual. As it is, the reader may sometimes feel there is too much name-dropping.

I do not think I should have realised that there was a place for some such book as this if I had not for many years taught much of the matter in it. I have done this at two levels. For twenty years I have had a graduate course, called, perhaps too grandly, 'An introduction to medieval and Renaissance bibliography'; the background of this was a list of books in

Edinburgh libraries (for how good they are see below, p.74), including a substantial section covering the scholarship discussed in what follows; latterly other colleagues have kindly assisted in this course. And ten years ago we began a remarkably tough undergraduate course in 'Theory and history of history'. This was started 'from an idea' (as they say in radio credits) of Dr Henry Kamen, then on the Edinburgh staff, but realised with the essential cooperation of my friend and colleague, Professor W.H. Walsh, and other members of the History and Philosophy Departments.

I must give my sincere thanks to Mr Tony Goodman for critical observations on this book, and likewise to the learned readers of the publisher for their perceptive observations. Of course I alone am responsible for errors of fact or judgment.

Edinburgh,   DENYS HAY
December 1975

1 Ancient Historians: Greeks and Romans

The chapter after this deals with another group of ancient historians, those whose writings form part of the Bible. The influence of the Bible on medieval historiography was to be far deeper than that of classical authors. Yet it seems sensible to begin with a short examination of the history written in Greece and Rome since from time to time during the Middle Ages, and with powerful persistence during and after the Renaissance, the writers of antiquity were regarded as models of both method and style. The word 'history' is itself, after all, a Greek word which came into European use through Latin. But it only occurs in the Latin Bible once or twice in the Apocrypha.

There is no need to attempt even a succinct account of classical historiography as such, partly because plenty of surveys already exist, partly because most classical historians are bad historians — or perhaps one should rather say that they were attempting to do something completely different from what is now regarded as the historian's task. This observation is less applicable to Greek writers than to Latin, but it was to be the Latin historians who were most influential in Western Europe down to the seventeenth century and many of their severer limitations were for long to frustrate the development of a sophisticated study of the past.

The three greatest Greek historians are Herodotus and Thucydides, who were both at work in the fifth century B.C., and Polybius, who lived in the second century B.C. Herodotus wrote about the war between Greeks and Persians which had ended in his boyhood, but he felt obliged to provide an elaborate geographical and social background to his work which takes him out of the contemporary world and out of his own milieu, thus compelling him to make comparisons (e.g.

between the chronologies accepted in Greece and Egypt) which in more propitious circumstances might have led him to a maturer sense of historical enquiry. In essence, however, Herodotus was a contemporary historian, differing from Thucydides only in that his canvas was much wider and he thus had to take great trouble to find out material which was not to hand. Thucydides, was, on the other hand, a statesman and soldier out of office, to be likened to Guicciardini or Clarendon and, like them, a severe and serious analyst of the events in which he had participated, the Peloponnesian war. Two centuries later Polybius came in many ways nearer to our modern notion of a historian: he was writing about a past which he had not witnessed; he was dealing with a problem and not merely telling a story or depicting a political situation. The period covered the years 221-144 B.C. and the problem was the rise in those years of the dominion of Rome in the Mediterranean area.

Rome never produced historians as inherently significant as these three Greeks.* But in the Latin west, Latin historians were later read as a part (admittedly not by any means indispensable) of the process of mastering the language, and we shall see that subsequently they were sometimes admired as models of the narrative genre. The notable Roman historians were: Caesar (d. 44 B.C.), Sallust (d. 34 B.C.), Livy (d. 17 B.C.), Tacitus (d. after 115 A.D.), and Suetonius (d. about 140 A.D.). The influence of these writers was exerted unevenly and Tacitus had to wait for the Renaissance before his work was rediscovered; indeed the emulation of Roman historiography as a mode of composition had in general to wait until the fifteenth and sixteenth centuries. It is interesting to note that the modern low estimation in which Latin historians are held was shown by the reading public of the Hellenistic world. Substantial portions of the historical works of the writers named have not survived; only of Caesar and Suetonius have we a fair amount of what they originally composed. There is every reason to suppose that the neglect which this suggests was

*It must be emphasised that in these pages I am not discussing the value of ancient historians as sources of information for the history of Greece and Rome.

envinced at at early date. It was the Romans who lost the missing Decades of Livy, preferring the epitomisers (Florus, for instance), and these epitomisers were also to be of use in the medieval world. This lack of interest of the latter day Latins for the best of their historians contrasts with the better preservation of the texts of Herodotus and Thucydides. If the text of Thucydides is admittedly incomplete this is probably because he continually revised it and it was never finished. Of Polybius only a small portion has survived. But the blame for this should presumably be laid at the door of the unappreciative Romans. All in all the respect of the Romans for their own past did not lead to a sustained interest in detailed narrative or analysis.

Roman historiography nevertheless had certain good features which should not be overlooked. Like many other historiographical traditions it derived from humble annals. (We shall encounter this process on two occasions in the medieval period.[1]) These annals are abrupt, undigested. They frequently related the important event alongside the ephemeral. It was the merit of the Roman historians, and notably Livy, to apply the canons of rhetoric to narration, to make the writing of history as serious an undertaking as any other form of composition. Hence the adornment of narrative with orations in both direct and indirect speech, the avoidance in the more classical writers of recherché expressions and unfamiliar words. The historian tried to grip his reader, if necessary in a poetical or mythological way, and was freer than the contemporary orator to deal with a large section of life. He could likewise regard his work as having a political and moral function. Polybius regarded it as axiomatic that 'The knowledge of past events is the sovereign corrective of human nature'. He added that this was the note 'on which almost all historians have begun and ended their work, when they eulogised the lessons of history as the truest education and training for political life'.[2] Livy's elaboration of this theme was to dominate medieval and Renaissance justification of the historian's activity.

What chiefly makes the study of history wholesome and profitable is this, that you behold the lessons of every kind of experience set forth as on a conspicuous monument; from these you may choose for yourself and your own state what to imitate, from these mark for avoidance what is shameful in the conception and shameful in the result.[3]

In a later phrase: history was moral philosophy teaching by example.

It was also meritorious that classical literary theory accepted that the historian must at all costs seek out and set forth the truth. Here the weightiest statements come from Cicero's dialogue on rhetoric:

> Who does not know history's first law to be that an author must not dare to tell anything but the truth? And its second that he must make bold to tell the whole truth? That there must be no suggestion of partiality anywhere in his writings? Nor of malice?

And in addition there should be a presentation not only moving but methodical:

> The nature of the subject needs chronological arrangement and geographical representation: and since, in reading of important affairs worth recording, the plans of campaign, the executive actions and the results are successively looked for, it calls also, as regards such plans, for some intimation of what the writer approves, and, in the narrative of achievement, not only of a statement of what was done or said, but also of the manner of doing or saying it; and, in the estimate of consequences, for an exposition of all contributory causes, whether originating in accident, discretion or fool-hardiness; and as for the individual actors, besides an account of their exploits, it demands particulars of the lives of such as are outstanding in renown and dignity.[4]

This, one of the few statements of the theory of history in classical Rome, not unfairly represents the best of Greek and Roman practice.

Yet when all these solid advantages of the ancient historians are put in the balance they seem to be outweighed by even more striking defects. Cicero said — it is a pretty obvious point — that 'the nature of the subject needs chronological arrangement'. Even today, the sequence of the years lays a heavy hand on the scholar. Earlier situations or pressures must be isolated and discussed before later ones. In the narratives which were to predominate in historical writing until a half-century ago chronology was even more important. Yet in classical antiquity there was virtually no system of chronology available to historians. In the absence of an era the clumsiest alternatives were adopted. The commonest reckoning of longish periods of time was by generations, but how erratic they may be appears from Herodotus where they are occasionally treated as lasting some twenty-three years, and at other times the more conventional third of a century. That Herodotus did some fairly sophisticated calculations with this blunt instrument is a tribute to his ingenuity, but would have been avoided if there had been a reasonable and recognised way of reckoning the passage of time. It is true that some Greeks used the Olympiad. This was a cycle of four years starting in what (in our terms) was 776 B.C. In using the Olympiad one had therefore to indicate which of the four years was being referred to. The Olympiad continued for centuries to have a shadowy official existence in Byzantium, and it is found (though rarely), along with other modes of calculating time, in the western Middle Ages. Livy invented a scheme of reckoning *Ab urbe condita*, from the foundation of Rome which, when transferred into modern reckoning, was supposed to have occurred in 753 B.C. But no one but Livy made much use of this era and even Livy himself often uses the more familiar reference to magistracies. Here is how Thucydides begins book II of his *History*. Let us remember that he is in most respects the ablest narrative historian of classical antiquity.

The war between the Athenians and Peloponnesians and their allies on either side now really begins.... The history follows the chronological order of events by summers and winters. The thirty-year truce which was entered into after the conquest of Euboea lasted fourteen years. In the fifteenth, in the forty-eighth year of the priestess-ship of Chrysis of Argos, in the Ephorate of Aenesias at Sparta, in the Archonship of Pythodorus at Athens, and six months after the battle of Potidaea, just at the beginning of spring....[5]

What Thucydides is warning his reader is that, after the initial indication of the exact date, he will be usually on his own, having to reckon the years for himself, season by season. And in reading ancient historians one is usually in doubt as to the year. It needs constant alertness not to lose oneself, an alertness one is usually spared by the careful apparatus of the modern editor. There were also stylistic pressures against littering the text with awkward references to archonships or consulates. 'This day was the fifth before the Kalends of April, in the consulship of Lucius Piso and Aulus Gabinius', is a sentence which must have seemed almost as ugly to Caesar in Latin as it looks in an English translation.[6]

Of course the annalistic framework within which even elaborate histories were written helped in such reckoning. History was about war and ancient war (like medieval war) tended to be an activity of the spring and summer. But to recall this is to encounter a further and perhaps more crippling limitation of ancient historiography and one which was to have unfortunate consequences in and after the Renaissance. For ancient historians did write almost exclusively about war and high-level diplomacy. This again is implicit in the passages from Polybius, Livy and Cicero quoted above. Polybius most explicitly states that history is a preparation for a full political life for important people:

> The young are invested by it with the understanding of the old; the old find their actual experience multiplied by it a hundred-fold; ordinary men are transformed by it into leaders; men born to command are stimulated by the immortality of fame which it confers to embark upon noble enterprises; soldiers, again, are encouraged by the posthumous glory which it promises, to risk their lives for their country; the wicked are deterred by the eternal obloquy with which it threatens them from their evil impulses; and, in general, the good graces of History are so highly praised that some have been stimulated by the hope of them to become founders of states, others to introduce laws contributing to the security of the race, and others to make scientific or practical discoveries by which all mankind has benefited.[7]

In his ponderous way, leaving nothing to chance or

imagination, Polybius is addressing the governing class of the Hellenistic world for which he and other ancient historians wrote their works. The general and the legislator should study history if they wish to be successful.

It is indeed remarkable that of the three Greek historians named above two were important public figures and only Herodotus can be described as a scholar. Of the Romans, Caesar's historical works are commentaries on his public career; Sallust, Tacitus and Suetonius were prominent politicians; and only Livy was primarily a man of letters. It is hardly surprising that such men wrote of and for their own small segment of society. They lived in a largely illiterate world and in their concern for writing they constituted an élite within an élite. Their concerns were not with cultural or economic matters. They took for granted their mastery of the world and the security of its social basis. For them public affairs were predominantly, almost exclusively, the only thing that mattered and by public affairs they meant the military conquests of Greek and then Roman imperialism and the struggle between prominent leaders and their factions. The poor, the merchants, even the spiritual leaders were more or less totally ignored. It is also to be expected of such authors that they should in the main concern themselves with events they had directly observed rather than with a remoter antiquity. Only Polybius, as I have noted, is to be reckoned as totally concerned with events before his birth. Livy, who begins with Romulus and Remus, acknowledges that his contemporaries would prefer the history of their own day (pref., 4). Such a concentration on the familiar did not encourage writers or readers to look at a larger social context. They took the facts of their small world for granted. They wrote about each other. The point is worth stressing, since the Roman dominions covered large portions of three continents and the generals and proconsuls occasionally give the impression of being exposed to fruitful contact with new civilisations. Herodotus did have such a curiosity and his account of Egypt is a remarkably interesting portion of his book; and Tacitus in the *Germania* gave the only account we have of the primitive northern tribes who were later to master so much of the Roman world. But in general the cultural ambience of the historians we have been discussing is extremely limited, their political circle narrowly circum-scribed.

Since they were talking about grand people they used grand language. The science of verbal communication was called rhetoric and the rules that applied in antiquity both controlled the form and largely determined the language in which exposition was couched. Cicero, it is true, exempts the historian from the rigorous conventions that governed speech in the courts but in practice there are many speeches, in both direct and indirect diction, in all classical historians, and the conventional shape and ornamentation of ancient artistic prose permeates their works. The question of speeches is indeed a complicated one. During antiquity, the Middle Ages and the Renaissance, many occasions presented themselves for oratory that were not to be found later. Councils and committees could not be briefed with duplicated memoranda but had to hear lengthy verbal summaries; ambassadors tried by persuasive language to capture the sympathy of the court to which they were sent; in wars where critical actions were often fought by small units, troops were harangued by their commanding officers. Nevertheless, the historians who tried to provide so much correct oratory did so following the prescription of Greek rhetoric, which divided the matter into three types — the judicial (for use in law courts), the demonstrative (of which laudatory speeches, funeral orations and other set pieces are examples) and the deliberative, this last comprising the addresses referred to above — in governing assemblies, battlefields and so on. A recent authority gives us an indication of what this meant to Livy:

> Of the surviving books ... by far the greater number of speeches are constructed according to the divisions of rhetorical theory. There is always a formal *exordium*, inserted by Livy himself if his source has plunged *in medias res*. The various methods of capturing the good will of an audience (*captatio benevolentiae*) can all be exemplified. A common form is a speaker's concentration of attention on himself ... as when Camillus in his speech opposing the projected transference of the capital to Veii, states in his

commencement that his return from exile is not from personal motives but to oppose the abandonment of Rome....[8]

And so to the end of the *exordium*. Then follows the 'statement of facts', the 'proof and refutation', and conclusion. [9]

Indeed the splendour of oratorical composition coloured all prose, and history more than most since the historian was allowed to use poetical language, employ unusual words, surprise with verbal paradoxes and delight with mazy patterns of phrases. For these adornments complicated lists of verbal devices were catalogued. In one celebrated manual of rhetoric we find 45 different 'figures of Diction',[10] which were of course the figures of speech which were to dominate stylistic prose in Latin and vernaculars almost to our own day; a selection of them was certainly drilled into pupils of some Edinburgh schools in the 1950s. Auerbach[11] has pointed out how the Roman historians from Sallust onwards took a more sombre view of life and expressed it in a gradually more colourful way. But he stresses how their view of life was uniformly aristocratic, how they looked down on the world and regarded the people with contempt tinged progressively with apprehension, until the process reaches its furthest development in the 'mannerism' of Ammianus Marcellinus, a general and historian who died at the end of the fourth century A.D.

It has seemed sensible to spend a short time dealing with ancient historians and with their rhetorical assumptions not only because of the influence they were to exert in the Renaissance and later but also because their influence was felt in many of the writings of the Christian Fathers; after all Eusebius, Jerome, Augustine and Orosius were roughly contemporaries of Ammianus Marcellinus and it will be argued that even the Venerable Bede's *Ecclesiastical History* is best regarded as coming at the end of the patristic and thus the classical tradition of historiography rather than at the beginning of a new medieval tradition.

It should not, of course, be assumed that all or even most of the Greek and Roman historians have been touched on. Many others have survived in even more fragmentary form than those mentioned, and one or two longer works, such as Plutarch's parallel *Lives* (written about 110 A.D. in Greek), were to encourage the trend towards ethical historiography in the Renaissance. Nor was Greek rhetorical theory purveyed solely by Cicero or by the treatise *Ad Herennium* so long ascribed to him. Quintilian (who probably died soon after A.D. 100), in his *Institutio oratoria*, produced a sensible manual on education which was neglected by his contemporaries, was unknown in the Middle Ages, but, when rescued by Poggio in the early fifteenth century,[12] proved very much to the taste of humanist educators and writers.

Finally, a word of warning should be addressed to those who did not heed the initial remark that classical historians were not trying to do what modern historians aim for. Those who did seek a wider framework in which to place their story found themselves tied up in singularly unproductive schemes of causality which, indeed, inhibited any desire to explain. Speculative concepts of a pattern in the passage of time were to be found: a notion of change through which the Ages of the World progressed — poetically enough — from gold through silver, bronze and iron: the verse of Hesiod is appropriately the fullest statement of the theme which is found occasionally in later writers. The idea of decline had more artistic attraction than the cyclical theories of Plato in the *Timaeus*, though this was adopted by Polybius. The Wheel of Fortune is introduced to account for rapid transformations, but this is a literary device, more or less devoid of interpretative significance. In fact these cyclical or other cosmic schemes play very little part in the work of ancient historians.[13] Their consciousness of significant social or constitutional change was not much developed and in any case they accepted, more or less tacitly, that what really motivated day to day events was human nature. The engine of change was essentially moral. Men acted well from good instincts and their baser appetites made them act ill. It was because of this assumption that history could claim to be a teacher. 'Testis temporum, lux veritatis, vita memoriae, magistra vitae, nuntia vetustatis', these phrases from Cicero's *De Oratore*[14] were acceptable descriptions of the art because of the eternal fame or infamy that the true historian could confer.

For those of us (we are getting fewer every year) who at school were obliged, usually for reasons no one explained, to struggle through some of Caesar's tricky *Commentaries* or the vapid sections of Livy or attempt to comprehend the complicated syntax of Tacitus in his *Annals*, it is salutary to remember how feeble was the tradition of ancient historiography. The three Greek authors mentioned had considerable merit. The Latins were a poor lot and it was the Latin writers rather than the Greeks who were to have the largest influence in the centuries ahead, indeed almost to our own day. For the educational ideals developed during the Renaissance absorbed, among other things, the doctrine that history made a man a good citizen. And with it came the study of the Latin historians. By the late nineteenth century they were admittedly used in teaching Latin rather than for their ethical message. We were not told at school why we should read them because our teachers themselves had forgotten.

2 The Bible:
Jewish and Christian Time

In the previous chapter no reference was made to the religious beliefs of Greeks and Romans since these had virtually no influence on the way they wrote history. It is true that myths regarding creation and a flood were current in antiquity and there was philosophical speculation about the meaning of the human story, of man's place in the universe, of his relationship with the Gods or with God. None of this, however, inspired the historians. As we noticed, they were nearly all both contemporary historians and moralists. They did not begin at the beginning. Nor were their writings regarded as constituting a significant portion of truth in any final sense, even if rules for civilised behaviour or public action might be inferred from their works.

For the Jew, history was on the contrary regarded as a manifestation of God's will. The history books of the Jew constituted a substantial element in his scriptures and facts, events in time, permeated even the prophetic literature in the Bible as well as the penumbra of poetry, proverbs and romance which sometimes entered the canon and sometimes did not. Above all there *was* a canon, an established list of books which were holy. This took a long time to be entirely clear cut — the contents of the Hebrew Bible did not become completely fixed until the end of the first century A.D. But from the seventh century B.C. certain parts of what was to be the Bible were already treated as authoritative, and by the fourth century B.C. the books attributed to Moses, the Pentateuch (Genesis, Exodus, Leviticus, Numbers and Deuteronomy), existed in much their present shape. These were the writings which told the story of Creation and of God's dealings with his chosen people. Genesis sets the tone in its opening: 'In the beginning God created the heaven and the earth'. The culminating act of creation came on the sixth day; 'So God created man in his own image, in the image of God created he him; male and female created he them'. History had started.[1]

The Hebrew Bible consisted of the Torah (the Law i.e. the Pentateuch), the Prophets and the Writings. The Law and the Prophets were accepted as being exceptionally holy. In particular the Mosaic books, the Torah interpreted by the priests, laid down the basic law of Israel. It was a collection of books which were largely historical, as was natural in a religion based on God's repeated manifestations of Himself in time. For the same reason the Prophets are largely historical in composition, especially Joshua, Judges, Samuel and Kings (the 'former' prophets); so are substantial portions of the Writings (e.g. Chronicles, Ezra and Nehemiah, which bring the story of the Jews down to the mid-fifth century B.C.). Within this large corpus of material it is difficult to separate history as we know it, or as the Greeks and Romans knew it, from prophecy or from myth, and it would not have occurred to any Jew that such distinctions had any meaning. In the event, the distinction between the act and the prophesying of the act was to be very important for later historiography, as will emerge in subsequent chapters. In Judaism, it should be remembered that prophecy was not merely foretelling the future. It was reiterating the divine imperative, recalling the people to their duties and indicating the character of the punishment that attended their disobedience.

By the time the canon of the Hebrew scriptures was more or less established (at the end of the first century B.C. or thereabouts) the Jews were scattered far and wide in the Middle East and the Mediterranean. The Diaspora was a long process. It was partly due to persecution and partly to the lively commercial sense of the Jews. It was to have many consequences — not least the way it facilitated the spread of Christianity. To be noted here, however, is the need experienced in the Hellenistic world in which Judaism had penetrated for a version of the Scriptures in a language familiar to the educated. This was at first Greek. Later it was to be Latin.

The Greek version is known as the Septuagint from a tradition that it was the work of seventy-two inspired translators. It seems to have been completed in the second century B.C. and contained the Old Testament much as it is known today. To speak of one Greek translation is perhaps misleading. There seem to have been three or four main variants, suggesting that translators felt free to improve or revise the text before them. In this way some peculiarly Greek concepts affected the text. Later than the Septuagint came the preparation of translations into Latin for use among communities with no Greek. These were probably made mainly in Italy where, although the well-educated were still bilingual in Latin and Greek in the first two centuries A.D., this was not true of the humbler members of society, including slaves, among whom Christianity was spreading. What experts call the Old-Latin Bible should perhaps rather be called the Old-Latin Bibles. No complete version exists and between the many fragments there are substantial variations. All of this was to change when the translation by St Jerome became authoritative. By that time for Christians a New Testament had crystallised alongside the Old.

The formative period in the establishment of a Christian canon was the late second century when controversy and schism racked the churches precariously developing in the central and east Mediterranean area. The four Gospels came first, then the Pauline Epistles. The Acts and the Book of Revelation were accepted as authoritative at much the same time. As with the Old Testament, there were in the New a number of writings which were sometimes regarded as canonical, sometimes not. And as with the Old Testament, a high proportion of the writings were history in the most literal sense of the term. In 367 St Athanasius listed the books of the New Testament as they are accepted today and the seal of Roman approval was given by Damasus, pope from 366 to 384. It was Damasus who persuaded Jerome to translate both Old and New Testament into Latin.

St Jerome's work dominated biblical scholarship not merely in his own day (he was born about 342 and died in 420) but thereafter. He was not only endowed with good Greek and Latin, at that time a rarer accomplishment in an Italian than

it had been, but also knew Hebrew. What began as a revision
of the Old-Latin version ended up as a translation of the
Septuagint, but from the Hebrew text. To this Jerome added a
Latin translation of the New Testament. The resulting work
was to gain gradual ascendancy over all other Latin texts until
at the Council of Trent it was finally described as the *editio
vulgata*, the Vulgate.[2]

The effect of the Bible on historical studies in Christendom
was profound. It was profound because it was regarded by all
believers, whether they could read it or not, as the word of
God. The Old and New Testaments must be taken together,
for it was through Christianity that the Bible influenced every
facet of European thought. Gradually the Jews who remained
indifferent to Christ were ostracised and isolated, playing a
very minor role in European intellectual life until much later.
It was nevertheless vitally important that the scriptures
adopted by Christians took in the whole corpus of the sacred
books of Judaism. The New Covenant was a fulfilment of the
Old. The entire history of the Jews down to the birth of Jesus
was a preparation for that event, which had been foretold
again and again in every book of the Old Testament. The
message of prophecy and continuity were hammered out by
the writers of the Gospels, by the apostles and in the liturgy.
Matthew 1:17 gives 'the book of the generation of Jesus Christ,
the son of David, the son of Abraham':

> So all the generations from Abraham to David are fourteen
> generations; and from David until the carrying away into
> Babylon are fourteen generations; and from the carrying
> away into Babylon unto Christ are fourteen generations.

In the *Magnificat* Mary's praise of the Omnipotent summarised divine control over the world; 'He hath holpen his servant
Israel, in remembrance of his mercy; As he spake to our
fathers, to Abraham, and to his seed for ever.' (Luke 1:54-5.)
And in the *Nunc Dimittis*, Simeon thanked God for fulfilling
his promise of salvation 'which thou hast prepared before all
people; A light to lighten the Gentiles, and the glory of thy
people Israel' (Luke 2:31-2).

St Luke in this last passage is quoting — or making Simeon
quote — Isaiah's words describing the evangelical role of the

Jewish race; 'I will also give thee (Israel) for a light to the
Gentiles, that thou mayest be my salvation unto the end of the
earth' (49:6; cf 42:6 etc). Proselytisers sometimes, sometimes
even conquerors and always indefatigable wanderers, the Jews
themselves stressed their exclusive relationship with God more
often than they did their hopes that eventually the Gentiles
would be converted. The Old Testament is full of tremendous
bargains between a God who is jealous and capable of terrible
anger but who repents again and again. To Noah after the
Flood, God made a promise never to destroy the world with
another deluge: 'I establish my covenant with you, and with
your seed after you ... for perpetual generations.' To Abraham
(Gen. 17:7-8) another divine statement confirms God's eternal
purposes:

> And I will establish my covenant between me and thee
> and thy seed after thee in their generations for an everlasting
> covenant, to be a God unto thee and to thy seed after thee.
> And I will give unto thee, and to thy seed after thee, the
> land wherein thou art a stranger, all the land of Canaan, for
> an everlasting possession; and I will be their God.

'All the days of thy life' is the term of the sentence passed on
mankind after the Fall, a sentence which condemned women
to sorrow and subjection, and men to sorrow and endless toil.
'For dust thou art and unto dust shalt thou return.'

This for Christians was the way 'sin entered into the world
and death by sin; and so death passed upon all men, for that
all have sinned'. So St Paul to the Romans (5:12). But the
Christian redemption was the end of that long episode.
Original sin remained, but by the sacrifice of His son, God
offered to all who believed a way of throwing off the crushing
burden of sin and a hope of eternal life. This was the new
covenant. And it was not made to the people of Israel but to all
men. God's role for the Jews may have been to enlighten the
Gentiles. For a Christian, God's plan involved abolishing such
a distinction. 'For there is no difference between the Jew and
the Greek', St Paul says, also in his Epistle to the Romans
(10:12), elaborating his earlier observation (2:11) that 'there is
no respect of persons with God'. Most startling is the way in
which St Paul summarises the Christian reversal of the Jewish

law when, in the Epistle to the Galatians (2:23-9), at a stroke he toppled the Ark of the Covenant and appropriated Jewish truth to Christian service:

> But before faith came, we were kept under the law, shut up unto the faith which should afterwards be revealed.
>
> Wherefore the law was our schoolmaster to bring us unto Christ, that we might be justified by faith.
>
> But after that faith is come, we are no longer under a schoolmaster.
>
> For ye are all the children of God by faith in Christ Jesus.
>
> For as many of you as have been baptised into Christ have put on Christ.
>
> There is neither Jew nor Greek, there is neither bond nor free, there is neither male nor female: for ye are all one in Christ Jesus.
>
> And if ye be Christ's, then are ye Abraham's seed, and heirs according to the promise.

It has been necessary to provide this quite inadequate summary of the essence of the Old and New Testaments because it provides the basic intellectual assumptions of all educated men in Christendom (or Europe — and in time much of the Europeanised world) down to the eighteenth century. Such assumptions coloured or even determined all speculation and not just theological or philosophical ideas. So far as history was concerned, we shall find that the Bible was perhaps less dominant as a guide or model than might have been expected. But certain aspects of the Jewish and Christian attitudes to the past deserve to be stressed, for they are reflected in much historical writing.

In the first place, for a Jew and for a Christian history was not repetitive or cyclical (as it had been for the few Greeks and Romans who thought about the matter). Nor was it a story of decline from a period of primitive innocence to one of degenerate corruption; and this despite the attractive parallels between the Age of Gold and Paradise, despite the analogy which some ancients and some early Christians drew between the ages of man and the ages of human history — for it was into an ageing world that the Redeemer had come. The Jewish and the Christian scheme was linear. It moved from a beginning, the Creation, to an end when a Messiah would rule. Some Jews by the first century B.C. expected the Messiah to rule as a king, to be an earthly monarch of superhuman powers. Other Jews accepted Christ as their Messiah but likewise accepted that his kingdom was not of this world. For the Jew who rejected Christ, the linear pattern had no discernible end, although an end there would have to be. For the Christian the end was, if not precisely in sight, at least determined. The doctrine of a second coming (parousia) left the duration of the Christian period vague and invited much speculation, as we shall see. But with the birth and Passion of Jesus, the Christian could be sure that time which had begun with the Creation would surely come to an end.

The linear concept of history not only involved the end of history, sooner or later. It had other momentous consequences. In some sense it involved a notion of progress, although this was totally different from the simple ideas developed in the eighteenth and nineteenth centuries, for it involved a progression to a divinely ordained conclusion.

More immediately important for the early Christian and medieval view of the past was the way Biblical history and its reflection of a divine plan could yield interpretations valid at any moment in the pre-Christian period as indications of the Incarnation. The concept of God prefiguring action is foretold in the Hebrew scriptures. A covenant implies a pattern of future behaviour however disguised; often there is no disguise at all, as when the Jew or the Christian looking at a rainbow knew exactly how that was a case of God displaying His promise in nature itself. For Christians such evidence was scattered through the Bible. Already in the New Testament the foreshadowing of many aspects of Christ's life has been identified. Jesus himself, faced with the attempts of the Pharisees either to trip him up or convince them 'with a sign' compared a future Descent into Hell to the three days Jonah spent in the whale's belly (Matthew 12:39-40). Later, according to St Luke (24:27), Jesus 'expounded in all the scriptures the things concerning himself ' ... 'beginning at Moses and all the prophets'. With the apostles anxious to spread their message among Jewish communities, comparison between Old Testament events and Christian events were not enough: the sign and the substance had to be treated as identical. For St Paul, Moses giving the children of Israel drink from the rock in Horeb was giving the same sacrament as the Christian received in the Last Supper; Christ *was* the Rock (I Corinthians 10:4, Exodus 17:6). Soon the science of typology — the study of types or figures by which God manifested in allusive or concealed gestures what was later to be concretely realised — was to dominate the exposition of the Old Testament by Christian apologists. This did not, of course, mean that the Old Testament or the Gospels were not history, the narration of events which had actually happened.

A text may itself be a historical narrative in form and substance, but may nevertheless be read either 'historically' or 'prophetically', that is to say as referring either to the past or to the future: a *story* about past events could be read as prophecy prefiguring things to come.[3]

Moses (for instance) did strike the rock but this prefigures a more momentous later event: 'and the Rock was Christ'. This way of regarding Scripture loaded it with a double dose of history, so to speak. But it could equally lead commentators to treat the literal or directly historical sense as either devoid of interest or of much less interest than the sense in which it could be read as a foreshadowing of the future. Allegory and analogy soon extended enormously the possibility of types, so that an ingenious and fertile commentator might find hidden meaning in any verse of the Old Testament. No one was better at such exegesis than the Greek father Origen (who lived from about 185 to about 254). Sometimes he seems to regard even straight Old Testament history as mythical or allegorical[4] and typology could, with concomitant emphasis on the moral and spiritual significance of Old Testament texts, turn at any rate that part of the Bible into a vast parable rather than an account of God's chosen people in time. Superhistory could become antihistory.

To some degree such an attitude characterised St Augustine. His capacity for moralising and allegorising was remarkable, combined as it was with a streak of rationalism derived from his knowledge of Greek philosophers. But he moved towards a concept of history which rendered an interest in the events which follow the Ascension of little real concern. The bishop of Hippo in North Africa (bishop from 395 until his death in 430) witnessed the so-called Sack of Rome by Alaric in 410. Like other intellectuals at the time he speculated on the role of the Eternal City. Like other Christian intellectuals he was compelled to relate the fall of Rome to the divine pattern of history. Old Testament typological references were admittedly not to be applied to the interval between the First Coming and the Second, but Rome, which had covered so much of the world with her civilization, could be regarded as a device for furthering the work of spreading the Gospels. The Greek Christian Eusebius, who for twenty-five years was bishop of Caesarea, ended his *Ecclesiastical History* (written about 323) with a paean of praise for the conversion of the Emperor Constantine and the era of religious peace it seemed to herald; earlier still Origen had associated the world rule of the Emperor Augustus with the moment when the Son of God was born. Against this there was, of course, another tradition — that Rome was one of the Beasts in Daniel's prophecy, one of the Beasts in the book of Revelations. Of these two views of the providential nature of Rome and the Roman Empire, St Augustine at first preferred the first. The events of 410 changed his attitude, but not to the second interpretation.[5] In his most influential work, *The City of God*, written over the period 413-26, he undertook to defend Christianity from the pagan accusation that the City had fallen because the ancient gods had been abandoned.

His answer, spread over a densely difficult and lengthy book, was in essence that the Fall of Rome, along with Roman imperial history as a whole, was a matter of total indifference to a Christian.[6] The only history which concerned a Christian was that enshrined in the Bible. With the Passion the division of society that mattered was between an earthly city and the city of God. This is far from reflecting an antithesis such as we nowadays express in the phrase 'Church and State'. These two cities were intermingled, their separation undetectable to ordinary eyes. The earthly city was the city of sin and ended in death. The heavenly city was the city of the righteous and ended in everlasting life. What mattered to men, the clever and learned as well as the simple, was to live virtuously, not to understand civil history. The city of God had always existed but was prefigured in the Old Testament, revealed in the New.[7] This in no sense implied a denial of the necessity of human government, based on the family.[8] But it did mean that the emphasis in Augustine falls heavily on the indifference a Christian should show to things of the world. The two cities may share a desire for peace, but the Christian's is not of this world. Man is a social animal: but a Christian should have a different, not merely a higher, aim. He is a pilgrim here below.

In the 'coruscating irrelevance', to quote J.N. Figgis' brilliant phrase,[9] of *The City of God*, it is hard indeed to find a brief passage indicating the message of the book which was intended to give an authoritative theological answer to what history is all about. But here are a few passages from chapter xvii of Book XIX:

> The families which do not live by faith seek their peace in the earthly advantages of this life; while the families which live by faith look for those eternal blessings which are promised, and use as pilgrims such advantages of time and of earth as do not fascinate and divert them from God, but rather aid them to endure with greater ease, and to keep down the number of those burdens of the corruptible body which weigh upon the soul. Thus the things necessary for this mortal life are used by both kinds of men and families alike, but each has its own peculiar and widely different aim in using them. The earthly city, which does not live by faith, seeks an earthly peace, and the end it proposes, in the well-ordered concord of civic obedience and rule, is the combination of men's wills to attain the things which are helpful to this life. The heavenly city, or rather the part of it which sojourns on earth and lives by faith, makes use of this peace only because it must, until this mortal condition which necessitates it shall pass away. Consequently, so long as it lives like a captive and a stranger in the earthly city, though it has already received the promise of redemption, and the gift of the Spirit as the earnest of it, it makes no scruple to obey the laws of the earthly city, whereby the things necessary for the maintenance of this mortal life are administered;

and thus, as this life is common to both cities, so there is a harmony between them in regard to what belongs to it.... Even the heavenly city, therefore, while in its state of pilgrimage, avails itself of the peace of earth, and, so far as it can without injuring faith and godliness, desires and maintains a common agreement among men regarding the acquisition of the necessaries of life, and makes this earthly peace bear upon the peace of heaven; for this alone can be truly called and esteemed the peace of the reasonable creatures, consisting as it does in the perfectly ordered and harmonious enjoyment of God and of one another in God. When we shall have reached that peace, this mortal life shall give place to one that is eternal, and our body shall be no more this animal body which by its corruption weighs down the soul, but a spiritual body feeling no want, and in all its members subjected to the will. In its pilgrim state the heavenly city possesses this peace by faith; and by this faith it lives righteously when it refers to the attainment of that peace every good action towards God and man; for the life of the city is a social life.[10]

It may seem unnecessary to spend so much time on a thinker who, in the end, denied the significance of temporal (as opposed to sacred or biblical) history. And in fact *The City of God* was itself not to be very influential among historians in the Middle Ages.[11] But there was a sort of history which St Augustine did find useful: the chronologies which displayed with incontrovertible proofs that Creation and the whole pattern of sacred history had a priority in time, whatever pagans might say. Here Augustine had notable predecessors and considerable influence in later centuries.

The Christian had almost from the start been faced with the older empires of antiquity, the account of whose successive dominions was available in highly sophisticated literary sources, not least Herodotus. Establishing that the Jewish history preceded that of other peoples was obviously necessary if the Creation in Genesis was to be credible. Among others who dealt with this problem was Sextus Julius Africanus who flourished in the first decades of the third century. His *History of the World* (Chronographiae) survives only in other people's writings, not least in Eusebius' *Chronographia* (*c.*303). This is in two books. One contains an epitome of universal history. The other, destined to be much more influential, was the *Chronici Canones*, which listed in parallel columns the rulers of the great nations of the ancient world, thus displaying the antiquity of the Jews; St Jerome translated the chronological tables into Latin in 380 and it was in this Latin form that it survived. Besides regnal years there was space between the columns to enter notices of important events. The tables begin with the birth of Abraham, and Augustine relied heavily on 'Jerome's chronicle' for chronological information.

Augustine encouraged another writer whose work was to be important, Paulus Orosius. At Augustine's request Orosius wrote a *Historia adversus paganos* (*c.*417). This was to be an elaboration in factual terms of the contention in *The City of God* that Rome had not fallen because of her abandonment of the old divinities, but because of the disapproval of the one true God. In the event the disciple did not argue his master's case. The *History against the Pagans* displayed the old tradition, which Augustine had abandoned, of a providential role for Rome, for the Empire, for Augustus. Dependent for factual information on Jerome (i.e. Eusebius), Orosius' *History*, like Jerome's *Chronicle*, begins with Ninus at which time Abraham was born, '3184 years after Adam, the first Man'.

In this hesitant way a Christian historiography emerged from the disintegrating classical world, owing extraordinarily little to the historians of classical antiquity.[12] Before looking at its achievements, attention should be drawn to a major advantage which it possessed and to a handicap inherited from the ancient world.

The advantage was that in the Bible the Christian writer had a model (the Greek Septuagint and New Testament in Eastern Europe and Asia Minor, the Latin of Jerome in the West) utterly different from the splendour of classical Greek and Latin diction. This is particularly the case, it seems, with the Latin scriptures, since Jerome found in the Old Latin versions already in use in the West a text familiar to Christian congregations and too well loved by them to be polished to any marked degree. (One is reminded of the constraints on the translators of the English Authorised version exercised by earlier translators from Purvey to Tyndale and Coverdale.) The Vulgate, to give it its later name, was thus even less affected by classical rhetorical devices than would otherwise have been the case and it acted for centuries as a model of *sermo humilis*, of simple or humble diction. This did not mean that it could not rise to ecstatic language when the need demanded — in the prophets like Isaiah, for instance, or in the Book of Revelations; nor that it could not command doctrinal niceties, as in many of the Pauline Epistles. But it did mean that the basic religious text was written in a simple language, aimed at simple people as well as at an educated priesthood. [13] This enormously affected patristic writing in Latin and, it must be observed, produced a two-way effect. The simplicities and directness of the Bible, which reflected the vocabulary and syntax of ordinary folk, were 'sanctified' by being in the Scriptures, so that to use scriptural language in other contexts ennobled such writing. Authors like Jerome and Augustine, who had been educated in the old manner (Augustine was repelled by the barbarous Latin of the Bible when he first met it), could and sometimes did resort to old stylistic conventions, and use vulgar Latin merely to shock or excite; and many of the old tricks of the orator were readily adapted to vulgar Latin diction, were part of the fabric of unsophisticated speech, for example, anaphora or repetition for emphasis. In no field was this truer than of history:

> But the Bible is written history; it was read or listened to by the vast majority of Christians. It shaped their view of history, their ethical and esthetic conventions. Both consciously and by a process of continued unconscious assimilation, Christian writers were influenced by it and modelled their styles on it ... the biblical and Christian substance was so overwhelming that rhetorical considerations became secondary.[14]

Equally, perhaps more, important were the human subjects of the Bible narratives. It is true that there are many grand personages, kings and pharaohs and high priests. But the Pentateuch is the story of a pastoral people, its most moving passages often dealing with squalid episodes (the drunkenness of Noah, for instance) or servants (when Abraham sent his servant for a wife for Isaac and he met Rebekah drawing water from a well) or even trickery and greed (when Jacob multiplied his cattle at the expense of Laban). Of course parallels to some of these episodes could be found in ancient classical literature: Ulysses was wily enough in all conscience. But one would not find in an ancient historian a great ruler like Solomon in all his glory being reproached for sins, nor Nebuchadnezzar, king of kings, eating grass as oxen, 'and his body wet with the dew of heaven'. Such humbling of the great comes, it is true, from the prophets but was regarded as historical for all that.

Above all, in the New Testament the narrative deals almost entirely with men of low rank, working men, tax collectors, beggars, prostitutes. The rich are regarded with suspicion. Rulers and magistrates are on the side of darkness and so are the priests. The style is imbued with humility in both the linguistic and the religious sense. In Auerbach's words:

> The birth of Christ in a manger in Bethlehem, his life among fishermen, publicans and other common men, the Passion with its realistic and 'scandalous' episodes — none of this could have been treated appropriately in the lofty oratorical, tragic or epic style. According to the Augustan esthetic, such matters were worthy of lower literary genres. [15]

And elsewhere Auerbach has analysed the narrative of Peter's denial of Christ, when he sat with the servants of the high priest and warmed himself at the fire.

> A scene like Peter's denial fits into no antique genre. It is too serious for comedy, too temporary and everyday for tragedy, politically too insignificant for history — and the form which was given it is one of such immediacy that its like does not exist in the literature of antiquity.[16]

The larger achievement in this revolution in diction, this invention of a new rhetoric, was of course of greater import than the mere historiographical; it liberated for literature of every kind a new and compulsive grasp of life. But for historians its effects were dramatic enough, for it enabled

them to introduce ordinary men and women as the central
characters in narratives of the past.

This enormous achievement was nevertheless limited by a
failure to produce an accepted era. We have observed the ugly
and unpopular procedures by which classical Latin and Greek
historians offered their reader chronological guidance —
generations, Olympiads, the computation from the Founding
of the City, names of magistrates, and often a mixture of all
these indicators of time.[17] The Bible offered no models here,
and for long the Fathers found no way out of the muddled
computations of the Hellenistic world. In the Scriptures the
only reckoning was by generations, those interminable 'begats'
which fill columns of the Old Testament and are found too in
the New (Matthew 1:1-17). A scheme of generations could be
made to yield a series of ages or periods, as we shall see, but it
was of small service for accurate dating.

The Julius Africanus-Eusebius-Jerome chronologies might
have been expected to make use of an era dating from the
Creation. In fact they favoured the Ninus-Abraham era but
when they reached the point when it became available, the
clumsy Olympiad was used. Orosius employed (not perhaps
surprisingly since he accepted the positive role of Rome in
Christian expansion) dates from the Foundation of the City
and, a more odd development, gave his early dates in years
before the Founding. Thus (I, cap. xix): 'Anno ante Urbem
conditam LXIII novissimus apud Assyrios regnavit Sardana
palus, vir muliere corruptior'. But he can as easily slip into
another scheme (II, cap. iv): 'Anno post eversione Trojae
CCCCXIV, Olimpiade VI ... urbs Roma in Italia a Romulo e
Remo ... condita est'. This was, of course, the result of using
parallel tables. Orosius did not respond to the obvious
possibility of making human time turn on the Incarnation:
'Igitur anno ab Urbe condita DCCLII natus est Christus' (VII,
cap. iii), and so on until the end of his chronicle. By this time
another unhelpful cycle had made its appearance in
documents, the Indiction. This was a fifteen-year interval
between the levying of taxes, which began in either 297 or 312
A.D., a result of the financial reform of Diocletian. (As used in
Christian documents, 297 is taken as the beginning of the first
indiction.)

The invention of the Christian era was to come five hundred years after the earthly life of Christ and the impulse behind it was liturgical not historical.[18] It was necessary to reckon in advance the date of Easter. Easter fell on a Sunday following the full moon following the vernal equinox so that the lunar and solar years were both involved. For convenience this calculation was done in cycles of nineteen years, for at the end of this period the solar and the lunar years were in agreement; in order to effect a recurrence of the day of the week the nineteen-years cycle (called by Christian calendar makers the Golden Number) had to be multiplied by 28. The result was the Great Year of 532 years. In the fifth century Victorius of Aquitaine constructed such a table and at Rome in 525 Dionysius Exiguus developed and defended this kind of Easter calculation. There was, however, a need for some dating by years when cycles as long as this were involved, or else confusion could easily arise. For his era Dionysius chose the date of the Incarnation, or Year of Grace. It took a considerable time for *Annus Domini* to be generally used as a means of counting forward; as for B.C., that was not regularly used until very much later.[19] By the early eighth century the Venerable Bede had produced an authoritative technical defence of the new approach to chronology (calculation of Easter and use of the Year of Grace) in *De temporum ratione*. The early ninth century saw documents in the West being dated by years A.D., although the older methods (indictions) were added — for safety's sake, one might say. Long before that, however, the chronicler was wedded to years calculated from the Incarnation. This annalistic type of historical composition was (as we shall see in the next chapter) a byproduct of the construction of Easter Tables.

The first centuries of the Christian era had thus produced a basis for identifying the new covenant as a way of reckoning time. They inherited from Jewish tradition a system of ages or eras of a rather different sort. Some of these have already been mentioned — the Creation, the birth of Abraham. They are:

1. From the Creation to the Flood (itself a kind of new Creation).
2. From the Flood to the birth of Abraham.
3. From Abraham to David.

4. From David to the Captivity.
5. From the Captivity to the birth of Christ.
6. From the birth of Christ until the Second Coming.

After this came a seventh age, when Time would be fulfilled
The parallel with the six days of Creation reinforced if it di
not inspire this scheme, which is partly laid out in St Matthe
(1:17), and which was elaborated by a number of writers fro
the second century onwards, culminating in St Augustine, wh
concludes the *City of God* (xxii, cap. 30) with a paean on th
Seventh Age, the Eternal Sabbath.[20] It dominated th
patristic division of the early ages and in due course it wa
enshrined in Bede. Throughout the Middle Ages and beyon
men accepted that they were living in the Sixth Age. For som
this was an invitation to determine when the Seventh Ag
would occur. For some it was a Sixth Age whose events were
on the Augustinian premise, of ephemeral interest. Fo
historians it was a convenient way, sanctified by usage, o
dealing with the sacred or biblical periods of time,[21] makin
them the critical moments not only for 'prophetic' but for a
history — for all history became true or 'prophetic' histor
Hence the early Christian historian attempting a genera
account of the story of mankind began with a summary of th
Old and New Testaments,[22] and then proceeded to narrat
the events of the Sixth Age. This six-fold division proved fa
more popular with sober medieval chroniclers than othe
schemes derived from Scripture and elaborated by theologian
and exegetes. These were the simple division of Jewish wisdon
where there were three epochs: an age before the law, unde
the law and under the Messiah (or, in Christian terms, Grace)
and the succession of empires, which drew its authority fron
the book of Daniel (2:31-45, 7:2-27) where four successiv
empires are referred to in a mysterious fashion, in th
prophet's interpretation of Nebuchadnezzar's dream and in hi
own vision in the time of Belshazzar. Christian historians wer
only tempted by this arrangement in so far as they ha
apocalyptic inclinations.[23]

Before we leave the Christian Fathers we must review thei
performance as historians. Some of their works were to li
heavily on future centuries as sources of information and a

models of what a Christian historian ought to be about. Let us remember their handicap: although an era, the Year of Grace, had emerged, they were mostly not trained to use it. Let us remember their advantages: they had abandoned the pomposities of the classical historical inheritance and could not only feel that facts were literally sacred, but they could also describe and discuss the lives and activities of ordinary men and women. From this point onwards history is taken seriously. As a result, the number of historical writings greatly increases and they are treated with a respect which contrasts with the carelessness which pagans displayed to pagan historians. The number of historians even for the early centuries of the Christian period is therefore large and in what follows only some of the more important authors can be touched on. In order of time the authors mentioned are: Eusebius, Orosius, Gregory of Tours, Bede and Einhard.

Eusebius' work on chronology, the *Canones*, which was translated into Latin by St Jerome, has already been mentioned. In his *Ecclesiastical History* he attempted something quite different. A fair number of manuscripts of the Greek text have survived and not long after its completion a Latin adaptation by Rufinus ensured that it was available in the West. The *Ecclesiastical History* is a substantial book, remarkable for the extensive quotations it gives of earlier writers, many of whom are only known through the pages of Eusebius. This emphasis on the identification of sources (transcription of earlier writers without acknowledgement has been common to historians of all periods) is due perhaps to Eusebius' conviction that he was engaged on a work which was not only serious but sanctified, and perhaps to a desire to impress pagan readers.

His work, carefully planned, surveyed the history of the Christian 'nation' from its beginnings to his own day when, with the victory of the Emperor Constantine, he considered that the days of trouble for the Church were over. There are ten books and the divisions are determined by a mixture of imperial and episcopal changes — in fact the division into books is often as perplexing as it is in Livy's *Decades*, which work had perhaps reinforced Eusebius' view that ten was a proper number. The emphasis falls decidedly on two periods. The first is the period of Christ's earthly ministry and the years

following it to the end of the first century — the martyrdom of
Peter and Paul — more or less to the point where he could no
longer rely on the *Jewish War* and *Antiquities* of Josephus (see
iii, 10)[24] The other most detailed account is devoted to his
own day. He was born about 260 and died about 340; nearly
half the whole is devoted to these years, down to the moment
when Constantine (whom Eusebius himself baptised) had
defeated his villainous rival Licinius.

Although his Greek style is said to be poor, Eusebius' history
is extraordinarily refreshing after the somewhat jaded and
aristocratic histories of classical antiquity. It is about
persecuted minorities. (There is a great deal of information on
the harrying of the Jews which they had, of course, deserved as
punishment for the betrayal of Christ.) In general, authority is
depicted with hostility. Main attention is paid to the spreading
of Christianity, to the confutation of heretical beliefs, to the
succession of bishops, especially in the greater sees (Jerusalem,
Alexandria, Rome, Antioch), to the recording of the
martyrdoms of saints.[25] The work is decidedly an ecclesiastical history and, when recording mere civil transactions,
relapses into abrupt annalistic form. Its unity and interest
derive from its defensive quality, due to Eusebius' identification of Christians as a group apart (a nation) although
individuals had been Jews, Greeks, Romans. Perhaps this
notion, too, came from Josephus. It is the work of a Christian
whose Church was, until the end, threatened with possible
extinction.

Eusebius' *Ecclesiastical History* owed much of its later
importance to its being available in a Latin version. This was
made, as noted, by a north Italian priest called Rufinus, who
lived from about 345 to 410. Rufinus did not stick closely to
the Greek original and in general abbreviated it. This is very
marked in the final book, where not only were the documents
omitted (Eusebius' long panegyric addressed to Paulinus and
the string of imperial rescripts) but the narrative itself was
streamlined.[26] This brevity was a merit in later ages when
men regarded these early centuries as a preface to the events of
their own epoch. For similar reasons the so-called *Historia
Tripartita*, which was designed to take the story on from
Eusebius' terminus of 324, managed to cover another century

by the translation into Latin of extracts from three Greek writers. This historical anthology emulated Eusebius' rich quotation of original sources and interest in episcopal succession but shared Rufinus' engagingly episodic approach. It was put together by Cassiodorus, the aristocratic Roman monk and writer who died about 580.[27] In this way an ecclesiastical history in Latin covering the first four centuries of the Christian era came down to be used by later writers.

This sense of a precarious existence here below is a mark of the other writers to be discussed in this chapter, for the conversion of Constantine was not the end of imperial persecutions and, in any case, as Christianity penetrated to the extremities of what had been the Empire it encountered pagan threats of a different and perhaps more persistent kind.

In the Mediterranean region another church history was composed by Augustine's disciple Orosius, whose views on the role of Rome in the providential spread of Christianity differed, it will be recalled, from those of his master. His *Seven Books of History against the Pagans* goes down to 417; he died soon afterwards. Compared with Eusebius (on whose *Chronicle* and *Canons* he relied heavily) he is a repetitive bore, grinding out his apologia for Christianity with complete conviction and a total lack of fire, save perhaps towards the end. For it is only in the last book that he reaches Christ and can rattle on to his own day. The earlier books summarise pre-Christian history in prophetic fashion, in order to demonstrate the providence that was to lead to the Incarnation. Orosius deplores historical works which do not begin in the Garden of Eden (I, i) but, in effect, like Eusebius and St Jermome, his effective starting point is Ninus, King of the Assyrians (I, iv). The work was destined to be very influential in the Middle Ages, partly because it was short, partly because it had ingredients attractive to non-historical prophecy, such as the four Empires (VII, ii), and partly because it had the prestigious association with Augustine, whose name figures on the first and last pages, even if he was dubious of the book's message.[28]

The handful of men with scholarly minds or who were inquistive about the past thus by the end of the sixth century had the makings of a narrative from Creation to their own day. The Bible story had been digested into chronologies which

fitted it into what was known of the ancient history of the other
kingdoms. This was the task of the Eusebius-St Jerome
Chronicle and Canons, and Orosius had put the story into an
abbreviated, jerky but continuous narrative. For the centuries
of the Sixth Age there were the histories, stemming from
Eusebius' *Ecclesiastical History*, which continued his account
of an embattled Church. Much of this was apologetic in tone.
All of it was 'ecclesiastical' in that it was concerned with
bishops as much as with kings, with heresies as much as with
rebellions, with church councils as much as with military
campaigns. Although all of this was available in Latin it was in
its original form mainly Greek. And in Byzantium, we should
remember, the level of literary culture of the fifth and sixth
centuries was higher than in the West. In particular the
models of ancient Greek historiography (much superior to the
classical Latin writers) were not forgotten. No Western
historian of this period achieved the sophistication of
Procopius (d. after 565), who wrote an elaborate account of
the wars fought by Belisarius on behalf of the Emperor
Justinian. The *History of the Wars* has naturally the faults of
the ancient historian. It is devoted almost exclusively to war
and diplomacy. It neglects the broader political and social
problems of the day; it even neglects the Church. Procopius'
narrative concentrates on great men, though it is evident from
his *Anecdota* or *Secret History* that for him the great were not
the good and he frequently descends with relish to discuss the
dregs of the population.[29]

Procopius aped Thucydides with confidence, though for
some time no other Greek writers followed in his steps. In the
Latin West men of letters were diffident, even when they
looked back to writers whom they admired. This diffidence is
hard to evaluate. 'I am too unlearned and ill-equipped with
Latin to undertake this task' becomes a commonplace[30] and
we find such disclaimers in Eusebius, Jordanes, Gregory of
Tours, Bede, Einhard and many others. In the case of
Jordanes it was no idle protestation and there is no need to
pause over his *History of the Goths*, written in the mid-sixth
century as an anthology mainly drawn from Rufinus and a lost
history of the Goths written by Cassiodorus.[31] But the other
three authors demand more consideration, for each was a

writer and historian of very considerable originality and talent.

Gregory was bishop of Tours from 573 to his death in 594. It was a time of chaotic and brutal public life, when the Franks were under a dynasty of newly converted Merovingians. (Clovis is supposed to have been baptised in 496.) The Arianism of many of the Germans who were converted to Christianity, the unredeemed paganism of many more, made a clergyman like Gregory genuinely share the world of Augustine and Orosius — a precarious region in a world threatened by wars, heresies and a sense of contraction both moral and economic. Hence it is hardly surprising that Gregory's *History of the Franks* opens with a brief synopsis (book i) of sacred history from Adam to the translation of St Martin in 442, and his concern with sacred history does not flag throughout the work. His hero is Clovis (a new Constantine, ii:22) but it was hardly possible to treat the role of the Merovingian rulers as fulfilling, as Rome had for Orosius, a culminating or at least decisive function in God's grand design. Much of Gregory's account is taken up with detailed narratives, with accounts of provincial saints and sinners, with pointless wars and pregnant prodigies. It is, however, vivid and direct. It captures the light and darkness, the conversation, the quick impulsive reactions of barbarous peoples. If Orosius offered a philosophy of sorts to Gregory, the New Testament conditioned his attitudes to writing:

> Undoubtedly the rhythm and the atmosphere of the Bible, and especially of the New Testament, are always present in Gregory's mind and help to determine his style. And they release forces which are already present in Gregory and his epoch... Gregory's literary Latin not only is decadent grammatically and syntactically, it is used in his work to an end for which, originally or at least in its hey day, it seemed little suited — that is, to imitate concrete reality.[32]

This has disadvantages. His language impedes logical exposition of facts; it is not economical or concise. But his ability to construct living dialogue and depict the rough and tumble of life that was far from courtly gave him enormous compensatory advantages. When he has analysed one of Gregory's episodes Auerbach writes:

It goes without saying that a classical author would have
arranged the material much more clearly — provided that
he had treated it all. For if we ask ourselves how Caesar or
Livy or Tacitus or even Ammianus would have told this story
it immediately becomes obvious that they would never have
told it.... Who are (these characters)? Not even tribal
princes, and during the hey day of the Empire their bloody
brawls would probably not even have elicited a special
report from the provincial governor.[33]

Gregory's real achievement is that, at the perimeter of the
Christian world, he has a grasp on actuality lost by the men
whose 'world views', based on Rome, Antioch or Constantinople, had been wider but usually more insubstantial. His
quaintness and his homeliness should not deflect us from his
serious purposes: 'it is the story of the barbarian settlement of a
Roman province seen not through Roman but Catholic
eyes'.[34] We shall constantly meet the modern proposition
that the artless writer is more valuable in some ways than the
artistic writer. Gregory's merit is that he is trying to say what
has not been said before and he has succeeded in establishing
the appropriateness of a new type of narrative.[35]

Bede's achievement is different but in its way no less
remarkable. He has occurred hitherto as the author of a book
on chronology.[36] There is no doubt that this and his
exegetical works were what earned him his reputation during
the Middle Ages as a great scholar. But among those of his
countrymen who were literate there is equally no doubt that he
was remembered chiefly as the author of another ecclesiastical
history. In his dedication (to the king of Northumbria) he
describes his work on one occasion as 'the ecclesiastical history
of the English people' (*Historiam gentis Anglorum ecclesiasti-
cam, historia ... nostrae nationis*).[37] It is to be doubted if
Bede could see any difference in the two formulations: the
English and their Church were identified with one another and
thus had a common history. His preface goes on with the time-
honoured classical defence of history: it presents the reader
with good actions to emulate, bad actions to avoid; he writes
for posterity (*ad instructionem posteritatis*). So much was
perhaps commonplace, and so probably was the protestation

of his inadequacy for the task — 'my bodily and mental infirmities'.[38] What is an innovation is Bede's careful description of what we would nowadays call his sources, and even that would be less remarkable (authors often hid behind authorities) if he had not in the event treated his sources with remarkably scrupulous care. In addition, he produced a work which is not merely an indispensable reference book for modern scholars (the same could be said of Cassiodorus' compilation and of many another indifferent work) but is still gripping to read.

It would be foolish to exaggerate Bede's virtues. His approach and much of his material came from obvious and established models. For example, Orosius prefaces his work with a geographical description and Bede follows suit. His narrative, especially in book I which runs from Caesar's invasion of Britain to 603, is largely a weaving together of passages from other writers but it includes substantial documents much as in Eusebius. Bede, like Gregory of Tours, was writing in a land where there were pagans and Christians who could revert over-night to paganism, where there were severe divisions between Christians (Pelagius, the Irish-English quarrel over the calculation of Easter). It was natural that he should feel involved in the uncertain world of evangelism, fortified by the miraculous, by God's ever-present protection.

Above all, Bede was fortified by the Bible. Echoes of it are found everywhere in his work and he specifically recommends it as a model of style.[39] It is true that for his day Bede was a man well versed in classical literature. There are moments when we find substantial exercises in direct speech,[40] but in general he writes with a directness and a simplicity which echoes the Bible, and especially the New Testament, again and again. Like Gregory of Tours, but with far better grammar and orthography, he produces passages of convincing dialogue,[41] and his ability to touch an anecdote with a mysterious poetry is best shown, I suppose, in the passage where a pagan Northumbrian nobleman speaks for the adoption of Christianity by comparing the secret of life to the sparrow flying from outer darkness to outer darkness through a great warm winter hall.[42] The story of Imma, who denies his earthly master as Peter did and like Peter cannot be shackled, has much of the magic of Matthew's Gospel and the Acts of the Apostles.[43]

It is a comedown to move from Bede, who died in 735, to Einhard, who lived from about 755 to 840 and whose biography of Charlemagne was completed about 830. But in a sense both Bede and Einhard belong to the past. The difference between them is that Bede belonged to a living past, a past with a future, whereas Einhard's biography was — despite its merits, perhaps because of them — a dead thing. There were scholars in the court of Charles the Great, who became Emperor of the West in 800, who consciously strove to recreate some of the glitter and grandeur of ancient Rome. They were among the first scholars in European history who in fact began treating Latin as a dead language. They tried to write as the ancients had written, though the world had changed.

Einhard was remarkably successful as a writer. 'There are sentences in Einhard of which Caesar and Livy would not have been ashamed.'[44] His model was the life of a king such as he found in Suetonius' *Lives of the Twelve Caesars*; that is, he treated Charles as a secular ruler and as a man rather than as a hero of the Church, which he could perfectly well have done either as warrior for Christ or as Christian emperor; the imperial coronation is not particularly emphasised (cap. xxviii). The choice Einhard made was, one must assume, deliberate, for there were hagiographical works in plenty by this time, as noted below, which a very different life of Charles might have imitated. But the life of Augustus by Suetonius which most influenced Einhard's approach is some fifteen times longer than the *Vita Caroli Magni*, although Charles in his way was as great a man.[45] Perhaps the book demonstrated that secular biography on the antique Roman pattern was inappropriate. Few other writers were to take Suetonius as a model in the Middle Ages.[46]

The saint's life, on the other hand, was soon to be a dominant form of biography and already by the time of Einhard hundreds of such lives had been composed. The impulse was partly scholarly (after all the New Testament is the first collection and a large literature regarding holy men and women soon formed the 'Christian apocrypha'). But

writers and men of the Church would not have been so
attracted by such compositions but for the enormous popular
veneration of martyrs. Their feast days were remembered in
the liturgy. Their relics formed the most precious possessions
of princes and churches. Molinier enumerates over 360 saints'
lives for Gaul down to the end of the eighth century;[47]
numbers for other parts of Christendom are proportionately
high. Some of these lives are trivial. Some are both intrinsically
important and well-written, as Bede's life of St Cuthbert and
his short but very interesting account of the abbots of
Wearmonth and Jarrow. These last were not saints' lives, but
they are introduced here because they established a manner of
writing the life of a great man which regularly became a
stereotype.[48]

Saints were often celebrated long before their lives were
written down in calendars and martyrologies, their lives
remembered rather than read. This should remind us of the
vast amount of oral history that must have circulated,
especially among the Germanic peoples in the period discussed
in this chapter. Something will be said later about the sagas.
Such stories must already have existed in the days of Bede and
Einhard, as may confidently be inferred from the Old English
poem *Beowulf* (eighth century) and from Einhard's report that
Charlemagne ordered such oral material to be written down
and so preserved. Such oral material doubtless also entered the
annals of the medieval chronicle, whose origins and early
development are discussed in the next chapter.

The really outstanding figure in the centuries just discussed
was unquestionably Bede. His *Ecclesiastical History* diminishes
the stature as historians, although it does not detract from the
influence, of Eusebius and Jerome. He has something of the
grand manner as well as of the grand convictions of the
apostolic age. Yet — like all the other writers discussed above
— his chronology in the *Ecclesiastical History* is hard to follow,
perhaps because of his sense of style, his classical aversion to
marring his prose with dates. In fixing the Christian era his
other writings had profound importance. The annals of the
Middle Ages were to owe much to the greatest Latin patristic
historian, for that is what Bede was, both through the
information in his *History* and his establishment of a way of
handling dates.

The characteristic annalistic chronicle of the Middle Ages did not grow out of ancient, biblical or patristic history. It was invented, and on a completely new pattern. Annals are the most primitive form of historical record and they are found everywhere. They were normally brief descriptions of events arranged under lists showing the annual changes in magistracies, or they were computed from the years of a king's reign. We saw that Thucydides used several of these annalistic devices in order to establish a date and they are to be found in many ancient writers. In Livy (II, xvi), for instance, we read 'Consuls M. Valerius P. Postumius. In that year a successful war against the Sabines. The consuls were victorious'. This is far different from Livy's normal way of writing up material[1] and it assumed that the reader who was interested knew or could find out when Marcus Valerius and Publius Postumius were consuls (505 B.C.).

To say that the medieval chronicle did not grow out of earlier historical writing is not to say that it did not derive important elements from antiquity, Greek, Roman, Jewish and Christian. The Bible provided basic chronology and influenced the kind of Latin employed, and Christianity, as we have seen, in the end provided an era, the Year of Incarnation.[2] Eusebius-Jerome drew from both the Bible and classical historians information about the history of the world before Christ, when the Sixth Age of the world began. All the general chronicles of a developed kind, for example, work within a framework of the Six Ages, though the diffusion of the arrangement is due to Isidore of Seville's writings.[3] This influential prelate (c. 560-636) wrote voluminously and transmitted, sometimes in a garbled form, much of the scholarship of the ancient world. The book for which he was most respected was the *Etymologiae*, a survey of the learning of his day.

Of all these inheritances and influences the era of the
Incarnation was the most helpful to later writers of history, for
it provided a fixed point in time round which all historical
events could be arranged in temporal sequence. By itself the
universal reverence of the birth of Christ would not, however,
have provoked further development of historical technique.
One might have expected a slow advance towards a type of
Eusebian narrative more plentifully supplied with dates
expressed as A.D., but otherwise trying to reflect older
historical styles. Jesus' birth was commemorated on Christmas
Day, a fixed date, 25 December. This was sometimes used to
begin the official year in certain places, since it was
conveniently if confusingly near New Year's Day, everywhere
regarded as the first day of the natural year.[4] But in fact
Christmas is a less important festival for Christians than
Easter, and Easter, being a movable feast, needed calculation
and provoked debate. We must now look for a moment more
closely at this question, which was touched on in the previous
chapter.

The early Christian churches had wide varieties of dates for
Easter and a wide variety of computations to justify their
different reckonings. It is not necessary here to rehearse the
complicated history of these developments which, as we noted
earlier, turn on the reconciliation of a date (soon established as
necessarily a Sunday) based on both the Hebrew calendar
(lunar) and the Roman calendar (solar). The solution was the
cycle of 19 years (which fitted the lunar cycle) multiplied by 28
years (which took care of the solar week and leap year) — a
total cycle of 532 years.[5] Many tables setting out a series of
Easters were constructed. The one which used the Year of
Grace as a way of checking the year was, we have seen, the
work of Dionysius Exiguus, who compiled it in Rome in 525.
The latest flare-up in controversy over the calculation of Easter
came in England, where Celtic practice encountered Roman
practice, with the certainty that in 665 there would be a major
divergence. Since the Irish (Scottish) and English churches
were mingled, especially in Northumbria, there was an urgent
need to resolve the differences between them. Hence in 664 at
Whitby a synod was held, described in detail in Bede's
Ecclesiastical History. Here the computation of Easter was

decided on the Roman method and to the elucidation of this
Bede subsequently contributed his *De temporum ratione* and
De temporibus, works which were to be extremely influential
throughout Christendom for centuries to come.

Traditionally the clergy who calculated Easter checked their
reckoning by reference to related material, such as the
Indiction. And Easter tables for long carried not merely the
Year of Grace and the date of Easter, but a range of other
information regarding the year. Thus a full table had columns
for:

1. The Year of Grace.
2. The Indiction (above p.26; the place of the year in a
   15-year cycle).
3. The Epact (the age of the moon on 1 January).
4. The Concurrent (the number of days between the last
   Sunday in the old year and 1 January in the new year).
5. The Lunar Cycle (the place of the year in the cycle of 19
   years, above p.27; also called the Golden Number).
6. The Paschal Term (The date of Passover, i.e. the
   fourteenth day of the moon preceding Easter Sunday).
7. Easter Day (preceded by 'c' = a common year or 'e' =
   embolismal).[6]
8. The age of the moon on Easter Sunday.

Much of this information was superfluous but calendars were
conservative and the calculations involved in finding Easter
were hallowed by the sanctity of the day itself. An example of
two entries from a late-ninth-century Paschal table of this kind
(taken from plate 1 in R.L. Poole's *Chronicles and Annals*[7])
will show the way the details were set out. (see facing page).

Lists like this [8] invited the insertion of historical items.
Indeed it has been asserted that Paschal tables contain such
items: 'Easter-tables *are* history, a historical record of the
annual occurrence of the greatest day in the Christian year'.[9]
This is of course an absurd paradox in that the tables set out
Easter for years ahead and it was only as these years rolled
away that the date became part of the past, part of history. It
is more to the point that great churches and great households
felt the need of such tables and found it natural to record
important events on them, with a brevity determined by the

TWO LINES FROM AN EASTER TABLE

Year	Indic-tion	Epact	Con-current	Lunar Cycle	Paschal Term	Easter Day	Age of the moon on Easter Day
DCCCCLXX [970]	XIII	XI	V	XVIII	vii Kal.' Ap.' [25 March]	c. vi Kal.' Ap.' [25 March]	XVI
DCCCCLXXI [971]	XIIII	XXII	VI	XIX	Id.' Ap.' [13 April]	e. xvi Kal.' ma.' [16 April]	XVII

space between lines and the width of the margin. To quote a
few such entries interlineated in the same page of the table
illustrated in Poole's book and discussed above, but omitting
the chronological and astronomical data:

A.D.
963   Otto the emperor [spent] Christmas at Pavia
964   Otto the emperor [spent] Christmas at Rome
965   Archbishop Bruno died
966   Otto the emperor [spent] Christmas at Pavia. Then he
      returned by way of Mont Cenis and Lukmanier

Laconic entries such as these seem to have been made on
Easter tables in the West from the seventh century and, since
the tables themselves were frequently lent or carried from one
centre to another, the annals on them also gradually spread
and were copied as copies were made of the Easter data. Then
we get annals where the entry regarding some public event is
flanked only by the Year of Grace and the date of Easter.
Finally we get annals in which are recorded only the year and
the event or events associated with it. A mark of such primitive
annals is the enumeration of the year even if there is no event
to place beside it. Many early chronicles display this feature.

There thus came into being a great deal of chronological
material, relatively exactly dated, which could be extended
backwards or forwards by writers anxious to write more
comprehensive or less rigidly annalistic history. One must
stress 'relatively' when one says 'exactly dated'. The moment
that events had receded a few years the events associated with
them could be misconstrued or miscopied by a later scribe.
And beyond that there was often ambiguity about when the
annalist began his year; this varied from time to time and from
place to place. A chronicle might thus conflate events from
two originals which had a different system of reckoning the
official beginning of the year.

Most of what follows in this chapter will be devoted to
writers who tried to make annals more comprehensive than
they found them. It is sensible therefore to remember that
calendared annals could lie behind historical works which were
in no sense annalistic. Of these the most signal example is
Bede's *Ecclesiastical History*. There seems to be no doubt that

the 'fixed dates' in the work derive from Easter table material and this is emphasised by the *recapitulatio* in book V, cap. xxiv, in which Bede provides a brief annalistic summary of his work running from Julius Caesar's conquest of Britain, 'sixty years before the Incarnation', down to 731 when 'Berctauld the archbishop died, Tatuin became archbishop of Canterbury, in the fifteenth year of the reign of King Ethelbald of Mercia'. Chronicles also form a part, C.W. Jones says an integral part, of Bede's chronological works, as a kind of practical demonstration of the theory.[10] The existence of Easter tables with historical events prior to Bede's *Ecclesiastical History* does not, however, make that work a 'medieval chronicle'.[11] Bede was following a loftier tradition. He was writing in the grand manner and doing it distinctly better than Eusebius, Orosius or Cassiodorus. He was to have virtually no successors. For centuries historical narrative was to be dominated by the annal.

It so happens that the progress of historical writing of this new type can be demonstrated extremely well from English material. The *Anglo-Saxon Chronicle* in its various forms typifies the development from the entry in the Easter table to the early medieval chronicle, being unusual in only one respect: it was written in English not Latin, the language in which continental annals were invariably couched. It has been argued that this early flowering of vernacular literature in Britain is not so much a reflection of a sophisticated society than of a society without adequate experience of Latin. King Alfred, traditionally associated with the origin and diffusion of the *Chronicle*, wrote gloomily about the state of learning among priests in his own day in the preface to his vernacular translation of St Gregory's *Pastoral Care*: there were few clergy who could read English, let alone Latin.[12] This, if not exactly a *topos*, is what was said of the clergy of Europe at all dates down to the eighteenth century. But it was probably truer of the dark days of Danish invasions in England than of most other times and places. At any rate, in Alfred's reign, if not at his express command, annals in Old English were assembled from earlier Easter tables, from Bede and from other sources, which became the kernel of the *Anglo-Saxon Chronicle*.[13]

The compilation of the earliest recension, which dates from

the mid- or late ninth century, was based on earlier Easter
table material, on Bede, on epitomised general histories and
on various lists of kings and bishops. From this material a
narrative jerks along, year by year, from the birth of Christ.
Down to the middle of the fifth century it contains brief entries
of continental interest, although the main emphasis is placed
on items regarding Britain. From Hengist and Horsa's invasion
(*s.a.* 449) onwards the centre of the stage is held by Britain;
events elsewhere are rarely recorded. I have called the entries a
'narrative' but this suggests continuous or connected exposition. What we have is a series of factual statements, normally
unrelated to each other so far as the annalist is concerned, even
if a connection is evident to the reader. Thus, in the Parker
manuscript:

634   In this year Birinus preached Christianity to the West
      Saxons.
635   In this year Cynegils was baptised by Birinus, bishop of
      Dorchester, and Oswald stood sponsor for him.
636   In this year Cwichelm was baptised at Dorchester, and
      the same year he passed away. And bishop Felix
      preached the faith of Christ to the East Anglians.[14]

Or, as an example of a wider vision:

803   In this year archbishop Æthelheard passed away and
      Wulfred was consecrated archbishop, and abbot
      Forthred passed away.
804   In this year archbishop Wulfred received the pallium.
805   In this year kind Cuthred passed away in Kent, and
      abbess Ceolburh and ealdorman Heahberht.
812   In this year king Charlemagne passed away. He reigned
      forty-five years. And archibship Wulfred and Wigberht,
      bishop of Wessex, both went to Rome.[15]

By the time the *Chronicle* reaches 935 the Danish attacks begin
and an account of the subsequent battles dominates the story,
gives it cohesion, leads to ampler entries.

The *Chronicle* in its earlier form was soon circulating from
its first home in Winchester and a bewildering series of
variants has to be studied by the student of Anglo-Saxon
England. The copies made elsewhere often betray their origins

by stressing events in a particular locality. An enormous
amount of expert scholarship has been devoted to identifying
the provenances and periods of composition of the six full tests
and the various fragments; versions now lost have been
reasonably assumed as archetypes. All in all in the ninth and
tenth centuries there must have been at least a dozen versions
of the *Chronicle* circulating in English in England.

The Parker manuscript, already referred to, is not only the
earliest. It displays as none of the others do a series of scribes at
work. There are eight distinct hands down to 955, and in all at
least thirteen. This demonstrates the contemporaneous quality
of the compilation; each writer recorded events as he lived
through them. The same is true also of the other manuscripts,
but they are all copies made in the eleventh and twelfth
centuries by scribes copying earlier exemplars, so that the
quality of the composition, its instantaneous nature, is not so
obviously displayed for earlier periods. The continuators (the
last text goes down to 1154) edited earlier portions, adding
details from other sources, usually with a particular interest for
the monastery where they were at work, so that we have
versions reflecting northern, west country, Midland and
Kentish preoccupations.

The *Anglo-Saxon Chronicle* begins with the first year of the
Christian era: 'Octavian reigned fifty-six years, and in the
forty-second year of his reign Christ was born'.[16] This was,
however, part of an epitomised world-chronicle inserted to
join the real matter, English history, to the beginning of the
Sixth Age, now widely known in England, not least because of
the section 'De mundi aetatibus' in Bede's *De temporibus liber*;
and the equation of the seven days of creation with the Seven
Ages of created Time, which Bede derived from Isidore and
Augustine and explained in his *De temporum ratione*.[17] We
do not find the five earlier ages referred to in the *Anglo-Saxon
Chronicle*, as they tended to be in other universal histories. But
one interpolation displays the itch to secure a link with the
beginning of the world. It occurs under the year 855 and it
gives the genealogy of Æthelwulf, king of Wessex. Such royal
genealogies are not uncommon in the *Chronicle* and in
continental compilations of this period. They actually go back
to a German legendary God, most often to Woden. But

Æthelwulf on this occasion has his ancestor traced back to the Flood and beyond:

> the son of Itermon, the son of Hrathra, who was born in the ark: Noah, Lamech, Methusaleh, Enoch, Jared, Mahalaleel Cainan, Enos. Seth, Adam the first man, and our father who is Christ. Amen.[18]

The liturgical overtones get very strong at the end of the list, but here and elsewhere in the *Chronicle* there are memories of an older folk literature, oral and pagan.

To summarise: the *Anglo-Saxon Chronicle* was
(a) based on Easter table annals, many of which were compiled in the seventh century;
(b) was continued from time to time as an annalistic record of important events, these continuations reflecting the interests of the area in which the compiler lived, or those of a patron such as a king;
(c) went back to the Incarnation by using epitomies based ultimately on such works as Eusebius and Orosius, and on one occasion went back to the Creation.

All of these features characterise the typical chronicle of the early medieval period, save that most begin by summarising in some detail the five ages between Adam and the birth of Christ. In some detail only, since there was no need to elaborate the story whose lineaments formed part of the services of the Church and indeed the decoration of ecclesiastical buildings.

It would be easy to produce series of examples of mature world histories. I shall content myself with an analysis of one of the most celebrated and influential of the earlier chronicles, that by Sigebert of Gembloux.

Sigebert became a Benedictine monk at Gembloux, a house not far from Brussels, before 1048. He then was sent to the abbey of St Vincent as schoolmaster and returned to Gembloux about 1070. He died in 1112. His life was entirely dedicated to writing and teaching, although as a propagandist he was involved in the polemic between emperor and pope, taking the imperial side. His most substantial work, the

Chronicon, is however non-partisan.[19]

This *Chronicle* begins in A.D. 381, that is at the point at which the Eusebius-Jerome *Chronicle* stops. In other words Sigebert assumes access to that work, just as he continues (in a series of modified forms) the annual enumeration of parallel regnal chronologies after the pattern of Eusebius' *Canones.* The work is prefaced by accounts of the northern peoples: the French ('our own people'), the British, the Vandals, the Lombards, Goths, Huns; that is, he puts the reader in the picture as it had emerged after the invasions and after the end of the Jerome epitome. These introductory passages are derived from the proper authorities more or less verbatim. Thus the account of the early Frankish rulers comes from the *Gesta Regum Francorum,* an early eighth-century compilation (which abridges part of Gregory of Tours), the *History Miscella* (a sixth century epitome), the annals which go under the name Fredegarius,[20] and Prosper of Aquitaine, who wrote an *Epitoma Chronicon* early in the fifth century. For early British history Sigebert quotes and paraphrases Bede; for the Vandals his text is Jordanes or Jornandes, *Romana et Getica,* an indifferent compilation of the mid-sixth century. For the early Lombards Sigebert turns to Paul the Deacon, the author of a *Historia Langobardorum* which was finished at the abbey of Monte Cassino in 787; this is a longer and somewhat more stylishly written compilation than the others mentioned. [21] And so on for the Lombards and the Huns.

I have catalogued the sources copied by Sigebert in his prefatory pages (all of them, it may be added, compilations similar in structure to his own — on which a further word below),[22] because it must stand for his procedure throughout his *Chronicle* until, in the mid-eleventh century, he reaches his own day and can regularly supply information from direct knowledge, occasionally also from accounts derived from witnesses older than himself. All in all Bethmann identified quotations from forty-seven narrative sources and from the lives of more than a dozen saints. These earlier writers are not digested. They are reproduced, sometimes a little edited; sometimes a little misunderstood, with resulting errors; very rarely conflated or digested, which is the modern process of the writer of elementary manuals and which we shall

occasionally see in the ampler chronicles of the thirteenth and
fourteenth centuries. When Sigebert finds an annalist who is
useful to him, then he sticks to him for a few years at a time,
but most annals are composed like mosaics, of brief excerpts.
Here is an example, chosen because each entry is short:

896   A sentence from the Metz annals; two sentences from
      the Saint-Vaast annals.
897   A sentence based on Liudprand's *Chronicon.*
898   Two sentences derived from Liudprand.
899   A sentence from the Saint-Vaast annals. Another
      from the Metz annals.

And so it goes on, occasionally an annal forming a lengthy
paragraph, as that for 900, when Sigebert retells (from
Liudprand) the story of Pope Formosus. But in most cases
Sigebert drastically abbreviates his source, though he does not
criticise it. This conciseness, this policy of stripping each entry
to a bare assertion, is even practised in the later part of his
Chronicle when the writer might have written much more
extended notices of the events of his own day. The entries for
1100-04 and 1107-10 are shorter by far than those for the
fourth and fifth centuries. The annal for 1104 reads simply:
'Crusaders take the town of Acre.' The annals for 1105 and
1106 are inflated by extracts from contemporary documents
and the last entry of all, that for 1111, is an extended record of
the famous 'reconciliation' of *regnum* and *sacerdotium* of
1110-11, when the Emperor Henry V compelled the pope to
surrender by sheer force. (Sigebert must have died thinking
that the Investiture Contest was over, whereas the ultimate
compromise was not reached until 1122.) In fact the
atmosphere of the early Easter-table entry is preserved
throughout and that Sigebert was highly conscious of this is
shown by the entry under the year 1063:

This year the great cycle of 532 years, containing 28
nineteen-year cycles which are absolutely essential to the
theory on which the date of Easter is calculated, came to an
end, having revolved from age to age back to itself without
error.

The regular brevity of Sigebert doubtless helped to make

him a popular chronicler. His editor Bethmann reckoned that over fifty subsequent writers took material from it, mostly directly, and Bethmann identified at least thirty continuators, that is writers of chronicles who used the narrative of Sigebert down to 1111 as their point of departure: 'a greater number than was provoked by any other chronicler except Martinus Polonus'.[23] Over 60 manuscripts of Sigebert's work are known to have existed and of these 44 have survived.

It would be possible to produce many works similar in construction and aim. Many are discussed in the surveys (such as those by Wattenbach and Molinier) which deal with the sources of medieval history. All would display a basis in annals, originating in Easter table material, reworking earlier entries to the point at which the compiler himself began to write of events with which he was contemporary. There are scores and scores of writers, nearly all at work in monasteries and many whose names we do not know. Just as Easter was celebrated solemnly, so by the twelfth century the great religious houses clearly regarded a chronicle as almost as important as the Easter table from which such compilations had arisen in the first place. To this sense of occasion we must also add a less reputable motive. By the twelfth century we have entered in Western Europe an era of written documents. It was no longer sufficient merely to affirm past transactions, especially those involving transfer of property; they had to be vouched for by documents. This led to many property-holders buying confirmation of their rights from higher authority. It also led to forged charters, in which conveyance of land and rights which had taken place earlier, sometimes centuries earlier, were provided with the appropriate documentation. (Sometimes such fabrications were doubtless totally dishonest attempts to obtain property by trickery; more often they were panicky responses to an altered view of law and, though technically forged, recorded perfectly genuine transactions.) Great churches in particular treated such records with intense reverence. They were sometimes copied out and bound up with service books. More often monasteries assembled their title deeds in collections called cartularies. These documents were normally arranged in chronological order. They could and sometimes did lead to narratives in which the documents were embedded. Two celebrated instances from twelfth-century England are the chronicle from Abingdon and the *Historia Eliensis*.[24] Such collections of charters forming a part of a narrative are found everywhere and, quite apart from the question of explaining or defending ancient territorial and other privileges, it was a fine thing to transcribe the rotund Latin in which kings or emperors had their diplomas composed. Such documents lent solemnity to the chroniclers' pages and will be found in the ampler narratives of a later age, such as the extended and mature chronicles discussed in the following chapter.

It would, however, be a mistake to leave the reader with the impression that narrative history down to the twelfth century invariably took the form of annals strictly conditioned by an Easter table framework. In the lively centuries which we call Dark and in the early Middle Ages we have abundant literary activity. It was restricted largely to clergy, especially to the regular clergy, for society as a whole was unlettered. But it contained all manner of adventurous intellectuals and two movements have been described as 'Renaissances' — the Carolingian and the Twelfth Century.[25] One example of an historian of the Carolingian Renaissance has come before us in the person of Einhard. An example of an historian from the Twelfth Century Renaissance imposes himself. He is Otto of Freising. Charles the Great's biographer had looked back for inspiration to the classical Roman historian Suetonius, who was to be admired and emulated in the twelfth century and later, as we shall see.[26] Otto of Freising was a much more unusual writer: he took his lead from St Augustine's *City of God* and was virtually the only medieval historian to do so.

Of course many medieval chronicles, based on Eusebius-Jerome and the Bible, began with the Creation. Many began with the Incarnation, as was natural with the Paschal annals and the use of the Year of Grace. All historical compilations of the Medieval west with pretensions to completeness accept the week of Creation as a pattern of God's disposition of time. The first five ages[27] usher in the sixth, with Christ's birth. Beyond lay the seventh age, or the eternal Sabbath. All of this was perfectly well-known, so well-known, indeed, that the pattern is often either taken for granted, or reference to it is perfunctory. Similarly, in general terms the chronicler was gratified when God rewarded the righteous and punished the wicked; occasionally God was observed to be doing that, although often his purposes were veiled in behaviour which seemed the very opposite. Hence all historians in the Middle Ages who provided us with prefatory remarks about their reason for writing almost without exception repeat the classical commonplaces that history is a preparation for life, that it shows the reader what good deeds to admire, what bad deeds to avoid. And of course practically all writers protest their unworthiness for the task. Otto of Freising does all these things. He writes:

> ... that the devout reader may observe what is to be avoided in mundane affairs by reason of the countless miseries wrought by their unstable character ...
>
> Nor do I think that I shall be justly criticised if, coming after such great men — men so wise and so eloquent [he is thinking of Augustine and Orosius] — I shall presume in spite of my ignorance to write, since I have both epitomised those things of which they themselves spoke so profusely and at length and have detailed, in however rude a style, the deeds which have been performed by citizens of the world since their time ...[28]

And so on. His devotion excuses his ignorance, he adds; he lacks 'proper training'. All of this is sheer window-dressing, a proper display of polite literature and polite self-depreciation. Otto's significance for us is due in fact to his being not only of royal blood but one of the best educated and learned men of his day. And above all the only historian who took Augustine really seriously.

Otto was born about 1114, his father being the margrave of Austria, his mother the daughter of Emperor Henry V; his brother married into the Greek imperial family. Otto was related to nearly everyone who mattered in Europe and, since he was the fifth son and destined for the Church, he was given the best education available. He was sent to Paris with a suitable retinue of sober young men. When he finished there,

probably in 1133, he became a Cistercian monk and soon after
wards bishop of Freising. In 1144 he accompanied his half
brother, the Emperor Conrad III, on the second crusade. H
died in 1158. His two historical works are really linked. Th
Chronicle or *The Two Cities* is a universal history running dow
to 1146. The *Deeds of Frederick I* overlaps the seventh book o
the *Chronicle* and covers the emperor's reign down to 1156.

The Paris where Otto studied was a stimulating place. It wa
the Paris where Abelard was teaching, along with othe
celebrated masters. His fellow pupils included John o
Salisbury, who also wrote some history.[29] At first a sort o
'humanism' characterised French scholarship, especially unde
the influence of the school at Chartres. But a university wa
growing up in Paris and the works of Aristotle, translated int
Latin, were revolutionising speculation, not least speculatio
regarding the nature of society and political obligation. Slowl
but surely an interpretation was to gain favour which radicall
challenged both Augustine's predestinarianism and his atti
tude to history. It is true that Augustine did not deny to Caesa
the things that were Caesar's; and he accepted that mar
developed a society based on the family. Nevertheless the *Cit*
of God dismissed the history of the earthly city as of littl
concern. If Augustine prompted Orosius to compile a survey o
earthly history it had a polemical end: to dispose of th
argument that Rome's disasters were due to Rome's adoptio
of Christianity. The chronicles we have touched on — th
Anglo-Saxon Chronicle, Sigebert's (and the scores of other
represented by these two works) — have none of this. The Pari
of Otto was moving away from it. It is therefore a surprise to
find Otto's *Two Cities* applying Augustine's views so thor
oughly. His work is based on a division in Nature which goe
back to the Creation:

> This is the city of God, the heavenly Jerusalem, for whicl
> the children of God sigh while they are set in this land o
> sojourn ... For, in as much as there are two cities — th
> one of time, the other of eternity; the one of the earth
> earthly, the other of heaven, heavenly; the one of the devil
> the other of Christ — ecclesiastical writers have declared
> that the former is Babylon, the latter Jerusalem.[30]

His work is to 'display the miseries of Babylon and also the glory of the Kingdom of Christ to which the citizens of Jerusalem are to look forward with hope'.[31] He does not really attempt to deny the relevance of history, of time, of the earth. His story is of miseries but these are usually perfectly explicable in terms of punishment of folly or sin; and optimism occasionally bursts out, especially when he leaves the epitomising of earlier authors and deals with his own day.[32] the kingdom of Christ is saved up for the apocalyptic eighth and final book, where he gathers all the evidence his well-stocked mind can find for an actual impression of heaven, a picture of Jerusalem the Golden. More than most chroniclers Otto stresses calamities; more than most he takes great trouble with his style; and his narrative is embedded in a self-consciously eschatological view of history. But in the last resort the bulk of it is a fairly conventional world chronicle, based on all the familiar authorities, who are transcribed or paraphrased as is most convenient. We must not exaggerate Otto's uniqueness.

Another characteristic form of historical writing at this time is the biography or group of biographies. As already noted, the saint's life was a much cultivated aspect of literature and there can be no doubt that it influenced biography in general. Some bishops were saints and rather more abbots, so that lives of the bishops of a town or of the abbots of a monastery might cross from biography to hagiography; a few later popes indeed became saints, although I count only five so regarded out of the 59 who reigned between 900 and 1200.[33] There were even a few secular rulers who were revered as saints. Such saints' lives were not historical in intention and so I do not discuss them here, however important some of them are as sources for modern historians; one thinks of St Godric of Finchale and the glimpse we get from his life of a merchant about 1100; one remembers the prominence of Thomas Becket in the public affairs of England and the Continent in the mid-twelfth century and the score of lives of him written everywhere from Italy to Iceland. But the pattern of the ideal saint's life can be readily applied to the story of prominent people who are not at all saintly. The saint as a child was often either at odds with his family who had secular ambitions for him which conflicted with his instinctive vocation or (and perhaps this was commoner) he had had an unregenerate youth, marred by moral turpitude as well sometimes by intellectual instability. Then came his adoption of a life of holiness, often following on a vision or direct communion with God or the Virgin. The holy man was now exposed to persecution and encountered, sometimes deliberately, temptation of all kinds. These he survived to the point at which he died and became the object of veneration.[34] How well such a pattern could be mirrored in the life of a prince! As a young man, the focus of resistance to his father the king, he is rebellious. As a ruler himself, he has his tribulations. He may survive them and, in acts of piety during his life and others embodied in his will, die as a model of the good governor. Moreover, the patterns offered by the saint's life encouraged writers to modify, if not to abandon, a strictly annalistic arrangement of their material in favour of argued episodes.

Just as there exist a bewildering multiplicity of annals and chronicles, so there are a largish number of works which are basically biographical and it is hard to select typical examples. There are continuing enterprises such as the *Liber Pontificalis*, which recorded briefly the lives of the popes; begun, it seems, in the sixth century it was to be continued from time to time down to the fifteenth and exercised a steady influence on the composition of similar collections of ecclesiastical biographies.[35] Or there are a few highly idiosyncratic works which are most enjoyable to read and are therefore fairly familiar. I am thinking, for instance, of the autobiography of Guibert, abbot of Nogent, who ended his days there in 1125, and of the Life of Abbot Samson or the *Chronicle* by Jocelyn of Brakelond, completed about 1203.[36] Two works which reflect more typical hagiography and were to be of more immediate relevance in subsequent historical writing are the Life of Louis VI by Suger, abbot of Saint-Denis, and the *Lives of the Kings of England* by William of Malmesbury.

The *Vita Ludovici grossi regis* certainly owes its shape and execution in some measure to the instinct prompting men to compose lives of saints.[37] Saint-Denis was the centre of the cult of the Capetian kings. Passages from the *Life of Louis the Fat* were read in the church on the anniversary of his death. Suger had been a monk there, and then an able assistant to the king before his election in 1122 as abbot, an election which was to consolidate the status of the church, lead to a Gothic style of architecture developing in north France, and above all encourage an alliance between the French king and his clergy from which the monarchy was to benefit greatly. Suger's biography of the king, written within a few years of Louis' death in 1137, contributed to the achievement of this last part of the programme. He makes it clear from the beginning of the *Life* that he is to 'celebrate the king and mourn his death', accepting also that one must be charitable not only to one's enemies but also to one's friends, that is to say that he will gloss over the king's faults.

So we shall acquit ourselves of a double debt ... of gratitude and love, and raise to him [in Horace's words] 'a monument more lasting than bronze' by writing of his devotion for the churches of God and his excellent government of the realm. The vicissitudes of Time will never obliterate the memory of these things, nor for such benefits shall ever cease the prayers of the Church from generation unto generation.[38]

And the *Life* concludes with the prayer that the Redeemer will place the king amidst the saints.[39]

Yet these aspirations of a religious kind, these sentiments bred of dependence and friendship, do not prevent Suger from writing a vivid and shrewd account of a remarkable reign, in which the French king began the long process of mastering his own domain and thus affording his successors a basis from which they were to master France. 'As opportunity offered, he administered wisely, bringing the disobedient to heel, and either garrisoning himself or raising to the ground hostile castles.'[40]

The most celebrated instance of this policy being applied was the long-drawn-out account of the destruction by the king of Thomas de Marle, *homo perditissimus*,[41] but over half the book is devoted to similar chastisement of perfidious vassals. Yet the larger scene is forgotten by neither Louis nor

his biographer. And the larger scene is France. The country
was threatened not only by internal dissensions, but by the
attacks and alliances of powerful and unscrupulous neighbouring princes. Here, too, Louis' vigilance was rewarded. 'In
modern times', writes Suger of the year 1124, 'or indeed as
long ago as one can look, France never had a more glorious
moment': she had frustrated the German emperor and the
English king.[42] Arranged in topical rather than annalistic
form, it was no accident that the *Life* was to form an integral
part of the national history of France.[43]

The book composed by another Benedictine monk,
William, who took his name from the monastery at
Malmesbury, is quite different. The *Gesta Regum Anglorum*
with its somewhat polemical supplement, the *Historia Novella*,
together form a continuous narrative of English history from
the coming of the Saxons down to 1142.[44] William of
Malmesbury, although presumably well-connected and certainly a friend of great men, was not a statesman but a scholar
of remarkable range — saints' lives, biblical exegesis, the *Gesta
Pontificum*. His history of England is remarkable on several
grounds. It has a degree of critical awareness greater than that
found in most contemporary chroniclers while yet displaying
relish for legendary material: it was (despite this, or because of
it?) relatively popular, some twenty odd manuscripts surviving:
and it proceeded by kings' reigns, a scheme which did not
catch on in England until the sixteenth century but which then
dominated English historiography down to our own day. The
model for a royal life was not difficult to come by. Clearly
hagiographical influences and lists of bishops (such as those
elaborated by Malmesbury himself in his *Gesta Pontificum*)
offered useful patterns, and some isolated royal lives already
existed (for Alfred and for Edward the Confessor). But, as
Giles pointed out in the introduction to his translation, the
clearest inspiration was Suetonius[45] which, as we have seen,
had prompted Einhard. Einhard, however, had written the life
of only one prince. Malmesbury, like Suetonius, undertook a
series, and this is particularly evident in the treatment of the
period 1087-1125 (William II and Henry I).

The originality of Malmesbury in subjecting his sources to
critical scrutiny is even more unusual than his division of his

narrative into kings' reigns.[46] His principal care was bestowed on the history of England down to William I's reign and he deliberately avoided annalistic narration. His famous disclaimer (II, iv) is worth quoting for such an observation would not be heard again in England until the Renaissance.

> To trace in detail the mazy labyrinth of his [Alfred's] labours was never my design; because a recapitulation of his exploits in their exact order of time would occasion some confusion to the reader. For, to relate how a hostile army, driven by himself or his generals from one part of a district, retreated to another ... 'to go round the whole island with him', might to some seem the height of folly: consequently I shall touch on all points summarily.[47]

He named his sources, whose value he shrewdly estimated, and in the prologue to book II he explained his devotion to ethics as taught by history (the ancient Ciceronian principle which, as we have observed, was never forgotten); and in the same place he explained that at his own expense he had acquired the works of 'some historians of foreign nations' and then 'studiously sought for chronicles far and near' bearing on British history. He is even prepared (with an apology) to sully his stylish pages with the barbarous names of the genealogies of the English kings — because St Luke recorded the genealogy of Jesus (II; ii).

Again we must not exaggerate. Malmesbury's 'research' is not what would be regarded as such by historical scholars from the Renaissance onwards. He may have eschewed the pattern of the Easter table for the early and interesting part of his work, but he reverted to the annal when he was truly coping with contemporary history in the *Historia Novella*. He structured early English history with great sophistication but as he progressed into the eleventh century (book III) the narrative was frequently that of a conventional world history, with digressions (as he occasionally called them) on, for instance, popes such as Gregory VII, heretics like Berengar of Tours, exciting tales such as the one about the two priests seduced by profane literature, one of whom returns from Hell to warn the other to become a monk. In book IV, ii a long excursus dealt with the First Crusade, providing also a pilgrim's guide to Rome,

lists of emperors and patriarchs of Jerusalem. Now the
Gregorian reform did have momentous consequences for
England as for Europe at large: but the significance of the
pontificate was totally ignored by Malmesbury. And it is only
at the end of the long account of the First Crusade that the
very minor consequences it had for England (Duke Robert of
Normany) are alluded to. Most conventional chronicles get
more interesting as they approach their own day. In broad
terms the opposite seems to be the case with Malmesbury, and
it is interesting to observe in the preface to book III his remark
on the need for charity towards William I, which echo the
caution, or the charitable suspension of criticism, which we
have observed in Suger. Having explained that he is himself
descended from both the English and Norman races he
deprecates the exaggeration to which racial bias has led
discussion of King William. So far so good. But he himself
proposes a middle course 'whereby I shall willingly and
carefully relate such anecdotes of him as may be a matter of
incitement to the indolent, or of example to the enterprising
useful to the present age, and pleasing to posterity'.[48] Rather
a come-down.

R.L. Poole sought to emphasise the difference between the
medieval *historian* and the medieval *chronicler* in his
influential little book, *Chronicles and Annals* (1926), on which
all subsequent discussions of medieval English historiography
depend. He based his generalizations on a passage from a third
rate annalist called Gervase, a Canterbury monk most of whose
work had been lost by posterity for reasons which are all too
obvious.[49] Gervase's literary diffidence, his employment of
the *topos* we have so frequently encountered, led him to
compare his limping offering with that of the prose
masterpieces of historians writing in the grand manner. Yet
this is, the moment one comes to reflect, a generalization
which had no application in the twelfth century. Nor can one
discern a difference between an ample annal and a meagre
chronicle. Bits of Malmesbury are not annalistic; often later
bits are, but are more thickly peppered with quotations from
his favourite Latin authors and were doubtless admired as
corresponding to what Cicero might have recognised as
history. The hierarchy of historical composition had been

clearly arranged about 600 by Isidore of Seville. It ran up from a note on the events of a day, through monthly summaries (or calendars), to annals and then history, which for Isidore comprised the survey of longer periods than a year. It was displayed carefully in books and dealt essentially with the present.[50] I do not know that Gervase is doing much more than elaborating this point in language as grandiloquent as he can manage, the implications being: 'I could perhaps have written history, but I am going to be a humble compiler.'

When he is introducing the 'first writers of history' Isidore mentions 'Dares Phrygius' who 'wrote a history of the Greeks and Trojans'. This survived in a fifth-century Latin version and was perhaps composed in that form at about that time, put together from scraps of older material. This chapter must conclude by referring to some additions to the materials available to the medieval chronicler derived from sources which we have not hitherto considered: mythical elements destined to have all sorts of developments quite apart from their function in history books.

Dares of Phrygia and Dictys of Crete (likewise only available in a Latin version, perhaps of somewhat earlier date than Dares) provided matter from which later writers could easily weave into their national traditions the Trojan origin of their first princes. In France this matter was first absorbed with 'Fredegar's' chronicle, whence it was to reach later compilations and later still the official history, to which I shall refer in the next chapter. Out of all this nonsense was to come Francus, the eponymous founder of the race of Franks.[51] Francus was to debase and confuse French history until the eighteenth century; Ronsard's worst poem is called 'Le Franciade'. But no European country was exempt from the bane of Troy, the 'Troy saga'. In Britain, the Trojan was called Brutus and he was naturalised, one might say, by Geoffrey of Monmouth who made him the substantial founder of the Britain about whose 'Kings' he was to write his 'History'. The Arthurian legends which Geoffrey wove (1138-9) into his 'History' were to be a subject of romance in England, France, Italy and everywhere else. And romance is the territory properly occupied by

Francus and Brutus, even if they are absorbed into chronicles
such as that late-medieval best-seller called *The Brut*.[52] I
Ronsard was to produce a stuffy *Franciade*, Spenser was to
produce a splendid *Fairie Queene*.

Let us remember the audience contained not only learned
clerks, but bored gentlemen, whose evenings needed the
entertainment afforded by the stories of the past, where great
names, remembered from childhood, could echo round the
hall after dinner. And the gentleman had servants. To this sort
of public the poets adjusted the Arthurian material
elaborating the heroic and the chivalrous. In similar fashion
the Trojan legends were enshrined in verse, the greatest work
being Benoît de Sainte Maure's *Roman de Troie*, written
about 1150. And historical memoirs contributed to the many
verse 'Chansons de geste' written down at this time and a little
earlier. They are about 'deeds' and there is no doubt that the
barons and their retainers who listened to the minstrel
chanting the heroic tales believed them to be recounting *res
gesta*, the events of the past. Charlemagne, Roland and Oliver
in the *Chanson de Roland*, Rodrigo in the Spanish *Poema de
mio Cid*, were indeed real people although their *gestes* were
raised to superhuman proportions; indeed El Cid died in 1099
(at about the time the Song of Roland was being written) and
the *chanson de geste* about him was written only some fifty
years after his death. Many of the stories told in these poems
were, we may feel, patently fictitious. But the fact remains
that Troy had existed and had fallen, that Hengist and Horsa
were invaders whom the valiant Britons resisted, that
Charlemagne had indeed crossed the Pyrenees with an army
All these heroic poems and scores more, for example the
Nibelungenlied, had the glow of epic ideal and the sharpness
of fact.

Many of these poems must have had an oral existence before
being written down. Northern Europe by the twelfth century
was also recording another variety of vernacular oral history —
the saga. The saga is prose, and it is the product of Norwegian
Danish and above all Icelandic historical experience. Many of
the sagas are authenticated history. All purport to be the
descriptions of actual events. Here again a long period of oral
transmission — in verse, later in prose — preceded the

recording of the tales in the twelfth and thirteenth centuries. These prose sagas are, even more than verse epics like the *Chanson de Roland*, based on true happenings and the *Heimskringla* (by Snorri Sturluson, written in the early thirteenth century) is a kind of biographical account of the kings of Norway down to the 1170s. This shares with the verse epics of France and Germany vivid dialogue and massively heroic actions; it is romance often and legend; but it becomes historical wherever the sources permit. It has been argued that behind the urge to recount heroic tales of kings and ancestors lies the emotional needs of emigrants. The massive and centuries-long shift of peoples which began in the late Empire and continued spasmodically until the eleventh century — or even longer, if we include the Crusades — produced a hunger for the old times, the old places and the old loyalties, satisfied by bards, later transmitted in tales and 'histories' naturally tending towards fiction.[53]

This literature in the vernacular, the *chansons de geste* and the sagas, represents a tendency for northern Europe to merge history with entertainment and perhaps partly accounts for the vast output of chronicles in the eleventh, twelfth and thirteenth centuries. In the broadest terms it is true to say that Mediterranean areas (apart from Byzantium) during this period are relatively poor in narrative historians, relatively rich in documents. The reverse is true of northern France, England, Germany and Scandinavia. There in both vernacular and Latin, history flourished. From the Easter table to the elaborations of Malmesbury and Suger is a major development. Just as it was reaching fulfilment some 'historical' material was entering the mists of magic and romance. This was to happen on many later occasions, when the process was more self-conscious than it was in the twelfth century (one thinks of Shakespeare's 'Histories', of Walter Scott's novels). Yet even on this early occasion, there were not wanting some observers who were aware of what was happening.

Baldwin VIII, in the court of Flanders (d. 1195), procured for himself an account in Latin prose of the story of Charlemagne. Composed with the aim of promoting the cult of St James of Compostella, this work purported to be the work

of Charlemagne's friend and counsellor, Archbishop Turpin;
it is nowadays referred to as the 'Pseudo-Turpin'. On his death
the Latin volume was inherited by Baldwin's sister, Yolande,
and her husband, Hugh of St Pol. They commissioned a
translation into French prose and the translator explained why
it had to be prose: 'No rhymed stories can be true. What such
tales say is all lies because they know nothing save by
hear-say.'[54] This and other vernacular versions of the
Pseudo-Turpin belong 'at once to hagiography, history and
fiction' and 'it directed prose towards historiography properly
so called and towards romance'.[55] It is as well to remember
the close links between history and story, between fact and
fiction. They are not readily disposed of.

4 Medieval Historiography at its Prime: from the Thirteenth to the Fifteenth Centuries

In the previous chapter we have identified the ingredients of the chronicle which was to reach its apogee in the later Middle Ages. These ingredients were a summary of world history drawn from the Bible, ancient history as epitomised by Eusebius-Jerome, Orosius, and then the material accumulated by Easter tables. This narrative from the Incarnation, that is the Sixth Age, was dated from that event and it led to elaborate summaries such as that of Sigebert of Gembloux. The abbreviated review given in previous pages omits, of course, those narratives of an exceptional kind, such as Bede, Gregory of Tours, Einhard. And we should remember that when one says 'the Bible', by the end of the twelfth century, although the Scriptures naturally retained their place in the liturgy, scholars turned regularly to the *Historia Scholastica* of Peter Comestor, a Frenchman who produced a substantial paraphrase of the Bible including much of the Apocrypha from the Creation to the end of the Gospels; the summaries and quotations were often accompanied by allegorical comments.[1]

This process of editing or copying earlier material was not unknown in antiquity and it was certainly demonstrated by Orosius and later by Cassiodorus. In the thirteenth century it continues as the main method of assembling general histories. Just as in the early centuries discussed above we had to select a handful from the hundreds of narratives great and small which were then composed, so in the heyday of the chronicle an even more rigorous selection must be made. Judged solely by their subsequent influence Vincent of Beauvais and Martinus Polonus deserve to be mentioned.

Both men were members of the newly formed (1220) Dominican Order of friars dedicated to combating heresy, committed to scholarship and consequently of great importance in the northern universities (especially Paris) where theology reigned as queen of the sciences.

Many members of the Order compiled manuals of various kinds. Vincent assembled an encyclopaedic 'mirror' — the *Speculum maius*. This was in three parts, one providing all doctrinal knowledge, one all information about Nature, and one a 'Speculum historiale', an anthology of extracts covering world history to the middle of the thirteenth century. He himself prepared an abridgement and both in its original form and in its abridged form it greatly inspired and informed later ages. In itself it had few merits. Its diffusion, the authority conveyed in it by its author's intimacy with Louis IX and the sponsorship of the Dominicans, all these factors made it one of the most widely known of medieval histories; there is no complete critical edition and it has not been properly analysed.[2]

Martin the Pole, or of Troppau in Silesia where he was born, worked in Bohemia, then at the papal court and died in 1279 as bishop of Gnesen. His *Chronicon pontificum et imperatorum* is poor and arid compared with Vincent. Perhaps for that very reason it had admirers. It survives in many manuscripts. It was translated into Czech, German, Italian and French. His work was from the beginning especially admired in Germany, not least because he adopted the succession of four empires, culminating in the Roman (i.e. the German).[3]

Vincent and Martin are indicative of one aspect of popular taste — the traditional desire among the learned for vast surveys and brief compendia. Such tastes were to outlast the Middle Ages. Other historical works were called for, however, and in this chapter we shall consider successively the great 'national' chronicles of France and England, the emergence of thematic narratives (crusades and chivalry), and the rise of a new form of annal in the town chronicle.

'Nations' is, of course, a misnomer for England and France in the thirteenth and fourteenth centuries. They were to try to destroy not only each other in the later Middle Ages but each nearly destroyed itself by civil wars — not only those of the fifteenth century, but those in the sixteenth and in the seventeenth centuries. Yet at the end of the fifteenth century, monarchy and the instruments of central government were stronger than they had been before the Hundred Years War, the Armagnac-Burgundian struggle and the Wars of the Roses — strong enough, in fact, to withstand those later upheavals which have been mentioned. Other areas of Europe had different fates. Italy and Germany were not to become unified states until the nineteenth century. Martinus Polonus, with his abstract narrative of popes and emperors, was obviously more relevant in those areas then he was elsewhere.

France and England as frameworks and subject matter for historical composition did not wait for the thirteenth century. The pages of Suger are devoted to French history, and so for an earlier period are those of Gregory of Tours. For England, even if Bede is excluded as writing in the Orosian tradition (though much better than Orosius), we have encountered the *Anglo-Saxon Chronicle*, the *Gesta Regum* of Malmesbury, not to mention Brutus and Arthur in the *History of the Kings of Britain* by Geoffrey of Monmouth. Yet none of these have the patriotic bite to them which we shall encounter in the great chronicle of France and the chroniclers working at St Albans. Such a tone could be savoured in very many other French and English writers of the later medieval period, but the bulk and quasi-official status of these two groups of compilers makes it appropriate to consider their work.

The *Grandes Chroniques de France* was in the end more than merely quasi-official; it was a formal expression of the Capetian sense of the French past. It began hesitantly in the twelfth century at Saint-Denis, the royal church *par excellence*. And the earliest elaborate component was the life of Louis the Fat by Abbot Suger.[4] The abbey was the first monument of Gothic architecture in France. It was appropriate that it should provide the most important monument to the greatness of the dynasty. By the end of the twelfth century the monks had collected a whole range of historical materials and, equally significant, a reputation among writers for authority and authenticity where the events of French history were concerned: 'un véritable laboratoire historique', says Molinier. A whole series of histories in Latin continued the story: Rigord, Primat, Guillaume de Nangis, the anonymous monk known as the 'Religieux de Saint-Denis', Jean Chartier. All of these composed lives of particular kings, histories of France under the monarchs from Louis VI to Charles VII — covering the period from the mid-eleventh century to the mid-fifteenth century. The pattern is not as uniform as this stark summary might indicate. Many of the known authors derive much of their matter from other notes and chronicles made in the abbey. There is a wide variety in the originality as well as the style of the various parts. Nor did the work proceed without gaps. These were filled in by various monks as best they could once the tradition of continuous narration was established: the early history of the monarchy was not filled in until the middle of the thirteenth century; several more or less unidentified hands patched together the short reigns between 1314 and 1350. And we must not forget that much other literary and historical work went on at Saint-Denis alongside the great chronicle of the kings. Guillaume de Nangis, for example, wrote a full scale general *Chronicon*, based on Sigebert de Gembloux and his continuators. And many other compilers were at work at the abbey in the thirteenth and fourteenth centuries.

The Latin chronicles assembled at Saint-Denis were, however, only the raw material for the French work known as the *Grandes Chroniques* which, being in the vernacular, had a more extensive public and dominated the historiographical tradition in France down to the sixteenth century and even beyond. The first French version associated with Saint-Denis was by the monk Primat, author of the chronicle (a continuation of Vincent of Beauvais) utilised in the Latin chronicles as mentioned above. In 1274 Primat dedicated to Philip III a long French history based on the Latin series but supplemented where necessary from other sources. This went down to the reign of Philip V. Later writers took the French chronicle down to Louis XI, and until 1450 a Latin and a

French version existed side by side. Then, at the year 1450, Jean Chartier ended his Latin chronicle, although he completed his French chronicle down to Charles VII's death in 1461. By this time the monastic chronicler charged with the compilation was remunerated by the Crown, a kind of primitive historiographer royal. For some time after Chartier, monks figure on treasury payments, but so far no official history from the later fifteenth century has been identified with Saint-Denis.

Innumerable manuscript copies were made of the *Grandes Chroniques*. They had imitators; stage by stage they were continued at some other centres and for other than royal patrons. When printing arrived the national story was early published (1493) and there were many subsequent editions under various guises — *Mer des histoires, Fleurs d'histoire* and so on. In this way generations of literate Frenchmen came to be indoctrinated not only with the historical history of France — slanted, it must be admitted, in favour of the French on all occasions when national prestige seemed to have been at stake — but also with the legendary history of France. The Trojan origin of Francus was more thoroughly implanted in French consciousness, we may guess, than the Trojan origin of the Romans was in ancient Italy. It did not produce an *Aeneid* in compensation. On the contrary, to criticise the myth could become lèse-majesté and when Nicolas Fréret addressed the Académie des Inscriptions, on his admission in 1714, on the origin of the French, his enemy Vertot secured the imprisonment of the young scholar in the Bastille because he had denied the historicity of Francus. No other European country was so bound together by an historical tradition as France was and the main instrument in effecting this was a collection of Latin chronicles, many of them pretty mediocre, turned into a continuous French narrative.

Compared with this the English 'school' at St Albans was less impressive, if usually composed of better contemporary historians. It also was utterly different, in being composed exclusively of Latin writers, in being extremely independent and critical of royal policy from time to time, and in the extraordinary amplitude of its treatment of early thirteenth-century history. Nevertheless the chroniclers of the abbey, at work at

least from the beginning of the thirteenth century to the
middle of the fifteenth, produced a narrative, beginning with
the Creation, of comparable size to the *Grandes Chroniques*.[5]

The first certain chronicler of St Albans was the monk
Roger Wendover, about whom little is known. He began to
write from direct observation (i.e. not depending on other
authorities) towards the end of John's reign, in 1214 or
thereabouts; he died in 1236. Until he reached 1214, and
especially down to the end of the twelfth century, Wendover's
work is a compilation of familiar form and there has been
much debate over the question whether he had a predecessor
at St Albans from whom this part of his *Flowers of History* was
derived. There is no proof of such a writer having been at
work, but in a rich and ancient house, with a large library,[6]
it would hardly have been surprising if a monk had put
together the familiar story from the familiar materials at some
date prior to Wendover's period of activity. At any rate, what
Wendover gives his reader is an annalistic survey of ample
dimensions, which aimed

> briefly to note the chief events of past times, and to give the
> image of our Saviour from the beginning, with the succession
> of certain kingdoms of the world and of their rulers, for the
> instruction of posterity and to aid the diligence of the
> studious hearer.

This preface adequately indicates the scope of Wendover's final
book, 'which treats briefly of the Old Testament, of the law of
God, through five ages of the world, unto the coming of the
Saviour'. In his second book, Wendover explains, he deals with
'the New Testament', commencing with the 'incarnation of
Christ'. In this there will be notices for 'every year, without
omitting one, down to our own times'.[7] The customary
Ciceronian defence of the historian should be noted in its by
now usual Christian guise: history enables men to be better
men; 'being admonished by past evils ... [they] may betake
themselves to humility and repentance, taking an example for
imitation from the good, shunning the ways of the perverse'.[8]

And off we move into extracts from Eusebius-Jerome,
Sigebert and the others. But in book ii we rapidly find the

emphasis falling on English history and then English sources predominate. Merlin and Arthur, Uther Pendragon, Guinevere and Modred come into the story from Geoffrey of Monmouth, the *Anglo-Saxon Chronicle* is an important authority and so, of course, is Bede. The entries of a general, non-British kind, are largely taken from Sigebert. A typical series of years runs like this:

A.D. 600 Theodoric reigns in France ... [from Sigebert]
A.D. 601 Pope Gregory sent a pall to Augustine ... [Bede]
A.D. 602 John, bishop of Constantinople, claimed to be universal patriarch ... [Sigebert]
A.D. 603 Augustine summoned a meeting of British (i.e. Celtic) bishops ... [Bede]

Obviously such an emphasis on English history — which is greater than can be simply demonstrated here, since the entries for England are habitually much longer and occur more frequently as time goes on — would not be found in book i, although we find there the Trojan material (Brut and so on) woven into the story and Caesar's invasion, which had already figured in Bede and the *Anglo-Saxon Chronicle*, is naturally emphasised. As Wendover reaches the twelfth century his narrative becomes much fuller and the stress on his own country becomes more pronounced (the story of the First Crusade is the last non-English episode treated in a substantial way). For the period from 1214 to 1236 Wendover's account is largely based on information acquired by him as a witness of events, well-placed in an aristocratic abbey one day's journey north of London, where news came quickly and important people often stayed. As a 'source' it is, of course, this portion of the *Flowers of History* which is used by historians of John's last years and for early years of Henry III. Wendover quotes a fair number of documents, including a text of Magna Carta.

When Wendover died Matthew Paris, who had probably been his assistant, became the chief historian in the abbey. His *Chronica majora* absorbed all of Wendover and went down to Paris's death in 1259. Paris's *Great Chronicle* absorbed Wendover, but in the process there was a good deal of the editorial adjustments which are a feature of this type of composition. In particular, Paris adds to Wendover's annals.

Sometimes the additions, which are significant for the period from about 1100 onwards, merely add a scrap of further information, sometimes a passage is rewritten to alter the emphasis, sometimes a document is quoted in fuller or more correct form. All the insertions Paris made become lengthier when he is revising Wendover's early thriteenth-century annals. From 1236 he writes an extremely lengthy series of yearly entries, with many documents quoted verbatim and others gathered in an appendix (the *liber additamentorum*). Although Paris's attention is frequently attracted to events in the papal curia and in France, although his interest in Frederick II is noteworthy, nevertheless the contemporary portion of the *Great Chronicle* concentrates overwhelmingly on the English scene — admittedly pretty exciting — and a good deal of attention is also devoted to Benedictine concerns and to St Albans itself.

Paris's persistent criticism of King John, Henry III, and the pope provide what little coherent argument his work has. Some have seen in this a deliberate 'constitutionalism', based on the lordly independence of a great monastic community. Some have felt that Paris's prejudices were simply based on a hatred of any administrative interference with his Order, his house, himself — especially taxation — and on the red-blooded loathing of a good Englishman for all foreigners.[9] The wide diffusion of Matthew's views or prejudices (which on second thoughts he sometimes toned down) was ensured by abstracts which he himself prepared (the *Historia Anglorum*, the *Flores historiarum* which for long went under the name of Matthew of Westminster, the *Abbreviatio* and others) and by the authority the St Albans chronicle had acquired in the later thirteenth century.[10]

Paris, somewhat bigoted, frequently dishonest in twisting the events and tampering with documents, careless as a copyist and as a supervisor of his scribes, was doubtless a not untypical monastic historian, although few intruded their personal likes and dislikes as much as he did. He was certainly admired by his brother monks and his *Great Chronicle* was continued, first of all to 1265, then (after a long interval) by Rishanger to 1323, and by Blaneford 1323-4 (or perhaps 1327 — the manuscript is defective). Another interval then occurs again and it is only in

and after about 1380 that Thomas Walsingham began to fill
the interval between 1327 and his own day. He did so in a
series of works — a *History of His Own Times* (1376-1392), a
Short History (1327-1422), and an epitome running from the
Creation to 1392. The parallels with Paris and Paris's
abridgements are obvious and Walsingham was conscious that
he was maintaining in this way an unbroken set of annuals.[11]
Walsingham was no Paris. His *Chronica majora* is relatively
brief compared with the oratorical and repetitious style of his
predecessor. One has the feeling that the impetus to compile
chronicles was growing weaker and indeed it was, and at other
abbeys besides St Albans. The composition of enormous Latin
annals, with related abbreviated versions, was no longer of
much interest to monks and not at all to the growing number
of laymen able to read English. Walsingham's work was
continued in an indifferent way down to 1440 when, after two
centuries, the annals stop. And not only the annals were
petrified by this date. The dozens of ancillary historical works
— memoranda, lives of the abbots, particular narratives such
as Paris's *Life of Offa*, or Walsingham's account of Norman
history (the pretentiously titled *Ypodigma Neustriae*) — these
all grind to a halt.

The contrasts between the *Grandes chroniques* and the St
Alban chronicles are evident enough and remain striking even
if we compare the Latin versions of the Saint-Denis chronicles
with the annals, large and small, which were put together at St
Albans. Most of the difference in tone must be attributed to
the irascible disposition of Matthew Paris, which coloured
his revision of Wendover and influenced Walsingham later on.
After all, Saint-Denis was a great Benedictine house and one to
whom the French kings owed homage (as counts of the Vexin)
and from whose monks they borrowed in time of war the
sacred oriflamme; Suger in his life of Louis VI does not forget
this.[12] In the Latin histories compiled at Saint-Denis there is
less royal propaganda than in the *Grandes chroniques*,
directed at a vernacular public which was steadily increasing
in size. And, although due attention was paid in the
Wendover-Paris *Chronica majora* to Brutus and Troy, as later
to King Arthur, this is balanced by substantial sections
recapitulating some of the main legends of pagan antiquity.

These last are discussed as 'fictions of the poets' (*de figmentis poetarum*) but they are there, and they remind us of the learned reader to whom to monastic chronicler was addressing himself.[13] Similarly Wendover began with Creation, while the vernacular *Grandes chroniques* began with the Trojan heroes.

The English-speaking public was catered for by a number of translations, often romantic, deriving ultimately from Geoffrey of Monmouth and more immediately from French verse chronicles. The most important group of those narratives, in considerable variety but with a common basis, went under the name of *Brut*, since they began (like the *Grandes chroniques*) with Troy and the conquests of Brutus, before becoming a mainly English history from the story of Arthur onwards. Translations of the *Brut* circulated from the 1330s and it was extensively copied, with appropriate continuations, until finally it reached print with Caxton's editions of *The Chronicles of England* in 1480.[14] It was through the *Brut*, through Trevisa's translation of Higden's scholarly *Polichronicon*, and the vernacular London chronicals that the English reader got his English history by the end of the fourteenth century. But before considering the town chronicle, there were other developments in the style and pattern of history writing in the later Middle Ages which must be discussed.

The histories dealing with crusading represent an historiographical theme which is circumscribed by an unfolding series of events as such and not determined by the chronology of the Seven Ages, or of a national epic (Francus and Brutus), or of the life of a king. It is also, despite the profoundly religious tone which crusading narratives acquired from the religious inspiration of the crusades themselves, in essence a secular, political theme. *Gesta dei per francos*, the conviction that the Moslems were wicked ('Christians are right, pagans are wrong', as the bard of the *Song of Roland* put it), the coincidence of crusading with the consciousness of the existence of Christendom — all of this cannot obscure the fact that the crusading narratives deal with tough and ambitious men, anxious for lands and titles in the Levant. In the early narratives there is, it is true, a certain apocalyptic spirit: 'The period was at hand of which the Lord Jesus every day spoke to the disciples ... If any man will come after me let him deny himself, and take up his cross, and follow me.' So begins the anonymous *Gesta Francorum*.[15] But the author is soon plunged in the detailed intrigues of the soldiers and the concentration on warfare and grabbing of lands and titles must have been gripping indeed to the warriors, their successors and the clerks who served them. Once established in Asia Minor the Latins found themselves part of a new political entity, wedged uncomfortably between the hostility of Byzantium and the pagan enemy in Egypt, from each of which the crusading states had been filched. This new world of war and diplomacy is described in the most elaborate of the narratives, the *History of Deeds done beyond the Sea*. This substantial book was written by William of Tyre, so called because he was made archbishop there in 1175. William had been born in Jerusalem about 1130 and was exceedingly well-educated at the universities of Paris and Bologna. His history, which in its literary allusions reflects his cultivated mind, begins with a rapid account of the Moslem conquests of Syria in the seventh century and proceeds quickly to the dominations of the Seljuq Turks and the First Crusade. Then he provides a detailed narrative down to his own death in 1184.[16] In general this is a straightforward chronicle, but a doom-laden tone is noticeable in the later sections of the book, where disasters are attributed to the corruption and unworthiness of the Christians and their leaders. And indeed some kind of an end was in sight for *Outremer*. In 1187 Saladin entered Jerusalem and the resulting crusade (the so-called third) failed to recover it.

The Fourth Crusade was even more exclusively an affair of gentlemen and merchants and it had its historian in a French nobleman, Geoffrey of Villehardouin. He was an important man, and his work is a vivid eyewitness account of the sordid episodes in which a large army of western soldiers, transported by Venetian ships and with the cognisance of Pope Innocent III, attacked Byzantine territory and finally in 1204 captured and sacked Constantinople itself, turning what was left of the

Empire into a colony, which was to shrink still further until another Greek dynasty again took control of the remnants in 1261. Villehardouin's narrative deals simply with the conquest of 1204, its immediate background and its immediate consequences. It has the urgent brevity but none of the redeeming naivety of the anonymous history of the First Crusade.[17]

Joinville wrote (or dictated) in French. His work was therefore directly accessible to the military men whose exploits he recounted. It was not the first time the deeds of the Franks were available in the vernacular. There had been a good many verse accounts, mingling the *chanson de geste* approach with the facts; the great work of William of Tyre had been translated and was very widely diffused — over twenty manuscripts of the French version having survived. And Villehardouin's contemporary, Robert de Clari, produced another (and less interesting) account in French of the capture of Constantinople. There is no doubt that this kind of military history was extremely popular in castles and courts — and details derived from these writings also entered the canon of the monastic chronicles of the twelfth and thirteenth centuries.

The Crusades, however, had virtually come to an end. From the thirteenth century only paid armies, and therefore small armies, were prevailed on to fight in the Levant. European sovereigns, who had intrigued in the Middle East during the Third Crusade, intrigued at home in the thirteenth century; by the fourteenth the literature of the crusade is a literature of propaganda, for the expeditions were small and ineffective. A new 'Turk' was moving ineluctably westwards. The Ottomans were to prove a more formidable aggressor than the Seljuqs. Even in the thirteenth century it was piracy and the protection of trade which was most evident in the activities of those (like the European Frederick II and Louis IX of France) who actually tried to support Christian interests actively; and a certain taste for the unusual, seen in Frederick II, was very evident in Louis XI's biographer Joinville, whose life of the king is a mixture of hagiography, shrewd political commentary and racy accounts of exotic peoples and places.[18] But the roll calls of baronial names are still there and the gentlemen of France, indeed of Western Europe, had clearly grown accustomed to reading about themselves and their ancestors.

I believe the habit thus formed lay behind the emergence of a
new genre of historical compositions, destined to have a longer
life than the chronicles of the crusades. In the fourteenth
century and once again in French, the deeds of the governing
classes were recorded in works which proved even more
popular than the earlier histories of Christian warfare. I refer
to the chivalrous historiography exemplified by Froissart and
his successors.

In fact Froissart was not the first of the line. He regarded
himself as continuing the work of Jean Le Bel, a canon of
Liège who died in 1370. Clergyman though he technically was,
Jean Le Bel was at home on the battlefield and fought in
Britain in 1327. His *Chronicle* covered his experiences as a
soldier and courtier and ran from 1326 to 1361. It was written
in good French prose and was neglected for long, we may
guess, because Froissart absorbed much of it in his own
narrative, literally copying Le Bel's text.[19] Jean Froissart was
also technically a clergyman. He was born at Valenciennes
about 1337 and had taken at any rate minor orders by 1361.
But for him too the Church was a status and neither a vocation
nor a career. Like Le Bel he moved freely among gentlemen
and nobles; like Le Bel he wrote amorous poetry; but he
wielded the pen and not the sword and was (rather like his
contemporary Petrarch) an early man of letters. Such a
position involved not only benefices in the Church, but
patrons, and again (like Petrarch) Froissart had a succession
of great folk to whom he was beholden, in whose interest he
slanted a little his narrative of nearly a century of war,
diplomacy and civil disturbance. Perhaps his first Maecenas
was the count of his native Hainault; his second was
undoubtedly Philippa of Hainault, the queen of Edward III of
England, to whom in 1361 he dedicated an early version of his
chronicle. Other grandees succeeded her (she died in 1369) as
protectors and sources of information, as successful candidates
for honourable mention. And in the last decades of his long
life Froissart travelled widely to seek out actors in his history
and was himself sought out by soldiers anxious to have their

deeds properly recorded. The changes in patrons and a
growing maturity as he became older led to various versions of
the work. Its immediate popularity led to large numbers of
manuscripts. All of this has posed daunting editorial problems
in producing acceptable texts of the chronicle, which covers
the years from 1325 (with a brief retrospect to 1307) down to
1499.[20] He died about four years later.

It will be noted that the dates just mentioned are derived
from English history: 1307 accession of Edward II; 1326 the
queen goes to France; 1400 death of Richard II. This
should make it plain that Froissart's French chronicle covered
much of English history. It was, indeed, a narrative which
embraced much of Western Europe, as the war between
France and England spread to allies in Germany, Spain, Italy.
Froissart's explicit aim was to record the war so that the
valorous deeds of armies should not be forgotten and so that
later generations would be inspired to comparable bravery.
His subsidiary aim was to please his readers and in this he
succeeded far beyond anything he might have anticipated. It is
still hard to put him down, so accomplished is his narrative.
Nor is the survey narrowly restricted to campaigns and
tournaments. In many ways it is the completest account we
have of the overall political development of Europe in the
fourteenth century: the popes at Avignon, the uprisings in
Flanders, the Ile de France, and England (1381), the Crusade
of Nicopolis, all find their place in Froissart's pages, naturally
viewed from the standpoint of one who was a courtier by
inclination.

Froissart thus produced what is in some sense a universal
chronicle. But he does not go back even in summary fashion to
Creation or Christ.[21] His story is essentially about what has
happened in his life-time to contemporaries, many of whom
had supplied him with authentic information. This information
he undertook to present with impartiality, and in general he
was fair and uncommitted (which is why controversy has often
arisen over his interpretation of this or that fact). Alert as
Froissart was to events other than military ones, the long story
in all its versions is one of adventures and battles, of the events
of the first half of the Hundred Years War and of the bellicose
truces which punctuated it. And the main *dramatis personae*

vere the nobles and gentlemen of France and the Low Countries, England and Scotland, Germany and Spain. Just as he story of the Crusades had in essence dealt with the noble varriors engaged in hostilities with the implacable infidel and he untrustworthy Greek, so the civil war between Christians vhich Froissart records is centered on the affairs of the same group in society and its resounding success is attested not only by the multiplication of manuscripts, but also by the succession of writers who emulated Froissart in the fifteenth century. They had, alas, neither his gift of vivid prose, nor his sharpness of judgment. Perhaps also they lacked his detachment, since hey were all more or less identified with the court of Burgundy.

Enguerrand de Monstrelet took up the tale at the point where Froissart stopped and his narrative runs from 1400 to 1444. His work in turn was continued by Matthieu d'Escouchy (as far as 1461) and by Jean de Wavrin (in a work styled *Anchiennes croniques d'Angleterre*) which ultimately reached the same year 1461. This work is overlapped by the chronicle composed by Georges Chastellain, written in and after 1453, which covered the period 1420-1474; there are gaps in the surviving manuscripts. Another Burgundian gentleman, Olivier de la Marche, compiled memoirs which span the years 1435-1488.[22] All these writers were men of action. They were laymen and wrote in the vernacular, mostly badly but sometimes (Chastellain is outstanding) well. Sometimes their courtly avocations — as squires of the body, as heralds — leads to an emphasis on ceremonial. And this is perhaps what is most 'Burgundian' about the writers so described. But 'chivalrous' is a better term, even if we are in the twilight of chivalry, even if the horse is on the way out as an invincible instrument of war, if not as a symbol of social superiority. Perhaps the last example of the genre is the *Histoire de Bayart*, written by an 'anonymous faithful servant' of this French soldier who fought in early sixteenth-century Italy,[23] although the Berners translation of Froissart into English at about the same time suggests that nostalgia was also found north of the Channel. But heralds seem to have been more active as writers in Burgundy and France than elsewhere.[24]

The chivalrous historians just mentioned (and many others

could have been added) were all men who were writing more or
less contemporary history, like the monastic chroniclers earlier
described. But unlike most monastic chroniclers, they were
frequently spectators or even actors in the spectacles and
actions which they recorded. They were engaged in diplomatic
missions, they recorded solemn ceremonies, they recorded the
deeds of the mighty. The narratives thus written have a social
cohesion denied to the monastic chronicle and at their best
they display an extraordinary verve and self-confidence. This
was based in large measure on a conviction of social superiority
which insulated itself as far as possible in a world of noble
heroism and regarded with contempt the 'vilain'. Villeinage
has in fact virtually disappeared as a legal status by the
fifteenth century in Western Europe. But the disdain of the
gentleman for his inferiors was sometimes paradoxically
intensified by the latters' financial success. Chastellain's
contempt for rich burgesses is well-known.[25]

Yet in many towns the burgesses were creating their own
history, in the form of narrative chronicles, of memoranda or
commonplace books, of private journals. The most influential
of such works were unquestionably the chronicles, for they
were soon to reach forms in which they were printed. But we
should remember the enormous bulk of more private
narratives — the *ricordanze* so plentiful in Renaissance
Florence and mainly aimed at the edification of the author
and his family, or the celebrated *Journal d'un bourgeois de
Paris* whose anonymity has survived intact despite its length
and its author's unguarded comments on the period 1405-59;
this *bourgeois* was in fact a clergyman of some kind. Such
works are invaluable to the modern reader and they testify to a
growing impulse to record the recent past in a new section of
the community and thus to a new market for a new type of
historian to supply. But such intimate documents are not
themselves history.[26]

Historical works in the vernacular satisifed the new relish for
public events in many. parts of Europe. They were, not
unnaturally, most in evidence in those areas where towns were
most in evidence — in Italy, in parts of the Low Countries and

Germany. The origins of the town chronicle were often to be
found in lists of civic office-bearers, changing annually and
listed with the year of appointment. Such lists of consuls or
mayors are then amplified by the insertion of scraps of local or
regional or national news and in time such narrative passages
come to dominate the whole. The continuator is at hand to
keep the story going and a tradition of historical composition is
established. The origin and early development of the chronicle
is thus in many respects similar to that of the monastic
chronicle; the latter's annalistic framework derived from the
Easter Table and the former's from the annual change of the
magistrates. Many examples of this *genre* of composition are
found all over Europe:

> In Italy the municipal chronicler appeared at Milan as early
> as the eleventh century, and from the twelfth to the
> sixteenth, not only in the largest towns of that country, but
> in those of minor importance the civic annalist lived and
> flourished ... the long series of chronicles written in city
> after city of Germany, split up into its innumerable states,
> with cities and leagues of cities, the importance of whose
> municipal records is indicative of the part they played in the
> history of the medieval Empire.[27]

The variety and importance of town chronicles is particuarly
evident in Germany because of the collection in one series of
the *Chroniken der deutschen Stadte*, a series which contains 36
volumes dealing with the fourteenth, fifteenth and sixteenth
centuries.[28] This publication displays historical activity of all
kinds. There are memoirs of a fairly intricate kind often
related to mercantile activity; there are annals derived from
the older chronicles. But there is no doubt of the wide
diffusion in Germany of an intense interest in history among
the bourgeoisie, especially in the bigger towns. In this divided
land, history was regionalised. But an intense nostalgia for the
good old days of the strong Empire persisted. It is reflected in
many local chronicles but it is especially evident in the large
chronicle of Hartmann Schedel. This was a Nuremberg
production, famous especially because the printed editions —
the first came out in 1493 in both Latin and German — were
splendidly illustrated with woodcuts which were greatly

admired and much copied. The German burgess was avid for
the past; but he accepted a very old fashioned view of it.

That this is less true in Italian chronicles derives in part
from the rejection by most governments in the peninsula of the
old imperial connection and the hostility of Italians to the
papacy. This induced an ambiguous attitude to Rome, ancient
and modern. The Roman emperor and the Roman bishop
equally disturbed the political scene in Italy and were resented
or manipulated as the case might be. At the same time the
Rome of antiquity exercised a fascination which was strong
everywhere in Europe but especially in Italy. This can be seen
in the finest of the civic chronicles, that by Giovanni Villani (to
1348), continued by his brother Matteo (to 1363), to which
Matteo's son, Filippo, added a few more pages.[29] Giovanni's
preface deserves an extended quotation since it illustrates aptly
the amalgam of the old general chronicle and the new civil
self-consciousness which he achieved:

> Forasmuch as among our Florentine ancestors, few and ill-
> arranged memorials are to be found of the past doings of
> our city of Florence, either by the fault of their negligence
> or by reason that at the time that Totila, the scourge of God,
> destroyed it, their writings were lost, I, John, citizen of
> Florence, considering the nobility and greatness of our city
> at our present times, hold it meet to recount and make
> memorial of the root and origins of so famous a city, and
> of its adverse and happy changes and of past happenings;
> not because I feel myself sufficient for such a work, but to
> give occasion to our successors not to be negligent in
> preserving records of the notable things which shall
> happen in the times after us, and to give example to those
> who shall come after, of changes, and things come to pass,
> and their reasons and causes; to the end that they may
> exercise themselves in practising virtues, and shunning vices,
> and enduring adversities with a strong soul, to the good and
> stability of our republic. And, therefore, I will furnish a
> faithful narrative in this book in plain vernacular, in order
> that the ignorant and unlettered may draw thence profit
> and delight; and if in any part there should be defect,
> I leave it to the correction of the wiser. And first we will

say whence were the origins of our said city, following on
for as long a time as God shall grant us grace; and not
without much toil shall I labour to extract and recover
from the most ancient and diverse books, and chronicles,
and authors, the acts and doings of the Florentines,
compiling them herein; and first the origin of the ancient
city of Fiesole, the destruction whereof was the cause
and beginning of our city of Florence. And because our
origin starts from very long ago, it seems to us necessary
to our treatise to recount briefly other ancient stories; and
it will be delightful and useful to our citizens now and
to come, and will encourage them in virtue and in great
actions to consider how they are descended from noble
ancestors and from folk of worth, such as were the
ancient and worthy Trojans, and valiant and noble
Romans. And to the end our work may be more praise-
worthy and good, I beseech the aid of our Lord Christ,
in whose name every work has a good beginning,
continuance and end.[30]

The Chronicle in fact begins with Noah's sons, and tells how
the giant Nimrod, Ham's grandson, ordered the building of
the Tower of Babel. The story then moves rapidly through the
Troy tales to Aeneas, the foundation of Rome and the
conspiracy of Catiline which led to rebellion at neighbouring
Fiesole. Then comes the destruction of Fiesole by Caesar and
the building of Florence — which would have been called
Caesarea, if the Roman senate had not intervened. And so
begins Villani's *real* theme, Florence and its vicissitudes
through the centuries. This of course involves many general
events. Emperors come and go. Totila ravages the city, the
crusaders establish themselves in the south and all the time
Florence gains in size and importance, in refinement of
government machinery, and in domination of the surrounding
territory. The names of the great families roll from Villani's
pen, as they were later to resound in Dante's verses. The
chronicle was not merely the story of a city, but the story of the
men and women who lived in it, their alliances and their feuds,
the churches where they worshipped, the walls behind which
they defended themselves, the public buildings in which

government was centred. The many passages in which Italian matters or events in the world at large, are discussed, should not be necessarily regarded as the persistence of the old universal chronicling tradition, though there is something of this about them. By the late thirteenth century Florence was a city whose trading interests covered the known world. Her merchants were used to intelligence reaching them rapidly from distant places and to guiding their commercial policies on the basis of a sound knowledge of the international scene.

Villani's scale of relevance can sometimes be seen very clearly, as in the paragraphs which touch on the early stage of the Hundred Years War. A brief account of Anglo-Scottish affairs in 1335 (XI, cap. xxxviii) ends with the comment: 'We will leave foreign matter for a space and return to our main business — events in and related to Florence.' The much longer passage 'about a great war which began between the king of France and the king of England' in 1336 (XI, cap. lv) ends in a similar fashion: 'We shall leave for a time the overseas matters and come back to the war we were having with Mastino (della Scala) of Verona.'[31] But Florence could not in fact regard the English invasion of France with indifference. The credit extended to Edward III by the companies of the Bardi and the Peruzzi helped to bring them to bankruptcy and since the firms had advanced the English kings their loan capital, it brought 'great danger to Florentines who had invested funds with them and great danger to the city itself' (XI, cap. lxxxviii).[32] The exact extent of the Peruzzi losses are quoted and this and similar details of a statistical kind give Villani's work a particularly concrete quality. Anything Florentine was treated with especial care and a few chapters beyond the ones just referred to comes the famous description of Florence at this time (1338), its wealth and the charges on it, its size in men and women and shops, the astonishment of foreigners approaching the city as three miles off they met the splendid buildings erected by citizens in the *contado* (XI, caps. xci-xciv).[33] Ten years later he records the beginning of what was to be the Black Death, from which he himself shortly perished (XII, cap. lxxxiv).

Villani's chronicle was not to be printed until 1537. The

reasons for this delay will be at any rate partly evident in the
next chapter. But his kind of historical narration, with its
mixture of the provincial with the general, its recording of
hundreds of names of important persons, its pride and its
patriotism, not unfairly represents the historical tastes which
prevailed in the towns of Europe in the later Middle Ages and
the sixteenth century. Yet it would be wrong to suggest that
there was cultural uniformity in this field, for nothing could be
less true. England and France offer conspicuous contrasts.

Despite the Anglo-French wars and the Anglo-French truces
and treaties, despite the shared chivalry and even despite
Froissart, the historiography of England and France steadily
drew apart during the fourteenth century.

Monastic history was written in both countries but activity at
St Albans, which had rivalled Saint-Denis in the thirteenth
century as a centre of great chronicles, dwindled almost to
vanishing point. The St Albans chronicle was revived by
Thomas Walsingham in the 1370s, but the resulting works are
thin indeed compared with the steady stream of writings at
Saint-Denis which culminated in the large-scale work of the
anonymous monk who covered the years 1380-1420.[34] The
standard historical work of fourteenth-century England was
produced by the Chester Benedictine, Ranulf Higden. His
Polychronicon, written in mid-century and continued by other
hands, became in Trevisa's English translation of 1387 the
nearet English equivalent of the *Grandes Chroniques*.[35] A
work destined to be hardly less influential was the *Brut of
England* which in its original French form, goes back to the
early fourteenth century[36] and which was also put into
English at the start of Richard II's reign.

The narrative sources for the two countries are, of course,
not restricted to the books just mentioned: very many others
will be found listed in the reference books and manuals. But is
is important to stress the absence in England of an official
historiographical centre, such as was provided for the French
Crown at Saint-Denis. This 'official' element in France was
to have important developments later on; and so in England
was the precocious development of the town chronicle.

In turning now to the fifteenth century we must firs appreciate that in England there was a sharp decline in the us of Anglo-Norman language, and although French was still viable vernacular in fourteenth-century England it was, despit its relevance in politics, declining in importance. There ar plausible tales in Froissart of linguistic difficulties encountere by English gentlemen on French battlefields.[37] Under Henr IV and Henry V the decline was rapid; it seems fair to say tha by then it was rare to use Anglo-Norman or French in Englan save on formal occasions. Doubtless the war with France which under Henry V and his brother Bedford had a bitternes that it had lacked under Edward III, encouraged this change the language of the 'natural enemy' must have attracted som of the odium attracted by all alien things in those xenophobi days. In any event, many a cultivated and travelle Englishman must have found it hard not to laugh, as Chauce did, at the sort of French spoken at Stratford atte Bowe English was rapidly becoming a much more self-sufficien medium; along with the international Latin of scholarship most needs were met without recourse to French, whethe Anglo-Norman or French French, if one may so describe th language of the north of France.

These developments made it unlikely that Froissart would b influential in England, at any rate in his own words, and eve bearing in mind that his treatment of the last years of Richar II had been fairly balanced. It is nevertheless astonishing ho uninfluential Froissart was. His *Chronicle* was just a important for English heroes as for French — perhaps mor important for the English; and a fair number of manuscript were available in fifteenth-century England. For a translatio we have to wait until the version of Lord Berners, printed b Pynson from 1523 to 1525, and reprinted in 1545: there is the silence until 1812.[38] It is true that through Polydore Vergi and the early Tudor chronicles much of Froissart becam embedded in historical tradition even before Berners' versio came out. But the absence of any chivalrous strain in Englis historians is striking.[39] Not one English writer befor Berners can be said to have drawn inspiration from the Middl Ages, save perhaps the so-called 'heralds' who have lef accounts of ceremonies at Yorkist and early Tudor courts.[40

It was very different in France. Apart from a number of smaller works such as *Le livre des faits du maréchal Boucicaut* and *La chronique du bon duc Loys de Bourbon*, a great series of chivalrous chronicles spans the fifteenth century: Enguerrand de Monstrelet, Georges Chastellain, Olivier de la Marche. Whatever their faults, whatever their novelties, as historians these writers were direct descendants of Frois-sart.[41] That some French critics have dismissed them as Burgundians' is a matter referred to below.

This, then, is the first and most striking difference between English and French historiography in the fifteenth century: chivalrous history is found flourishing across the Channel; in England it is not found at all. The other remarkable difference between the two countries is the development of the town chronicle in England and its virtual absence in France, save for a few places in the south. Something has already been said about the London chronicles (above p.72). C.L. Kingsford estimated that about forty different compilers were at work in fifteenth-century London, and the *Brut* was also by now a city chronicle. These chronicles, more or less full, more or less up-to-date, were clearly a regular item in the houses of well-off citizens and were regularly available among the stock of scrivener or bookseller. The Londoner liked reading about his town. He accepted happily a background of history based on the *Brut*, but he was mainly interested in the events of his own day and of the preceding generation. National events displayed him as responsive to official pressure and jingoist, in line with other English writers of the period. This civic history was almost but not entirely confined to London. Civic records are given greater prominence and permanence in many towns in the later Middle Ages and this could border on the chronicle, as in the *Diary of the Corporation of Reading*, begun in 1413.[42] The most impressive, and the earliest, of the genuine town chronicles outside London is Robert Ricart's *Maire's Calendar* of Bristol. He was town clerk from 1479 to 1503 and wrote — apparently independently of the London chronicles — a series of annals which are relatively full from 1447 to 1492.[43] Such local histories multiply in the sixteenth century until they merge with the antiquarian interests of a later age.

However, when France is looked at what is striking is the relative absence of such works. Molinier records published civic chronicles in three places only: Béziers (the work of the *escudier* Mascaro); Montpellier (*Le petit Thalamus*); and Bordeaux ('la chronique des coutumes de Bordeaux').[44] On examination only the Béziers and Montpellier documents resemble a true city chronicle — containing lists of consuls together with notes of other events of importance. There are, i seems, other local records of similar structure, as yet unpublished.[45]

The real surprise is the absence of any chronicle tradition in Paris. We now know that Paris in about 1400 numbered some 80,000 souls; that is, it was twice the size of London.[46 Kingsford was inclined to attribute the flourishing historiography of London to the revolution of 1399.[47] Certainly that event and the victories of Henry V in France, which bulk large in the chronicles, often in the form of ballads, were surely inclined to start men off scribbling or demanding a history book from the stationer. But Paris saw upheavals no less catastrophic; a darkening feud between Burgundy and Orleans; an English invasion and occupation of the capital; and a final triumph over the enemy in 1453. Moreover Paris produced, as London did not, both statesmen and demagogues of real significance. There are no Londoners like Étienne Marcel or Simmonet Caboche. On the other hand Paris was effectively managed by a royal *prévot* and had no magistrates to compare with the mayor and sheriffs of London; political tensions in London for long had been self-generated rather than only reflecting (they did this as well) the troubles in the country at large.[48]

These are not the only differences between the historiographical traditions of two neighbouring lands, whose political fortunes were to remain inextricably connected. But they are the most important, and were to colour the reception of the new historiography of Renaissance Italy as this crossed the Alps in the sixteenth century. To this new style of viewing the past we must now turn.

5 The Humanist Historian in Fifteenth-century Italy

For nearly a century the Renaissance has been generally regarded as a watershed in the intellectual as well as the artistic development of Europe. When Burckhardt published his *Civilization of the Renaissance in Italy* at Basle in 1860 the work was a relative failure and of interest only to a handful of specialists. For hundreds of years, indeed from the Renaissance itself, the fine arts and *belles lettres* had been accepted as stemming, in their 'modern' forms, from the innovations of the fifteenth and sixteenth centuries. But the notion that an even wider transformation of ideas then took place, although hinted at by Goethe and Stendhal, and even asserted stridently by Michelet, needed the persuasive scholarship of Burckhardt to gain acceptance. This it did slowly but surely. Indeed it may well be felt that Burckhardt's essay was in the end too influential, for it argued that the transformation extended to political activities, to the physical sciences, to every aspect of 'life' — and this is manifestly not the case. All of this was complicated by the assimilation of Renaissance 'humanity' to nineteenth and twentieth century 'humanism'.[1] *Humanitas* = the 'humanities' in the Renaissance meant education in 'grammar, rhetoric, history, poetry and moral philosophy, and the study of each of these subjects was understood to include the reading and interpretation of its standard ancient writers in Latin and, to a lesser extent, in Greek'.[2] Professor Kristeller's definition cannot be overemphasised. After the Renaissance became associated with 'the Greek spirit' early in the nineteenth century, the confusion between Renaissance 'humanism' and the modern variety has increased. This is

partly because of the widespread use of the word 'humanism'
by students of the Renaissance — defensible enough in itself, I
dare say, as a portmanteau word more familiar nowadays
than 'the humanities' — and partly because the contemporary
humanist muzzily feels he is descended from the heroic thinkers
and artists of the centuries around 1500. The contemporary
humanist is almost invariably some kind of ethical pragmatist,
an unbeliever who believes in the necessity of virtuous action;
the humanist of the Renaissance was a teacher or practitioner
of the humanities as identified above, and almost without
exception he was a Christian.

It is necessary to utter these preliminary warnings before
turning to historical writing and research during the
Renaissance, especially since for some time the period has been
regarded as witnessing the birth of modern attitudes to the
past. The 'modern historian' takes shape in Italy in and after
the mid-fourteenth century, so runs the story, which (as we
shall see) has something to commend it. Apart from
Burckhardt's doctrine of Fame, which led him to emphasise
Italian developments in biography and in the celebration of
states (part II, iii; part IV, v-vi), the great Swiss historian
clearly preferred the earlier chronicles of the medieval type
(Villani's work, for example) to the frigid style which was to
deprive the humanist historian of realism: 'the manner of Livy
— that Procrustean bed of so many writers' (part III, ix). It
was, however, another Swiss writer (who, like Burckhardt, had
been a journalist) who set the seal on the critical efforts of the
Renaissance for historiography. This was Eduard Fueter in his
Geschichte der neueren Historiographie (Munich and Berlin,
1911), who began his survey with Petrarch and ended it with a
severe assessment of Burckhardt himself, whom he characterised as a dilettante, a criticism Burckhardt, who hated
pedantry, would not have minded in the least. Fueter's book is
the only grand survey of historiography that merits still to be
treated with respect. For the greater part he had read the
books he was talking about. His judgements were astringent
but founded on fact. His approach was schematic, aiming at
the identification of principles and the establishment of
'schools', but his treatment was so thorough that we still mostly
move among the categories he accepted. One of these was the

significance for history writing of the Italian Renaissance.[3]

So influential has Fueter's analysis of humanist historiography proved that it must be summarised. He argued that with Salutati (chancellor of Florence 1375-1406) and his disciple' Leonardo Bruni (chancellor 1427-44) the new manner of writing history 'entered the Florentine foreign office' and he described the new manner as being on the one hand consciously artistic and on the other geared to propagandist purposes. The artistry lay in a Latin which aped the best rhetorical precepts of Cicero and the best rhetorical practice of Livy. And the propaganda element was a deliberate attempt to persuade one's fellow citizens of the superiority of their state in all respects, not least in matters regarding government, and convince their enemies of the righteousness of the Florentine cause. Fueter naturally saw the dangers of the apologia; he shrewdly noted also the limitation of topics capable of treatment in the grand manner — that kind of literary snobbism we have already noted in classical historians. Beyond that, an adherence to literary purism led humanist historians to use absurd anachronistic phrases to describe objects and institutions for wich there was no classical word. But Fueter found compensations. The Latin-writing 'official' historians were at any rate reflecting the lively preoccupations of their republic or their prince, and they had jettisoned the lumber of Empire and Papacy. They were (so he argued), if not pursuing a consciously 'lay' method or espousing an explicitly secular philosophy, at any rate uninterested in the miraculous and the legendary. This freed them for a calm appraisal of the cold politicians who dominated the Italian political scene.[4] Some modifications of this picture must necessarily be made, but it remains the earliest and in many ways the soundest introduction to the subject. Fueter made no secret of his feeling that much of the humanist's approach was empty and verbose, a searching for literary effects. But, granting even this, he made less allowance than was proper for other and positive innovations.

The first of these is undoubtedly the acceptance of a new division of the past. Of old, as we have seen, historians of the Christian era had worked usually to the pattern of seven ages, of which to all intents and purposes they were only concerned

with their own — the sixth age, the previous five having ru
from Creation to the birth of Christ, and the seventh lying i
the future, that seventh age when history would come to a
end, at any rate in a way incomprehensible to men.[5] Now w
find new divisions being invented. They are groped for in
fumbling manner in the Trecento. Petrarch's sense of intimac
with Cicero and Augustine made him preternaturally sensitiv
to the gulf which separated his own day — the metaphysica
programmes of the schools, the literary ideals of the vulga
versifiers, the logic-chopping of lawyers — from the eloquenc
of the golden age of Rome, from the lofty moral precepts c
antiquity, from that union of literature with beauty of bot
form and content to which he himself instinctively inclined
Boccaccio, his contemporary, was even more explicit in hi
sense of a literary revival after centuries of barbarism. Neithe
man was in any significant sense a historian. Each was th
harbinger of a notion of Renaissance which had as it
complement the notion of a Middle Age or Middle Ages.

The concept 'Renaissance' took longer to acquire a
accepted terminology than the concept 'Middle Ages'.[6] Th
metaphor of rebirth is frequently found in fifteenth-centur
writers to describe their sense of identity with antiquity but i
was so overloaded with Christian mystery (one must suppose
that it could not easily acquire a merely literary or historica
connotation. 'Renewal' (*renovatio*) was a good Bible word; bu
it had been worked to death in political as well as exegetica
contexts. The awareness of a rebirth of ancient values, literary
artistic and ethical, was vivid from the early decades of th
fifteenth century, especially among Florentines. It was no
made concrete, so to say, until the casual use of 'rebirth
(*rinascita*) by Vasari in 1550, when he applied it to the fine art
of painting, sculpture and architecture. Long before thi
Italians had groped their way to a naming of that trough o
time between the ancients and the new 'moderns', thos
moderns who felt more at home in antiquity than in th
intervening centuries: *media tempestas* (1469), *media aeta*
(1518), *media tempora* (1531) and so on down to the *mediun*
aevum (1604) which was in the end to triumph, not leas
because it yielded in Latin and the vernaculars the convenien
adjective 'medieval'. That some of these coinages came fron

he north of Europe is an important aspect of the diffusion of Renaissance values. But the essential ideas and the essential words were Italian in origin. Petrarch wrote with contempt of he 'shadows' or 'dark age' which intervened between antiquity and his own day. The phrase *media tempestas* comes from a etter in the edition of Apuleius published in Rome in 1469. And in about 1450 Flavio Biondo published his *Decades*, a history of the world from the fall of Rome to his own day. He aimed to be the Livy of the period we call the Middle Ages, although he only intermittently made the effort to command Livy's style.[7]

In this crab-like way Europe, and the world which derives its educational and cultural values from Europe, acquired the tripartite division of time: Ancient, Medieval, Modern. This extraordinary simplification traps us all. In antiquity and the Middle Ages men regarded themselves as moderns. The humanists changed all that. They made Cicero and Vergil ancients; they made Héloise and Abelard medieval; they made Petrarch, Shakespeare, Burckhardt moderns in a new and confusing sense.

With the creation of a new series of epochs came a sense of anachronism which was also new. 'Autres temps, autres moeurs' was a concept which had little real meaning in antiquity and none in the Middle Ages. The role, the costume and the ambience of the heroes of antiquity were displayed by historians, illuminators and sculptors exactly as they would have appeared if they had been great men in the twelfth or thirteenth century. Aristotle was depicted as a doctor in the schools, and no one regarded his doctrines as in any sense reflecting a world that had perished. 'One must not be surprised', wrote Émile Mâle of a statue of Abraham at Rheims, 'to see Abraham in the armour of a thirteenth-century knight'.[8] 'The Middle Ages did not envisage classical antiquity as a different civilization or a lost Paradise'.[9] For instance, the Nine Worthies — Hector, Alexander, Julius Caesar, Joshua, David, Judas Maccabaeus, Arthur, Charlemagne, Godfrey of Bouillon — were represented as though they were contemporary with one another, a series of chivalrous *milites*. True, the artists and the writers sought for exotic effects, and happily introduced splendour and mystery

into their imaginary worlds. But it is not until we reach the
fifteenth century and Italy that we encounter a genuine
attempt to recreate the character of the past age. 'Recreation'
seems the right word to describe Mantegna's archaeologically
exact details in those of his pictures which displayed antique
scenes — as in the 'Triumphs of Caesar' at Hampton Court.
The process of identifying congruities or conformities proper
to one age and not to another took a further step in the
sixteenth century in the self-conscious preoccupations of artists
and architects faced with the task of completing buildings
begun in the old Gothic or Byzantine manner — the facades o
the cathedrals at Florence and Bologna, for example. In the
debates over St. Petronio at Bologna, for example, we see
deployed all the problems of periodization as applied to styles,
and in his history of the artists Vasari reveals his own
preoccupation with the same problems. It is interesting to note
that such awareness of anachronism did not face the northern
artist until much later.[10]

Historians in Italy were slower than artists to seize the full
implications of what was in a sense a step towards relativism —
the awareness that matters past must be viewed *non
semplicemente ma, come s'usa dire, secondo che* — the
secundum quid of the schools, 'having regard to place, time
and other similar circumstances'.[11] And one reason fo
hesitation was obvious: such an attitude might well imply a
moral relativism, too, and thus endanger the traditional
defences of history as a discipline which, as we shall see, were
repeated with new conviction during the Renaissance. The
only work which at times betrays a preoccupation with
historical propriety is Lorenzo Valla's polemical attack on the
validity of the so-called 'Donation of Constantine', written
when he was a servant of Alfonso of Naples in order to
embarrass the pope. Some passages in this pamphlet suggest
the kind of antiquarian preoccupations of a painter like
Mantegna, but Valla's main contention is the absurdity o
supposing Constantine would have been fool enough to divest
himself of such power, or the pope fool enough to keep so
momentous an event concealed in contemporary sources.
These points had been already made more than once, though
not with Valla's sharp command of vitriolic Latin, nor with his

long additional argument that the language of the Donation was corrupt and confused. This, of course, is one of the inconsistencies which most strikes the reader of the Donation today. But Valla's invective really misses the truly interesting matter of how and when and why the forgery took shape. Instead it is really a diatribe against the temporal powers of the papacy. He was not, that is to say, considering the historical aspects of the problem in depth.'[12]

Nevertheless the declamation, even if it was flogging a dead horse, even if it sheds no light on eighth-century Italy when the Donation emerged, even if it does not lead on to much immediate application of philosophy to history, it yet does represent a modest step towards a consciousness that the world of the ancients was characteristically different from the intervening centuries of shadows, and not merely because the quality of Latin composition had been ruined by the influx of barbarians and barbarism. It was, of course, much more difficult for Italians in the *quattrocento* to appreciate how different their times were from those of the palmy days of the Roman Republic or the early Empire. Their sense of affinity with antiquity went with an incomprehension of the thousand years that had intervened. Even Machiavelli can write as though the invasion of Italy in and after 1494 was part of the *Völkerwanderungen* which had flooded Italy in the fifth century with Goths and Lombards.[13] But then Machiavelli was a sociologist *avant la lettre*.

The old didactic purposes of the historian, derived from classical writers and cherished during the Middle Ages, were naturally of great interest to Renaissance historians, all the more so since they were by no means unaware of the counter-claims of moral philosophy and poetry, recently advanced by Boccaccio and Salutati, from a firm basis in ancient doctrine. Leonardo Bruni's preface has (besides other things) those justifications with which we are familiar. The great achievements of Florence should not be regarded as of less significance than those of the ancients: recording them should be of the greatest utility to both statesman and private citizen. If the men of antiquity derived benefit from their experiences, how much more conducive to prudence would be a conscientious history covering matters in many epochs showing what may be shunned and what followed — the example of outstanding men firing the spirit to the exercise of virtue. Bruni also remains true to traditional form in protesting his own incapacity for the task. But he has overcome his aversion to the unravelling of obscure events and coping with ugly terminology and has accepted the challenge. Besides, 'this narrative will also throw light on Italian history'.[14]

These sentiments are repeated by nearly all humanist writers of history in the Italy of the fifteenth century,[15] as they had been in Europe at large in the past and were to be in the future. The position of the historian had, however, markedly changed since the medieval chronicler assembled his annals. The humanist educator put history high on his list of priorities because he was teaching a new lay governing class and it was axiomatic that the experience of ancient public men was relevant to their successors. It is worth quoting Pier Paolo Vergerio, whose *De ingenuis moribus* is one of the earliest and most balanced statements of the humanist educational programme:

> We now come to the consideration of the various subjects which may rightly be included under the name of 'Liberal Studies'. Amongst these I accord the first place to History, on grounds both of its attractiveness and its utility, qualities which appeal equally to the scholar and the statesman ... And history provides the light of experience — a cumulative wisdom fit to supplement the force of reason and the persuasion of eloquence.[16]

Poetry might deal in untarnished Truth, but it could beguile the scholar and sometimes even seduce him in a way which the pages of Livy and Sallust could not; no one ever became a good magistrate or even a useful citizen by reading Ovid. The Renaissance historian thus belonged to a great pedagogic tradition which had become enhanced by being associated with an élite, associated *again*, for the scholars of fifteenth-century Italy, like their Roman predecessors, regarded literary or spoken communication, or rhetoric, as the supreme human skill. History as a literary genre had thus to be devoted to the interests of statesmen (i.e. war and diplomacy) and it had to be eloquent. As for the standing of poetry, one could go further than Vergerio, who had urged its fundamental plan in the curriculum. One could argue that it had an absolute priority among created disciplines. Valla, in the preface to his official history of Alfonso V's father, met the challenge of poetry by asserting that in Latin culture annals had been composed before poetry and (if they really existed) Dares and Dictys wrote their histories before Homer had written his poems. He then invoked the very argument that Salutati had used in poetry's defence. The Scriptures, Salutati had said, were poetical; Valla pointed out that the Scriptures were largely history — Moses and the Evangelists 'are to be termed nothing other than historians'. As for Truth, the Truth of poetry, history was founded on the truth of fact.[17] One must not make too many inferences from these bold statements. Valla was not treating the Bible 'as a history book', nor did his life of King Ferdinand of Aragon live up to the intelligent and 'vigorous' (the word is Gaeta's) promise of the preface.

This reservation must, indeed, be applied to humanist historical theory in general. It is all too easy to look only at the intentions of authors in their prefaces or at the doctrines of the schoolmasters (or, more often, of those who were telling the schoolmasters what they should be about). Yet, embedded again in the canonical prescriptions of Cicero, there was sound enough advice about the structure of historical works and we must constantly refer to the passage already quoted from *De oratore* if we are to comprehend what the humanist historian is about. Cicero repeatedly urged that the mere possession of eloquence was relatively unimportant. The writer or orator had to have something to say,[18] and for the historian his argument or theme was fairly precisely laid down (above p.4). The narrative must be chronological and the region described; campaigns must be analysed and explained and their consequences estimated; important characters must be given detailed treatment.

> Then again the kind of language and type of style to be fol-
> lowed are the easy and the flowing, which run their course
> with unvarying current and a certain placidity, avoiding
> alike the rough speech we use in Court and the advocates'
> stinging epigrams.[19]

A 'smooth' style, as it was to be described later, was what was
required for a narrative dealing with what mattered: great
public events and great public personalities. Noble statesmen,
noble debates, noble wars and dignified and dramatic
diplomacy — that was the history which demanded the artistic
treatment prescribed by Cicero.

To Cicero's injunctions the Renaissance added those of
Quintilian. Quintilian's *Education of an Orator* (Institutio
oratoria) had not been unknown in the Middle Ages, but it
had been available only in mutilated or incomplete versions, or
through the pages of anthologists. The full text became
available at the end of the fourteenth century and soon
circulated widely, mainly through the discoveries of Poggio. In
general Quintilian, who (unlike Cicero) had actually been a
teacher, supplemented rather than supplanted the latter and
was to be most influential with grammarians like Valla and
Perotto. As far as his discussion of history is concerned he
provided an interesting, almost paradoxical, comment:

> History, also, may nourish oratory with a kind of fertilising
> and grateful relish. But it must be read with the conviction
> that most of its very excellences are to be avoided by the
> orator; for it borders closely on poetry, and may be said,
> indeed, to be a poem unfettered by the constraints of metre;
> it is written to relate not to prove; and its whole nature is
> suited, not to the pleading of causes, or to instant debate,
> but to the transmission of events to posterity, and to gain the
> reputation of ability for its author. And for this reason it
> relieves the tedium of narrative by words more remote from
> common usage, and by a more bold employment of figures
> of speech.[20]

Given the *Kleinstaterei* of the peninsula it is hardly
surprising that the result of the counsel of Cicero and
Quintilian was a multiplicity of apologetic histories advancing
the cause of republics and dynasties, and intended also to
further the reputation and career of the writers concerned.
The first and in many ways the most distinguished of these was
The Twelve Books of Florentine History by Leonardo Bruni of
Arezzo (Aretino), written between 1415 and 1444, with which
Fueter rightly began his discussion of what he somewhat

misleadingly called sometimes the 'rhetorical school' and sometimes the 'first Florentine school' (in distinction to Machiavelli and his contemporaries).

Bruni's history must be judged by Renaissance standards.[21] Compared with the narrative patterns of a later period or indeed of the Middle Ages, the distortions dictated by the elevated style can be not merely irritating, but a positive impediment to understanding. Chronology is subordinated to fine phraseology. Hardly a year is mentioned by its date, and the story progresses, based though it is on the blow by blow annals of his sources (mainly Giovanni Villani), in a dense and repetitious confusion of 'at about the same time, in the same year, next year, the following summer' and so on. Without the help of a modern editor one flounders.[22] But while there are some periphrases designed to avoid calling a spade a spade, owing to Bruni's desire to use classical terms, such tricks should not be exaggerated. Classical Roman warfare resembled fairly closely most aspects of the fighting described by Villani and so translated both comfortably and fashionably into Bruni's rolling Latin periods. And medieval chroniclers in any case frequently used classical names for Christian monuments, e.g. those of Rome, as Bruni delighted to do.[23] There are absurdities of nomenclature which demand an alert reader, as when Giano della Bella appears grotesquely as 'Ianus Labella' and Salvestro de' Medici as 'Medix'. Such nonsense was, however, to be even more pronounced in later humanist writers, and was the price paid for the cultivation of a stylish Latin, designed to win friends and influence people. We must not allow such incidentals to distract us from the achievement of Bruni's work. It was a unified history of Florence of an extremely sophisticated kind.

This may be seen by comparing it with Giovanni Villani's chronicle. Villani begins with Noah and writes a history of the world in which Florentine affairs loom larger as time goes on. He stops at 1348 when he died, a victim of the Black Death. Bruni begins with the foundation of the city by Sulla's veterans, thus disposing of one of the legends of Florence — a foundation by Julius Caesar. He ends with the death of

Giangaleazzo Visconti in 1402. Both these points are clearly polemical. The foundation in the republican period (which, incidentally, was probably nearer the truth than the legend had been) made Florentines the heirs and custodians of Roman republican tradition, enemies of the 'tyrant', pledged to resist oppression and proclaim the virtues of a free commune. The city had indeed been facing just such a threat to its liberty from Giangaleazzo, duke of Milan, who had surrounded Florence with a chain of cities recognising his lordship and harbouring his garrisons. The *History* is thus organised towards an argument, frequently lost to sight in the detailed narrative but always there in the background. In practice the annalistic framework often obtrudes, partly because Livy was Bruni's model and Villani his principal source. If we feel that the genre was condemned to sterility because it exposed a self-destructive literary doctrine, this is not how contemporaries saw it. They saw it as a long defence of Florentine policy, especially in its foreign connections, a long condemnation of Florence's enemies, and all in the most genteel and cultivated manner. It was primarily about war and diplomacy. But that was what politics was about in antiquity and in the Renaissance. Bruni had in fact produced a better organised narrative history than any surviving from antiquity, except Thucydides.

It is, moreover, important not to allow the prominence of armies and ambassadors to conceal other aspects of the work. To a considerable degree it is a balanced history of Florence in the later thirteenth and fourteenth centuries. This means that, although Bruni's narrative does give great prominence to the external relations of Florence — the relations of the city with Frederick II, Charles of Anjou, Manfred and the popes — some discussion of the internal and constitutional evolution of the city was unavoidable, even if the author was led to minimise its part in his history. The events of 1266-7 which saw the establishment of the 'second popular government', and above all the crises in and after 1289, are given extended treatment.[24] The constitution of 1292 (the Ordinances of Justice) which first saw the creation of the 'form of the republic which we have used for 130 years', with one of Bruni's famous set pieces, the speech of Giano della Bella, is the culmination of a substantial account of domestic history. Practically all of this is derived from Villani (though not the speech) and it is certainly a more elaborate account than that found in Machiavelli's *History of Florence*, although Machiavelli accused Bruni of brevity or silence in discussing the internal history of the city.[25] On the other hand, the Ciompi rising of 1378, while its importance is stressed, is dealt with fairly summarily.[26] And overall there is no doubt that Bruni dwelt longer and most happily on external affairs — treaties, embassies, warfare — rather than on internal developments, and tended to keep the two as separate as possible. 'Haec foris. Domi autem ...'[27] represents a fairly common transition.

The *History* of Bruni was immensely successful. Although he was a native of Arezzo he was accorded civic honours for this work and his long service as chancellor.[28] He was honoured by a civic funeral when he died in 1444. Manuscripts of his *History* were kept in the Florentine chancery and the government commissioned a translation into the vernacular by Donato Acciaiuoli. Moreover, he was succeeded by other humanists — Marsuppini, Poggio, Bartolomeo della Scala, of whom the last two both wrote the history of Florence. Even better evidence of the impression this new type of history made on contemporaries is the way the princes and other republics of Italy took up the fashion as a matter of policy. Just as ambassadors were now figuring as permanent features of the Italian political scene (especially after the Peace of Lodi in 1454), so the well-written narrative displaying the antiquity and the victories of a dynasty or a ruler imposed itself. As Fueter rightly points out, what had been composed spontaneously at Florence had to be commissioned by the rulers of other Italian states. Valla's life of the father of Alfonso V of Naples has been mentioned. The Visconti dukes of Milan were celebrated by Pier Paolo Decembrio and the Sforza by Giovanni Simonetta. Platina was commissioned to write the history of the Gonzaga of Mantua and at Venice the signory employed Sabellico (Marcantonio Coccio) and Pietro Bembo as the first of the historians of the republic. Indeed the humanist history of Venice was official in the full sense from the start and long remained so.

Only the better known writers have been mentioned in the

previous paragraph. There were scores more of lesser ability or
lesser repute. It would not be true to say that every princely
family or every independent city had had by 1500 a flattering
portrait of its past prepared by a judicious humanist. But
many had, most of them mercifully destined to be forgotten.
Unless such works were translated they were soon of little
interest. Donato Acciaiuoli's Tuscan translation saved Bruni's
History from oblivion: the translation was published in 1473;
the original text not until 1610.[29] If Simonetta's interesting
work (he wrote it in retirement after Ludovico il Moro seized
power in Milan) appeared in a bowdlerised version in 1479, it
owed its further influence to the translations of Cristoforo
Landino (1490).

Nor must we suppose that older forms of composition were
not found alongside the polished works of humanists. Dozens
of annalists were at work in Renaissance Italy who had no
pretension to the grandeur of classical Latin, who envisaged no
public beyond perhaps their own family. Chronicles could
sometimes be very elaborate — as with the most original of the
Milanese writers, Bernardino Corio, who wrote in Italian a
Patria Historia when he was a protégè of Duke Ludovico. And
private *ricordi*, *ricordanze*, memoirs, diaries abound, more
especially perhaps among the intensely literate and numerate
Florentine businessmen. To these the historian today turns
avidly, regarding such sources rightly as offering more than
the frigid papers of the humanist scholar, whether or not
working expressly for a patron. Likewise the historian
nowadays is infinitely obliged to the biographers of the Italian
Renaissance, for instance Vespasiano da Bistici (no humanist)
who wrote the lives of the men he had encountered doing
business as a Florentine bookseller, and Paolo Giovio (most
certainly a humanist) whom Fueter calls a journalist — and
Fueter, who was one himself, was in a position to recognise the
type. Giovio, though his shrewd opinions are valuable on the
characters of his own day (he died in 1552), represents much
that is somewhat comical in the humanist. Besides a series of
biographies and his *Elogia*, linked with the portraits displayed
in his *Museum* or library, he wrote a history of his own day in
forty-five books. This was deliberately designed to have gaps in
it: 'he was glad that his work, like Livy's, should survive in

fragmentary form and for the rest only in epitomes (he wrote his own *periochae*). His contemporary history became a sort of 'artificial ancient ruin'.[30] The most celebrated piece of Renaissance journalism is also so described by Fueter;[31] although in his rigid system it is subordinated to the category 'memoirs'. This is the autobiography of Aeneas Sylvius Piccolomini, Pope Pius II, which an English version has made familiar to a generation of students.[32] Here again we are dealing more with the stuff from which history is made than with history itself. As a historian Pius was hardly successful or important; as a diarist and pamphleteer, none better.

There was, however, one unit in Italian public life unlike all others — the papacy, an autocratic monarchy which just escaped becoming a dynasty. Similarly Rome, where after the mid-fifteenth century the popes almost invariably resided, was no ordinary town. It was the City, *Urbs* with a capital letter, home of martyrs and city of monumental remains. The institution and the place both compelled historiographical innovations which were in their way to be of more lasting influence than those we associate with the humanists writing in communes and courts. It would have been strange indeed if the papal curia had not bred historians, since it was increasingly staffed by men steeped in the new learning. From Nicholas V (1447-55) onwards Rome became steadily more important than any other Italian centre as a focus of literature and scholarship. Popes might sometimes be personally uninterested in any patronage or in any patronage which did not offer immediate self-advertisement, but the momentum in Latin writing, in art and in archaeological research was such that even a disaster such as the Sack of Rome in 1527 barely halted it.

Much of this activity at Rome (and by the early sixteenth century elsewhere in Italy) was archaeological in the broad sense, though as yet not really distinct from a zest for collecting and copying admired objects. As such it will be mentioned again towards the end of this chapter. The historical activity associated with Rome and the Papacy stems from two remarkable servants of the curia, Flavio Biondo of Forlì (1392-1463) and Bartolomeo Sacchi (1421-81), known from his home town of Piadena as Platina. These two North Italians were, in different ways, to be very influential in the centuries ahead.

Biondo — chorographer, philologist, antiquary[33] — broke two of Fueter's basic rules for humanist historians. He wrote about those out-dated medieval relics, the Empire and the Papacy, or at any rate he wrote about Europe and Italy in the Middle Ages, as we have seen.[34] And he was not 'rhetorical'; while his Latin was good he seldom strove for fine effects as he should have done, although Fueter quite erroneously claimed that Leonardo Bruni would not admit him as an acquaintance. Pius II was also superior about Biondo's style, but even the Italian epitome of Biondo's *Decades*, a translation of Pius's abbreviation, did not save the work from fairly swift oblivion (a matter to which we shall have to recur).

How can one briefly describe the *Decades*, this first general history of Medieval Europe? Some hints there are in what he himself says, but mostly we must infer what he is about from his treatment, remembering that *Decade* I runs from 412 to 754 A.D., II from 806 to 1410, III thence to 1439 and the two books of *Decade* IV run through 1440 to 1441. For the modern sections Biondo tells us that he was writing 'Italian history'.[35]

He hardly tells us in the work itself what precisely he intends to cover in the earlier portions. It is, he says at the start, to cover the deeds of the thousand and thirty years since the Goths captured the city. It is from the fall of Rome that a new epoch must be dated: Livy's history was called *ab urbe condita*; and his (we may infer) *ab inclinatione imperii*. But the Roman empire was a bigger affair than Italy itself. And so the story is at first filled by 'those things which happened in the former provinces of the empire beyond the Alps and outside Italy', where, he laments later on, the rule of Rome is a thing of the past. The scope of the first eight books of the first decade (i.e. to about A.D. 600) may fairly be described as an account of the former provinces of the empire, with the stress laid on events in Italy. He summarieses this himself by saying he has described not only the decline of the empire, but also the devastation of Rome and Italy.

Soon, however, we may detect a change in the author's aim. Already in book ix of the first decade he explains that much could be written of the former provinces — Gaul, Spain, England, and the rest. But they all continue in independence, and his prime task is the decline of Rome. Yet Rome was now the heart of another kind of universal state: the *orbis christianus* is mentioned — very significantly he abandons the dating *ab inclinatione imperii* at this point — in 'the year of the incarnation of our Lord 700'. And the first decade ends with a frank disclaimer of any intention of a general account of the Franks. Later on we are told that the deeds of Otto I outside Italy are beyond his scope. Thereafter, though we have references to the provinces, the wider horizon might be described as Christian rather than imperial: it is as an extension of Christendom that Charlemagne's campaigns are presented; it is for this reason that the relief of the Holy Land is described as the finest deed of any pope, and this explains the very full account of the Crusades in the Middle East and elsewhere. From the fourth book of the second decade to the end of the eighth book, from the Council of Clermont to the fall of Acre in 1291, the non-Italian material is virtually restricted to accounts of the Crusades.

Before Biondo reaches the third decade and the events of the fifteenth century he has, of course, begun narrowing his interest to that intensive concentration on Italy which, as we have seen, he himself recognised as his aim in the later books. How did he view Italy? What is the range of his interest in Italian affairs? There are some tantalising glimpses of a general interpretation of Italian history. In an early passage of the *Decades* Biondo consoles himself for the shame of the fall of Rome by contemplating the rise of a new Italy: let us be encouraged by narrating the beginnings of the new cities, the glory of the splendid people, which were to restore to Italy her lost dignity: Venice, Siena, Florence, and the rest re-establish for Italy the glory of fallen Rome. But this proves a dead end. Biondo does not deal adequately with any city save Venice, whose origins (nor surprisingly in view of his intimacy with Venetians) are discussed at some length. The rest are merely mentioned, if at all, in a perfunctory line or two. Another theme, rather more substantial this time, is the need for peace in Italy. He seems to have accepted that the barbarian invaders of Italy soon became Italians: thereafter Italy is disturbed either by foreign attack — by aggressive Greeks under Justinian, later by Germans and French — or by domestic warfare. This deep-rooted desire for *pax in Italia* accounts, of course, for the panegyric on Theodoric which Machiavelli later helped to form into a significant strand in Italian historiography. Popes are praised for their efforts to secure peace in the peninsula: so Honorious III and so, in his own day, Martin V, who attempted to pacify the papal states when he failed to secure a more general settlement; Benedict XII, on the other hand, is rebuked for having legitimised the tyrants of Lombardy — however wise it may have seemed at the time. The schism of 1378 is stated to be a disaster for Italy as well as for the whole of Christendom. The poisonous rivalries of Guelf and Ghibelline call forth a stinging passage: *ea infausta rebus Italiae nomina*. The scourge continues to our own day, Biondo goes on, and Italians treat each other worse than they had formerly been treated by the barbarians: town against town, region against region, one section of the population against another group — only Venice has been spared this competition for territorial power in Italy.

Yet such passionate moments do not represent a steady argument and when Biondo comes to the events of his own day in the third and fourth decades alarums and excursions become his theme. The third decade represents a different kind of history in more ways than one, and it is in fact the case that it is more stylishly composed, more 'humanist'. But we should be wrong to think that the concentration on war was a product of Biondo's humanist aspirations. It was, unhappily for him and his contemporaries, the true condition of his times in the Italy which was now his main theme. 'Italy was now quiet', he writes of the peace of April 1428, 'and this had happened seldom enough in previous centuries'. But the peace lasted only four months and later on Biondo describes such a period as 'rather an interval between upheavals', and notes that the lull corresponded to winter months when campaigning was suspended. The whole work ends with the peace of Cavriana in the autumn of 1441. But this terminus represented nothing very significant for Biondo.

Original as the book was, we must not exaggerate its sophistication. Biondo's method of work was not really in any sense an innovation. One can, if one tries, list a fair number of 'authorities' quoted by him. But essentially he is a modest enough medievalist. Richer than some earlier chroniclers in his range of late classical and patristic material, and alert to ways of securing information for his own day, he was for earlier periods in the last resort the victim rather than the master of his sources. He does not take all his materials and spread them out in a fundamentally reconstructed story. Rather he has one main source and sticks to it, using other writers for supplementing his narrative. Thus Paulus Diaconus supplies the skeleton of his narrative of the fifth century. The account of the Goths comes from Procopius, largely it seems from the version of Leonardo Bruni. Then he reverts again to Paulus Diaconus down to the mid-eighth century. From the ninth century down to the Crusades his main account is drawn out of Tolomeo of Lucca, who, with Villani, is the basis for the rest of the second decade. These main sources partly account for the emphasis which the history of Biondo has from time to time; we may reflect that, doubtless involuntarily, he thus transmitted fairly truly the changing horizons of earlier periods.

The other historian in the Roman curia needs less space because his work is much better known. Platina's *Lives of Jesus Christ and all the Popes*, unlike Biondo's *Decades*, was an early publishing success and has been steadily reprinted over the centuries as well as translated into many vernaculars.[36] The reasons for this sustained popularity are not far to seek. Platina enshrined in the new manner the old material on the popes and this had a continuing relevance for those faithful who were curious about the history of the Church.[37] But he was also far from uncritical of the Church, especially in his own day, and this gave his work an attraction for protestant readers after the Reformation. The *Lives of the Popes* thus had the best of both confessional worlds, a fate which befell very few books, and its biographical structure — one pope's life after another — facilitated continuations which (rather like the annals of the medieval chronicler) tacked on subsequent popes' lives to Platina's account which ended in effect with Paul II. It is of some interest that Platina is the first historian mentioned in this book to see his *magnum opus* in print. It came out at

Venice in 1479.

Platina was a protégé of the Gonzaga family of Mantua
before (and indeed after) he came into papal service, and he
had cut his teeth, so to speak, on a history of Mantua which
has little to commend it. His history of the popes was, however,
precluded by its very nature from singing the praises of a
dynasty. Popes were elected not hereditary monarchs and the
basis of their authority was in the last resort, or perhaps by the
fifteenth century one should rather say 'in the first instance',
religious: 'Thou art Peter and upon this rock I will build my
Church'. Platina was cautious, therefore, in dealing with the
mysteries of early Christianity. He had been accused of pagan
practices under Paul II and then protested his firm if
conventional belief in the Christian faith.[38] It is nevertheless
the case that as he entered the post-patristic period he became
more sceptical of traditional tales and of pious legends.

The work is remarkably well balanced considering the
temptation Platina must have had to expatiate on the popes of
his own life-time. Two-thirds of the space are devoted to the
popes before Boniface VIII (1294-1303) and only a modest
fifth to the popes from Martin V, elected by the Council of
Constance in 1417, down to the end of Paul II's reign. It is, of
course, to these later *Lives* that historians have devoted much
attention and they have had most influence on later
interpretations of the Renaissance papacy. And model lives
they are, in many respects. They usually begin, when his
information is adequate, with a sketch of the new pontiff's
election and background; they proceed to a narrative of his
pontificate; they end with a sketch of his character and of the
notable men of his day. Platina was well-informed, knew the
scholars and prelates of his day extremely well and his polished
account is both an agreeable and an important source. His
sharp account of Paul II is a good instance of the unwisdom of
the prince attacking an historian and then relenting; it is only
in our own day that the rehabilitation of Paul as an
enlightened patron has been accomplished.

For earlier periods Platina was, however, no better than
Biondo as a critic of the sources, as a historian in the modern
sense of the term. Like Biondo he accepts his authorities with
no more than the reservations of common sense. His three

main sources are the *Liber pontificalis*, the *Historia ecclesiastica* of Tolomeo of Lucca, and Flavio Biondo's *Decades*, books I and II. The first of these was an uneven compilation of popes' lives begun in the seventh century and continued in subsequent times and with uneven results down to the early fifteenth century. This has been described as the backbone of Platina's own work, which is itself a new and polished 'Book of popes'. Tolomeo of Lucca was at work on his history early in the fourteenth century; it was much used by some of the compilers of the *Liber pontificalis*. The first two books of Biondo's *Decades* were used not in the original but in the more stylish paraphrase of Aeneas Sylvius. Of course Platina consulted and quoted from many other writings from the New Testament down to writers like Bruni and Poggio in his own day; indeed his references are most various for the early centuries and for the fourteenth and fifteenth. But for the bulk of the *Lives of the Popes* Platina stuck to his main authorities, transcribing, with sometimes hardly any but stylistic changes, page after page. If he encountered an obvious clash he occasionally tried to correct it. If he found an obvious gap he occasionally tried to fill it. Sometimes error stared him in the face and he corrected it. But his procedures are very much Biondo's and they remind us of the way in which the more elaborate medieval chronicles were composed.[39]

He was well placed to get at the books he needed for, like Tolomeo of Lucca a century and a half earlier, he was custodian of what was rapidly becoming the best collection of books in Christendom, the Vatican Library. He also had at his elbow the rich records of the Secret Archives — but there is little indication that he turned to this source as much even as Bruni had turned to the papers of the Florentine Chancery. Platina looked for narratives of the past, and for narrators of the contemporary scene. Nor did he really (*pace* Fueter) treat the papacy as an institution. Take as an example his jumbled account of papal finances, which we find in his life of Boniface IX:

Then, either because he feared the power of the Visconti or because he wished to extend the power of the Church the pope imposed for the first time the practice of paying

annates by ecclesiastical benefices: the new holder paid half
the annual income of his benefice to the papal treasury
(*fisco apostolico*). Some however attribute this new device
to John XXII. Everyone accepted this customary levy except
the English who only allow it in respect of bishoprics ...

The muddle here over when such taxation began, and between
annates and the common service levied from prelates, shows a
total lack of interest in a central aspect of papal administration. As for the moment when such fiscality began, the
records of the *camera apostolica* were at Platina's elbow had
he wished to find out. It was the case, and it deserves respect,
that the Donation of Constantine had sunk without trace:
Valla had here an attentive reader, even if he was a papal
official. And yet there is no discussion of the growth of the
Papal States, on which the power of the pope now depended
more than ever before.[41]

If Platina's originality tends to be exaggerated, it remains
true that overall the *Lives of the Popes* is a valuable digest,
even for those events for which it has no independent
authority. Like Biondo, Platina is writing about the past, and
if we treasure in both authors the sections devoted to their own
times, this is because we are going to them for our purposes
rather than for the purposes they had in designing their books
as they did. It is salutary to compare an account of Innocent
III's pontificate in a modern handbook with Platina's
summary at the end of this pope's *vita*:

He issued many decrees to regulate the behaviour of both
the laity and the clergy. He composed books on the euchar-
ist, on baptism, on the wretchedness of human life. He
preached sermons suited to the season and the feast. He
blamed as purveying false doctrine a book by Abbot
Joachim and he condemned the errors of the heretic
Amaury who was later burned at Paris with his faction ...
The pope also delighted in the virtue and scholarship of
St. Dominic (from whom the Order of Preachers had its
origin) and the holiness of St. Francis (founder of the Friars
Minor). Some say that Gratian the compiler of the
Decretum and Papias, who made a Latin vocabulary, lived
at this time. There is no doubt about Papias; but there are

authorities who place Gratian under Alexander III. And lest one might think that Innocent overlooked works of piety, it should be recalled that by his initiative and at his expence the hospital of Santo Spirito was established and largely endowed, so that pilgrims, the sick, foundlings and orphans might be succoured. He adorned the altar of St. Peter's with mosaic as is indicated by his picture and inscription in the vault ... In all regards he stood out as a man of the highest qualities, worthy to be reckoned among those popes who were saints.[42]

No one would quote this passage nowadays as a source of information; it is all derivative, and some of it is wrong. But this happens with modern textbooks, and on the whole Platina gets the measure of the pope fairly enough.

As already observed, there were still scores of chroniclers at work in fifteenth-century Italy who operated in the old annalistic way. We must not assume that the canons of humanist historiography were rapidly or universally adopted. It would, however, be true to say that with the advent of the sixteenth century there was to be an increasingly assured position only for the more or less polished narration of the humanist writer, as well as a smaller but significant public for antiquarian scholarship, itself closely related to humanist interests and skills, but addressed to specialists. In a sense, these erudite researchers were not writing history as such, but their studies of ancient buildings, of coins and medals, of inscriptions all contributed grist to the historians' mill. Nor must we compartmentalise too much. Biondo wrote two books on ancient Rome, the *Roma instaurata* and the *Roma triumphans*. The first was a description of the physical appearance of the ancient city — an early exercise in what we would describe as archaeology; the second dealt with the religion, government, armies and customs of Roman Rome, a 'companion to Latin studies', it might nowadays be called. These were seminal works,[43], and so was the *Italia illustrata*, the first chorographical treatise of the Renaissance. In this short but extremely influential work Biondo described Italy province by province, indicating the towns (especially with reference to their ancient names) and the great men of each region.

Works such as these were bound to be overtaken by subsequent scholarship, archaeological [44] or topographical.[45] In subsequent chapters we shall have to consider some of the consequences of this development in technical research, both in Italy and elsewhere, for it culminates in works of permanent value which in some measure have not had to be revised and replaced and so forgotten. But it was not only the *eruditi* who fell into oblivion as later and better studies came along. Only a tiny handful of scholars looks at Bruni's history today or at the other humanist historians mentioned above. Even when translated they have virtually no interest save to specialists.

Yet by the end of the *quattrocento* Italy had produced two approaches to the past which were to be models for countless historians and researchers for two centuries. For anyone interested in the past it was possible to choose between writing history as a form of artistic literature and writing history without such pretensions as an enquiry into origins, real or supposed, of places, artefacts and institutions, at any rate those of antiquity. Between these two modes the old annalistic compiler, the local chronicler, gradually grew less and less important. He survived everywhere but tended to conform with the new patterns by aiming to please the public with agreeable and undemanding works or to please fellow antiquaries by producing 'collections' of monuments, authors, *objets d'art* or *de vertue*. The opposition between history designed to attract and persuade, and history which wrangled about *minutiae*, did not preclude the former from possessing considerable merit, nor the latter from the discussion of matters of substantial importance. And, in practice, it need hardly be said, there was never so sharp an antithesis as has been suggested here. For instance, the propagandist and popular historians of the late fifteenth and sixteenth centuries lean very heavily on Flavio Biondo's *Decades*, usually without acknowledgement. But history as it was to develop by the decades around 1800 was to depend on an amalgam of the two approaches, which was not to be accomplished until the Enlightenment.

f the writers discussed in the previous chapter are scarcely
ead today, many of the authors who were at work in the
ixteenth century are both more accessible (because they wrote
n vernaculars) and better known (because widely translated
nto other vernaculars). This is notably the case with the two
great Florentines, Niccolo Machiavelli (1459-1527) and
Francesco Guicciardini (1483-1540), who are familiar to
generations of university students and to a still wider public all
over the world. Machiavelli is, of course, especially admired
now, just as he used to be especially notorious in earlier
centuries, for *The Prince*.

Fueter distinguishes Machiavelli and Guicciardini, together
with one or two much less important historians, from their
Latin-writing predecessors (Bruni, Poggio and the others) as the
second Florentine school'. But it is an arbitrary distinction,
and false in that it suggests that the two men inaugurated a
new approach to historiography, which they did not. Bruni
and other humanist historians established a genre of
composition which was to be influential for centuries, long
after their works themselves were forgotten. The vernacular
histories of Machiavelli and Guicciardini did not lead on to
other similar writings; their time of influence was to come in
the late nineteenth century when scholars writing histories of
Florence or of the Italian wars depended greatly on their
works. At first sight it is surprising that one must contrast
Machiavelli and Guicciardini with Bruni and his 'school'.
Machiavelli and Guicciardini, like their predecessors, were
public servants, administrators, used to being at the centre of
political action. Moreover, in broad terms they accepted the
humanist principles (those of rhetorical tradition) for 'true'

history. Yet the nature of their approach to the past w
different and one must associate this at any rate in part wi
the character of their involvement in affairs. Bruni, much
he advocated the 'active' life, was in no real sense a man
action. His contribution to Florentine policy lay to a sm:
degree only, we must suppose, in his influence as chancell(
considerable though that must sometimes have been, a
much more in his production of pamphlets, dialogues a
other writings designed to demonstrate the values whi
underlay the Florentine way of life, and of the great *Histo*
which reviewed the past in political terms, from t
foundation of the town in the Roman republic to the defian
of Visconti Caesarism in his own day (cf. above p.8*
Machiavelli and Guicciardini, while obsessed with t
problems of Florence, produced histories void of su
polemical purposes; they accepted a republican Florence
axiomatic.

The major historical studies of both men were writt
(unlike those of Bruni and Poggio) after they had ceased to
practising politicians and administrators. If Machiavelli h:
continued as a chancery official instead of being tortured ar
exiled to his property outside Florence in 1512 it is m(
unlikely that we should have had any of the great prose work
The Prince, the *Discorsi* and the *History of Florence*.
became a historian because he was prevented from being
politician by the recovery of Medici power in Florenc
Subsequently the Medici refused to give him serious emplo
ment despite the *History of Florence* which was written for t
Medici pope Clement VII, just as the last Florentine republ
refused to employ him in 1527 (because he had tried
ingratiate himself with the Medici) — a final deception whi(
surely precipitated his death. The story of Guicciardini
different but the upshot not dissimilar. After decades of pap:
service as a top official in the papal territories and as a
organiser of papal armies, Guicciardini might well hav
expected to have become an important, even the al
important, political figure in the Medici court which w:
established when the republic of 1527 collapsed in 1530. But h
was soon put out to grass, and so we have the great *History* (
Italy, begun in 1538 and intended for publication, as w:

Machiavelli's *History of Florence*. It is these two works — and not the many other writings of these men[1] — which shall be considered here.[2]

Both works reflect the authors' attempts to conform to the literary ideal of history, with careful composition, set speeches and elaborate battle scenes. But in each case the author's practical experience and his view of life is evident beneath the carapace of the humanist manner. Machiavelli had a gift for sharp observation derived from his experience as diplomatic agent. He was used to composing incisive despatches which analysed a situation and urged a course of action. Even more important, he was constitutionally addicted to politics as a subject for science. He felt, not that the past moulded the future, but that it contained lessons which, when mastered and applied, would enable statesmen to make the sort of future which they wanted, would enable them to frustrate the blind operations of Fortuna. It was in this spirit that Machiavelli surveyed the early history of Florence and would, doubtless, have surveyed the town's internal development in the later fifteenth century had the *History* not been commissioned by Clement VII. As it was, the later books dealt mainly with Medici foreign policy, a much less contentious field than home affairs, for Machiavelli had no desire to overpraise the incipient Medici principate.[3] A good example of the way he made his *History of Florence* yield political wisdom is the repeated illustration of the failure of mercenary armies: 'fighting was reduced to a trade so vile that any peddling captain, in whom the mere ghost of ancient valour had reappeared, would have laughed them to scorn, to the amazement of all Italy who in her folly paid them respect'.[4] Machiavelli genuinely believed that his citizen army could be created and that it would be effective. This optimistic conviction that all one had to do was to tell one's contemporaries the truth for them to alter their ways is found in all his writings and not least in the Florentine history.

If Machiavelli was an optimist, Guicciardini knew that in any crisis in public affairs whatever a statesman did would be wrong. This too is a general proposition, to be sure, but it holds out no hope for the future and, as he knew, it cannot be proved from events of the past. His *History of Italy*[5] surveyed

the peninsula from the French invasion down to the death o
the second Medici pope, Clement VII, in 1534. His scope i
therefore exclusively diplomatic and military. This accorde
well with the precepts of Cicero. It also fell well within the
first-hand experience of Guicciardini himself, author of man
despatches and reports. Machiavelli's canvas covers a longe
period and in theory aimed at a less conventional approach
After a brief account of early Florentine history, the perio
covered was from the late thirteenth century to the death o
Lorenzo de' Medici in 1492. It was his intention, he wrote, t
remedy the defects of Bruni's work down to 1434. Bruni ha
neglected the internal history of the city and Machiavelli woul
put that right, and then from 1434 he would pay equa
attention to domestic and foreign policy.[6] In fact, with the
rise of the Medici in 1434, about halfway through the *Histor
of Florence*, the emphasis Machiavelli placed was mainly o
foreign affairs, partly perhaps because, as a republican, h
had no desire to describe the gradual ascendancy of th
Medici, partly no doubt because this enabled him more readil
to follow rhetorical practice, that 'graver and more elevate
style' which he told Clement VII he would adopt in the event
which followed Lorenzo's death — events he would not live t
relate.[7]

Neither author has any use of protestations of the mora
value of history.[8] They both undoubtedly felt that it ha
political worth, that statemen could benefit by understandin
the network of interlocking events which made up the face o
destiny, of Fortuna, which made or marred all. Both writer
accepted that in the Italy of their day the political scene wa
composed of rotten and corrupt states, whose future lay in th
hands of strangers and barbarians.

> If the deeds of our princes at home and abroad are no
> worth studying for their valour and dignity, as were those o
> their ancestors, yet they have other attributes which are no
> less worthy of consideration … If in the following descrip
> tion of the affairs of these corrupt communities one ha
> nothing to relate of the fortitude of their soldiers, the valo
> of their captains or the patriotism of their citizens, on
> will see with what deceit and with what craft and guile th

princes, soldiers and leaders of republics have achieved for themselves a reputation they have never deserved.[9]

Guicciardini had an equally scathing view of the contemporary scene, but had no illusions about it being capable of improvement. Writing of the year 1508, after the barbarians had begun to dominate the land, he says:

> The diseases of Italy were not such, nor their forces so little weakened, that they could be cured with simple medecines; rather, as often happens in bodies overflowing with corrupt humours, a remedy employed to cure disorder in one part generates even more pernicious and dangerous ills ... For although there had already been, for fourteen years in Italy, so many wars and so many changes of State, yet because these things often ended without bloodshed, or else the killings took place, for the most part, amongst the barbarians themselves, the people had suffered less than the princes. But now ... there followed throughout Italy, and against the Italians themselves, the cruellest accidents, endless murders, sackings and destruction of many cities and towns ... [10]

Despite the conventional titles of their respective works their range is wider. Machiavelli explains at the beginning of book VII that it was impossible for him to confine his history to Florence; to do so would make his narrative less intelligible. In similar fashion, the last seven books of Guicciardini's history (1421-34) are different from what goes before. 'The events after 1521 are part of the general European struggle between the French King and the Hapsburgs; the Italian rulers were no longer initiators of events but rather were subject to them'.[11] And of course Guicciardini at this time was at the very heart of the political action. The dominant concern in both authors with diplomatic and military events thus, in a sense, distracted them from the sort of history of a town, a dynasty, a state, which had developed earlier and was to form the pattern of future historiography, at any rate as far as a general cultivated public was concerned. And as for analysis of events, this was done almost entirely through analysis of the interplay of the powerful or weak personalities of the men who mattered. All

were exposed to the blind actions of Fortune. Against thi
heroism and stoic resignation enabled an individual to retai
honour and dignity — though not dignities of power or wealth
as both men found out. Machiavelli's *History of Florence* is
less ambitious, and a less attractive work, although the earl
books, discussing the internal scene in Florence prior to th
crisis of 1420-34, are more genuinely 'historical' in our moder
sense of the word. His embarrassed praise of the Medic
contrasts with the terrible portraits of the two Medici pope
given by Guicciardini (XVI, xii).And his evasion of discussio
of events after 1494 preclude him from using, as Guicciardin
did, personal experience.

Both men, however, display the sharp observation of th
trained diplomat and administrator and it was this that gav
their writing its novel pungency. Guicciardini's use of se
speeches, his careful rearrangement of the narrative int
twenty books because this was a more perfect number, hi
proceeding a year at a time — all these tributes to a Livea
model and to humanist tradition are not the essential parts o
his work. This work, and to a lesser extent Machiavelli's, deriv
from the world of despatches and action, from an absorptio
in politics which dominated them and which, when they wer
deprived of participation in events, flower out in narratives o
the past and (in Machiavelli's case) prescriptions for th
future.

The two men have no real successors in Florence, or indee
elsewhere, for a considerable time. The statesman in disfavou
writing his memoirs was, of course, to recur. More inter
estingly, we can find an example before we encounter th
'second Florentine school'. Philippe de Commynes (1447
1511), in his *Mémoires*, compiled (ostensibly for an Italia
humanist friend to rewrite in noble Latin) an account o
France and Burgundy under Charles the Bold, Louis XI an
Charles VII which in its way has been as influential with late
historians as have the writings of his two celebrated Florentin
contemporaries.[12] While Commynes followed a rough
chronological pattern his *Mémoires* are not in any true sens
narrative history; and they are closely related to his ow
experience. They begin in 1464 when he entered Charles th
Bold's service and they go down to 1498 when, with the adven

of Louis XII of France, he was dismissed. Whatever his original intentions may have been, he shows early and regularly a didactic impulse, a desire to teach princes and men of public importance some of the lessons he has learned in his career as councillor first to the duke of Burgundy and then to the king of France. And to drive his points home he is capable of adjusting awkward facts, though the work as a whole cannot be regarded as self-exculpatory despite its bias, despite its 'discontinuous' character. He 'has no intention of organizing his recollections either chronologically or thematically to show the evolution of events'.[13] He was thus different in this regard from Machiavelli and Guicciardini, as he was also in his larger acceptance of divine providence in the scheme of things. All three men were Christians but there is no doubt that religion meant far more to the author of the *Mémoires*.[14]

What we witness in these writers is the emergence of a new secular administration, the dynamo of government in Europe in the sixteenth century and after. Such men were not readily expendable and normally survived changes of dynasty or other political upheavals. Hence the literate and professional councillor, ambassador, secretary usually died without committing his experiences to paper: he was too busy being busy. The sequence of memorialists is therefore sparse, and it is obvious that many possible writers imposed on themselves self-censorship. Thus, despite the obvious attractions to the men of affairs, all by now educated in the new manner, of humanist historical canons (literary good manners, concentration on diplomacy and war), successors to the two Italians and the Frenchman are seldom impressive. Fueter describes the 'disciples' and 'successors' of Guicciardini and Machiavelli; they were a poor lot, mostly Medici placemen in Florence or in the service of a state like Venice. As for the French, Fueter surely greatly exaggerates the effects of Commynes on the mediocre historical works of Martin and Guillaume du Bellay, Blaise de Monluc and Pierre de Bourdeilles (abbé de Brantôme). These sixteenth-century Italians and Frenchmen were soldiers, diplomats, courtiers, lacking the edge of Commynes and the penetration of Machiavelli and Guicciardini.[15] It is not until we reach the seventeenth century, with perhaps de Retz and certainly Clarendon, that works of stature by statesmen reemerge.[16]

Far more important reflections of sixteenth-century tastes in history were shown by the continued popularity of late medieval chronicles and a steady 'translation' of such material into humanist forms. This phenomenon is common to nearly all parts of western Europe, but it is perhaps most evident in states governed by princes, whose autocratic behaviour rapidly increased after 1500. The developments alluded to took varied forms, but some generalizations may safely be made.

The continuance of affection for the older traditions is very evident in England, where a succession of early Tudor writers — the compiler of the *Great Chronicle*, Alderman Fabyan, Edward Hall — lead on to Grafton, Holinshed and Stow at the end of the Tudor period.[17] This was tribute to the lively life of the capital and to the desire of leading citizens to read about themselves and their ancestors in the immortality of the printed page, just as they had coveted manuscript accounts somewhat similar in effect to the family histories of Venice, or in Florence the *priorista* (a list of the family's office bearers). But the itch to find familiar proper names in the annals of the past was not confined to burgesses. Long lists of knights and gentlemen taking part in wars, invasions and tournaments were gathered in by the industrious chronicler. In England this process of vulgarising history was supported from the mid-sixteenth century by a rapid development of dramatic pieces based on English historical themes. John Bale's *King Johan* is the fruit; they culminate in Shakespeare's 'Histories' but do not end there. This trend was accompanied by a series of poetical effusions, heavily moralising, of which the best known was a sequence of limping effusions known collectively as *The Mirror for Magistrates*.

However lightly we treat it, in its time the *Mirror* was thought of as a profoundly serious book, and its readers were right to think so. This explains why the book was so often added to, so often imitated, why the line of the progeny of the *Mirror* extended well into the seventeenth century, and why men should still wish to read it when much better poets were at work.[18]

In the *Mirror* Fortune and Providence struggled, much as they had in Machiavelli and Guicciardini; the solution of the dilemma was a notion of divine retribution, somewhat erratic in operation, which operated with theatrical results, especially from the deposition of Richard II. The first exponent of this interpretation of English history was the Italian, Polydore Vergil.[19]

Vergil was in England after 1505 as the familiar of Adriano Castellesi, and as his deputy in the office, diplomatic rather than financial, of Collector of Peter's Pence.[20] He had a literary reputation, was scholarly by inclination, and thus an obvious author for an up-to-date history justifying the Tudors in Latin to the Latin-reading humanists of the courts of the West. Vergil's work is well known and there is no need to rehearse his sources (mainly obvious ones, strictly followed) or his influence, which was greater abroad than at home, as was intended. The large work was published half-a-dozen times at Basle and Leyden and every European historian depended on it for the facts of English history prior to the sixteenth century. At home, those who read it read it in Latin, for the English translation that was made for the second edition was not published until the nineteenth century. Good Englishmen (and Welshmen) loathed the debunking of Brutus and Arthur, regarded Vergil (after the break with Rome) as a papist interloper, and were oblivious of his contribution of a theme to recent English history, as well as a retelling of a familiar narrative in the medium of neo-classical (but not frantically ambitious) Latin. Vergil had lists of gentlemen at battles, he named the mayors, and very occasionally 'digressed' to discuss institutions or political problems. Something of this filtered through to Hall and Holinshed and Shakespeare: it would be possible here and there to trace back a glowing line of a verse to the remorseless periods of the author of the *Anglica Historia*. But the main message of the work was the monarchy. After the earliest period is disposed of, Vergil proceeds to a book to a reign, saving up biographical details of other great men to a concluding paragraph in each book. This, and the providential pattern already referred to, were his main structural contributions to English historiography. As for presentation, he offered his adopted country a model of stylish narrative, comparable with Italian work.

Many of the first humanist narratives of trans-Alpine
countries were composed by visiting Italians and for a time it
was exceptional to have history in the new manner composed
by natives. England offered a striking exception. Thomas
More wrote his life of *Richard III* at about the same moment
that Vergil completed the first draft of the *Anglica Historia*
(1513). More wrote both a Latin and an English version.[21]
The latter appeared in John Harding's *Chronicle* (1543) and
the other suitable collections; the Latin did not appear
until the Louvain *Opera Omnia* of 1565. More's reading of the
ancient historians (Tacitus, Suetonius and especially Sallust)
gave him his approach, and he doubtless had recourse
occasionally to chronicles for narrative detail. But his work is
more truly 'classical' than Vergil's, for it is written out of his
head, so to speak, and almost certainly not as a result of royal
prompting; it is contemporary history by an Englishman,
stretching his historical limbs. Vergil's account, on the other
hand, is the conclusion of a long survey, much tied to rewriting
medieval material. It is interesting to note the self-censorship
which led More to avoid publishing and also refrain from
writing about Henry VII and which equally deterred Vergil
from publishing his account of Henry VIII's reign (to 1537)
until 1555, when he was back in Italy.

In France, too, there was an Italian at work, Paulus
Aemilius of Verona (d. 1529). Far more of a stylist than Vergil,
he had a far more ordinary mind. He was also slower.
Beginning work in 1489 he had only reached the thirteenth
century when he died. His anodyne and respectful account of
the mythological origins of France, his deference to the
dynasties of French monarchs, his sustained speeches in *oratio
recta* and *obliqua* (later published separately, so great was the
admiration they aroused) — all ensured that his work would
find continuators to bring it up to date and a number of
mediocrities had the necessary Latin to do this. Nor was there
need to hesitate regarding publication: by his death books i-ix
had appeared (Paris, 1517 and 1528). Even more than the
Anglica Historia, Aemilius's *De rebus gestis Francorum* laid its
imprint on refined historiography in France, both in Latin and
the vernaculars.[22] There was no equivalent to Thomas
More.[23]

Aemilius in France, Vergil in England — the expatriate Italians working in the courts of the north can be multiplied, though they scarcely equalled Aemilius for style nor Vergil for critical ability. Filippo Buonaccorsi (1437-96) is the first humanist historian writing in Poland. In Hungary a little later we find Antonio Bonfini (d. 1505). Lucio Marineo of Sicily (Siculo), who died in 1533, published at Alcalà in 1530 a work intended to present Spain's Roman origins. And, more important, if only because of his subject — the discovery of the New World — Pietro Martire d'Anghiera, who died in Granada in 1526; the first complete edition of his *Decades de orbe novo* was published in 1530. Vergil, indeed, ascribed the spread of humanism to the Italian wars: '... good literature, both French and Greek, was expelled from Italy by the disastrous wars ... and betook itself across the Alps, pouring into Germany, France, England, Scotland'.[24]

This is, in fact, true if one looks at the literature and not at the men of letters. The names just mentioned are only a fraction of those who, outside Italy and in the sixteenth and seventeenth centuries were captivated by humanist history and practised it. The principal humanist historians in the Spanish kingdom, in Scotland, above all in Germany, were natives, not imported Italians. A very long list indeed could be compiled of such scholars and Fueter devotes a substantial section of his survey to them. They were particularly numerous in Spain and Germany. In both these countries there was what might be termed 'a reception' earlier and more diffuse than elsewhere. Fueter ascribes the survival of the medieval chronicle approach in Renaissance Germany to the absence of any coherent political pattern in the area and the survival of a weak Empire. Yet, as already observed, medieval chronicles, only very slightly updated in manner, survived elsewhere, and it is far more likely that the divisions of Germany, the strong urban cultural centre, and the growing power of the greater princes, provided a cultural background in certain senses parallel to that in Italy and equally conducive to the exercise of good Latin. The resulting works were not destined to be of much long-term significance. The best writers — Jacob Wimpheling (1450-1528), Beatus Rhenanus (1486-1547), Albert Krantz (1448-1517), Johann Turmair (Aventinus, 1477-1534),

Willibald Pirckheimer (1470-1530) — have been the subject of much research by students of German humanism.[25] But, for a long time at least, these men and all they originally stood for, including patriotic emotions whether to Germany or one of its provinces, were warped by the influence of the Reformation. This did not happen in Spain and there the steady stream of native humanist historians marches onwards, gathering strength as the union of Aragon and Castile became more of a reality under Charles V. Here again one can usefully refer to Fueter, where there is a helpful discussion.[26] The most celebrated of the polished works on the peninsula is without doubt Juan de Mariana's imposing and often reprinted *Historiae de rebus Hispaniae libri xx*(to 1516. Mariana lived from 1535 to 1625 and his great work began to appear in 1592; he himself produced a Spanish version. The work was continued by others and, both in Spanish and Latin, had great influence both in Spain and on the Continent in general.

Fueter compares the Jesuit father Mariana's history of Spain with the Protestant Scotsman George Buchanan's *Rerum Scoticarum historia*, published in 1582 at Edinburgh as the author lay dying. Buchanan was the towering figure in Scottish humanism: professor at Bordeaux, tutor to James VI (later to be James I of England), and from time to time deeply involved in the politics of his country. His history was frequently reprinted and, like Mariana's for Spain, gave European scholars for a century their picture of Scottish antiquities and Scottish history.[27]

With the Jesuit and the Calvinist we have moved across the Reformation which at first glance might seem to have exercised the most profound effects on historiography. Effects of an important kind it did have. It turned scholars with a quite new critical awareness towards the early courses of early Church history, it concentrated their attention for the first time on the history of an institution rather than the history of territories or their rulers, and it led to an examination of the evolution of doctrines — to the history of ideas. It also for a time led to embittered and violent interpretations of the past in Germany and elsewhere.

Though Reformation historiography does not begin with the 'Magdeburg centuriators', the scholars so described were its most impressive early manifestation. Headed and inspired by Matthias Flacius Illyricus (= Vlach from a town in Istria), a team of Lutheran scholars compiled an entirely original work.[28] A translation of the title page of the *editio princeps*, vol. i (Basle: Oporinus, 1560) will set out the scheme on which the work was planned:

> The Ecclesiastical History of the perfectly conceived church of Christ, as to situation, propagation, persecutions, periods of peace, and as to doctrine, heresies, ceremonies, government, schisms, councils, important individuals, miracles, martyrdoms, religions other than Christianity, the political position of the Empire, all comprehended in a clear manner according to centuries; compiled with great diligence and honesty from the best historical, patristic and other writers, by a group of studious and devout men at Magdeburg.

The title should be regarded seriously, for it represents the sections under which, century by century, the history of Christianity was laid out. That is to say, each century had chapters devoted to the public state of the Church, its doctrinal development, and so forth. Nothing remotely comparable had been attempted earlier and the systematic manual side of it remains with us almost to our own day, in such a work (for instance) as Johann Gieseler's *Lehrbuch* or *Compendium* (first ed. 1824-5, but much reprinted and translated), which still figures in the standard bibliographies and is indeed still useful.

The division into centuries was a new device and indeed the subsequent frequent use of *centuria*, meaning a hundred years, which is not classical, derives from its employment by the Magdeburg centuriators, even if they were not the first to employ it in this precise sense. Fueter is very rude about the word, which he regards as a concept derived from the annal but much more damaging.[29] I suppose a hundred times more damaging! But it would have been asking too much of sixteenth-century scholarship to analyse the past by 'organic periods'. The fact that we still arrange our historical teaching and research by centuries, still talk of 'nineteenth-century' phenomena, use such an expression as *fin de siècle* (with all its absurdities), shows that Flacius had hit on a worthwhile term. It may be added, in praise of the format and presentation of this very large work, that it was beautifully printed in highly legible double columns, amply provided — and on an entirely new and scholarly scale — with *corrigenda* and *addenda*, and very thoroughly indexed. It was among the first books to put nearly all of the capabilities of the printing press at the disposal of a learned public.

Quotation of reference material is also impressive. This makes, as we have already observed,[30] for ugly Latinity and it was far from unusual, even in humanist writings of the purest sort. A work like Lorenzo Valla's *Elegantiae* is peppered with interruptions such as 'ut Terentius', 'teste Prisciano', 'et Accius in octavo didascolion'.[31] So the centuriators, save that they frequently skip any attempt at weaving an authority into the text by an 'ut' or a 'teste'. It is, however, the range of their material that impresses. From two adjacent columns of the first volume (*Cent. III*, cap. iii) I note Nicephorus, Vincentius, Henricus de Erfordia, Sabellicus, Bede, Reginus, besides many references to Eusebius, as was to be expected in an early part of the work. Now it is worth noting that the compilers (who copy out regularly documents of some length, especially from Eusebius) are not by any means dependent on writers such as Nicephorus of Constantinople and Reginus of Prüm (both late eighth to early ninth century), Bede (d. 735, see above pp.34-6) or Eusebius (early fourth century, above pp.23, 30), who might all in a sense be regarded as patristic, as exempt from the errors and biases of the medieval papist chronicle. The references to Vincent of Beauvais (above p.64), to Henricus de Herford (d. 1370), another Dominican, and to Sabellicus's *Enneades*, a worthless poetical effusion on world history written in Venice about 1500 — these are more surprising names to encounter and testify to the genuine attempt of the compiler to gather material from every available source. To this end Flacius himself made several journeys to libraries in foreign (mainly Protestant) lands and so did his colleagues, especially Mark Wagner.

The team work involved and the ransacking of sources and of libraries for fresh sources were both major innovations in historical work. The collaboration of a group of scholars to produce a coherent work was in particular an original attempt to attain completeness and authority which was not to be repeated on a significant scale until the nineteenth century. Men of letters corresponded, of course, but it was to be a very long time before they worked together as Flacius and his friends worked. That Flacius was the dynamic spirit behind the whole enterprise is clear from its termination with the thirteenth *Century* at his death in 1575.

Having remarked on the pioneer character of the *Centuries* it is only right to note that the work had a sharply polemical interest. It was a Lutheran (in later editions it acquired Calvinist overtones) demonstration of the decline and corruption of the Church under the papacy. Therefore it was on the basis of good and bad that the authors judged events and ideas, institutions and individuals. Saints were fine when martyred by infidels, suspect if beatified by due canonical process. The medieval chronicles and charters were scrutinised, not in a spirit of scientific enquiry, but in order to condemn the popes (and all the clergy they were supposed to control) out of their own mouths. Sceptical procedures found, as we have seen, in a few writers such as Biondo and Valla, were only of interest when they demonstrated the falsity of some hoary prop to papal power such as the Donation of Constantine (Cent. IIII, cap. vii). All the myths which discredited the papacy and which displayed superstition and incredulity, were recorded without a blink — Fueter instances 'Pope Joan' as a good example; anyone who resisted the Church became a morning star of the Reformation. 'Universal history became again a battle between God and the Devil'.[32] It can easily be imagined how this monumental battery of anti-papal weapons could be turned by protestants against the Roman anti-Christ, how welcome the secularising tendencies of the work were to the princes of Reformation Europe.

Scholarly and polemical, it was a formidable challenge to Rome, and it was not until Cesare Baronio began work that a satisfactory alternative account appeared of what must now be called the Middle Ages. If Flacius was a son of the Reformation, Cesare Baronio (1538-1607) was a son of the Counter-Reformation. His inspiration was St Philip Neri and he joined the Congregation of the Oratory in Rome. He was intensely devout and ascetic and much of his scholarly work had therefore to be done at night, when his priestly duties were over. His scholarship was multifarious and he was an obvious choice as a Roman Catholic alternative to the centuriators. In 1596 he became a cardinal and the next year librarian of the Vatican.[33] The compilation of a monumental account of Church history, the *Annales ecclesiastici*, could not fail to have its controversial aspects, even within the bounds of the Roman obedience; for example, discussions of the papal relations with the Normans in the eleventh century led to the Spanish resenting consideration of their rights in the Kingdom of Naples, and this involved much additional work, particularly painful as Baronio was himself a Neapolitan by birth.

But the enemy to be combated was protestantism. The preliminaries of the first edition, indeed, have an 'appendix' addressed 'ad lectorum extra catholicam' and several distinguished protestant divines were won over by the patient honesty of Baronio, his earnestness and application. He certainly surpassed the centuriators in the extent of his quotation from and of original documents, to which he had privileged access as librarian; the early volumes of the work contain many pieces of epigraphic evidence — coins and medals are discussed and illustrated. Nor was he gullible. Like most serious scholars by this date, he rejected the Donation of Constantine and many other traditional bits of papal apparatus. References to authorities are even more plentiful than in the *Centuries* and, useful device (though not his own invention), the exact location of the text quoted was removed to a marginal note instead of encumbering the text. Like the *Centuries*, the work was well indexed.

It was immediately and immensely successful among both protestants and catholics.[34] There were many reprints and compendia, the latter being widely translated. The first two volumes (1588, 1590) were printed on the presses of the Vatican; later editions had the honour of being issued by Plantin (1589-1609) and Moretus (1596-1610). Above all it was continued. Bzovius carried the story down from 1198, where Baronio had ended (vol. xii, 1607), to the year 1572. Later others took up the task, notably Rinaldi (1646-77) and in the nineteenth century Theiner; meanwhile many other scholars had revised and enriched the work, notably G.D. Mansi (1692-1769).

The familiar sight of Baronius-Raynaldus-Theiner on our library shelves, and the recourse which is still had by scholars to the *Annales*, is certainly a portent of a new continuity in scholarship but it almost certainly exaggerates the importance of Baronio's original research. He was thorough and by his own lights fearlessly honest. Yet the *Annales* was in many regards as tendentious as the *Centuries*. Baronio treated patristic and medieval error with suspicion, seeing potential heresy on every hand. Nor was the annalistic form an improvement. It is interesting that in practice Baronio often accepted a scheme of centuries in his larger volume organisation. But within each volume we creep forward a year at a time, within each year are numbered paragraphs, with marginal titles, discussing events as nearly as possible in chronological sequence. Of course some discussion of topic and problems does occur, but it occurs despite and not because of Baronio's plan. And this limitation, of course, governed the activities of his continuators. Hence what we have is a chronological reference book, which, in its annalistic way, remains useful, but which is less intellectually stimulating than the subjective treatment of the *Centuries*.

The Reformation had thus produced an original work in the *Centuries* and a manual with a future in the *Annales*. However, many writers of Church history worked within a nationalist framework and their books, some of which remain useful, are discussed in the next chapter. In the long run, I believe, the effects of the Reformation on European histor-iography were not to be vitally important.

Vast as was the output of historical works in nearly every part of Europe during the sixteenth century, it is important to remember that the public avidly consuming vernacular histories, the smaller public relishing Latin writings, were not without critics who warned against trusting any accounts of the past. Such scepticism was attracted to history at any rate partly because the confessional conflicts had encouraged distortion

and bias, and partly because national traditions had been
severely disrupted by political divisions acquiring religious
affinities (e.g. Catholics, Huguenots and 'politiques' in France
cut across the traditional unities of the patriotic past). There
were, moreover, philosophical temptations towards Pyrrhonism, reflected in the writings of Giovanni Francesco Pico
della Mirandola and Agrippa of Nettesheim; the latter's works
also reflected the medieval mystic's conviction that human
reason was fallacious, if not irrelevant, in the basic concern of
man with his immortal soul. From such roots doubt could
draw rich substance. The most revered authorities could be
called in question. 'If Herodotus was the father of history, he
was also the father of lies.'[35]

How easy it was to debunk the pedantic historian was shown
in sparkling style by Sir Philip Sidney, in his *An Apologie for
Poetrie*:

> The Historian, scarcely giveth leysure to the Moralist ... but
> that he loden with old Mouse-eaten records, authorising
> himselfe (for the most part) upon the histories, whose great-
> est authorities, are built upon the notable foundation of
> Heare-say, having much a-doe to accord differing Writers,
> and to pick trueth out of partiality ... curious for antiqui-
> ties, and inquisitive of novelties, a wonder to young folkes,
> and a tyrant in table talke, denieth in a great chafe, that any
> man for teaching of vertue, and vertuous actions, is compar-
> able to him. I am *Lux vitae, temporum magistra* ...[36]

And so with the Ciceronian tags. So that the historian's claim
to be a moralist is false. And in any case he is 'tyed, not to what
should be, but to what is, to the particular truth of things, and
not to the general reason of things' ... 'The best of the
Historian, is subject to the Poet'. The historian, based on
falsity, cannot deal with the ideal.

The lead in rebutting such criticism was taken by French
scholars. For this there were several reasons. The long
tradition of Gallicanism, that is the notion that there had
always been a French Church with its own characteristic
institutions independent of the pope and Rome, was clearly an
historically-based position and was deeply embedded in the
French legal profession. Hence the attraction for some

Frenchmen of an attack on the Roman law, which had in many parts of Europe begun to subjugate other, older (and generally customary) systems — the Roman law either in its medieval form (*mos italicus*), or rejuvenated and 'purified' by Renaissance scholars Italian and French (*mos gallicus*). The tensions of cultural rivalry which produced everywhere later on 'battles of the books' also manifested themselves in France earlier than in Germany or England.

The validity of historical scholarship had also to be maintained against the more insidious charge that, since the genre was literary, it was therefore a branch of oratory. This was an assumption widely held by humanists, as we have seen. But the orator's task was to delight and persuade and it was not hard to show that delight and persuasion were far from being compatible with the gritty and glowing events of the past. The old doctrine that 'history was philosophy teaching by example' could surely only be true if great stress was laid on avoiding bad examples, for there were more such in the annals of the past than there were good ones; it was the wicked who prospered, as it still is. As for the *laudatio*, the *elogium* — patriotic accounts of countries fulsomely loyal and uncritical puffs of princes — were they not a distillation and essence of bias?

The defence of historical reflection as a valid and necessary activity was undertaken in the 1560s by a Spanish Dominican called Melchior Cano, and by two Frenchmen, François Baudoin and Jean Bodin.[37] That Cano was a Roman Catholic, Baudoin a protestant and Bodin (probably) nothing at all, illustrates the irrelevance of the Reformation at least as far as the historians were concerned, or perhaps one should say as far as the discipline of history was concerned, for in essence what was being achieved was the detachment of the subject from its subjection to conventional rhetoric. A new attitude to law as a comparative study combined with a new attitude to history as a subject with its own rules of evidence and its own lessons, distinct from if not in conflict with those of conventional humanist ethics. For Bodin history was basic to an understanding of government and therefore remained an essential ingredient in the training of a man of affairs, of anyone with public responsibilities.

The way that Baudoin and Bodin refuted the Pyrrhonist
arguments was by an analysis of the authenticity of source
materials, divided into primary and secondary;[38] and by
arguing that the artefacts, written books, archives, laws etc., of
the past were integral to that past and illuminated each other.
Bodin went further with his *Methodus and facilem historiarum
cognitionem* (1566).[39] He discussed the internal evidence of
reliability (absence of bias, refusal merely to entertain) and
urged sceptical appraisal of the interests which an author
might be subjected to. Clearly these might vary with time and
circumstances. No one was wholly good or bad and so no one's
statements could be taken as utterly reliable: '... the
standpoint is more clearly psychological (with Bodin) and
there is a corresponding shift of emphasis from the judgment
of an author as a whole to an estimation, from the bearing of
his interests, of his attitude towards different topics'.[40]

Both Baudoin and Bodin aimed at the provision of a proper
history, of a history of a universal kind, calm, judicious,
embracing all public aspects of human affairs. The ideal for
such men and their contemporaries was not Thucydides or
Livy or Caesar. It was Polybius, detached and writing truly
ecumenical history. Bodin, of course, actually produced such a
work in embryo in the later chapters of his *Methodus*, and in
great elaboration in his *Republic* (first edition of his French
version 1576, of his Latin 1586).[41] Bodin's *Republic*,
important and influential though it was, nevertheless hardly
falls to be considered here. It belongs to the historiography of
sociology or politics. His *Methodus* or 'Teach yourself history',
on the other hand, was the blueprint for centuries of historical
activity. It not only evaluated the historical activity, and
provided a measure of reliability, it not only ended with a
bibliographical list of historians, arranged in time and by
countries, but in every way it was to be an invitation and an
encouragement to the production both of source material (as
we would term it) of every kind and of the composition of
serious work based on research in such materials — as opposed
to the glamorous, glittering histories with which historians
writing on humanist principles had often tries to dazzle their
admiring readers. History was to be difficult and technical.
Much of the activity of the scholars of the seventeenth and

early eighteenth centuries was a response to this programme.

It is in the light of this kind of sophistication that we must view the most remarkable of the French books of the sixteenth century, *Les Recherches de la France* by Étienne Pasquier. Pasquier (1529-1615) was a Gallican lawyer, chiefly famous among his French contemporaries as the advocate who defended the Sorbonne against the Jesuits in 1565. His historical research is original and interesting because he assembled over the years a series of chapters each discussing an institution or a problem in earlier French history. The work began to come out (he tells us in the prologue to Book I) in 1560, but he regularly added to it and the final version, which appeared in 1621, contained ten books and a total of 308 of Pasquier's 'recherches'.[42] Much affected by the recent revolution in the teaching of law, anti-Romanist (but not anti-Catholic) in his religion, and living through the dark days of the Religious Wars, Pasquier was one of a number of cultivated Frenchmen who turned for support and consolation to the past. In many ways he was the most unusual. To read the contents of his second book, published in 1565, is to be reminded of Muratori's *Antiquitates* (below pp.176-8), for in this group of 'researches' he discusses, more or less systematic- ally, the origins of some of the great institutions of France: *parlement* (very much Pasquier's home ground), the *chambre des comptes*, the council, the estates, the treasurer and so on. But the rest of the book lacks this coherence, doubtless because of Pasquier's political stance as a *politique*. The third book, on the Church, while it contains some shrewd observations, is marred by Gallican prejudice. The fourth book is a miscellany of antiquarian notes (rather like another contemporary work, Camden's *Remains*, first published in 1605). The fifth and sixth books are more conventionally historical and narrative; they contain a few remarks which throw light on the author's personal attitudes, but are spoilt by being rather jerky and anecdotal. In the seventh and eighth books Pasquier discusses the history of the French language, sections which still command the interest and respect of modern philologists. Book IX deals, again with a fair amount of coherence, with the University of Paris and its faculties, and with civil and customary law in France. The final book reverts to early

French history and consists in its entirety in an examination of
the case against Queen Brunhilde (done to death in 613),
defending her against the many charges laid against her.
Again this, while it does not fit into the book unless one
regards the collection as pretty ramshackle, as it often is, is not
without its interest. It shows a careful reading of such sources
as were available and a deployment of what the author calls
(p.919) 'le sens commun', a faculty of which he was plentifully
supplied and which was to be an important ingredient in later
historiography.

There is no question but that Pasquier (and a few of his
friends) set up a higher standard of scholarship, notably by
referring to particular sources — though often in ways which
made verification very hard, especially in the case of
documentary as opposed to narrative material.[43] Yet he
lacked the sort of expertise that such work demanded. He
lacked good texts and he lacked methods for validating them.
Nor does it seem reasonable to compare him, as has sometimes
been done, with Montaigne, either as a stylist or as an
introspective or as a scholar. But he is a portent of the
enormous strides which French historiography was to make in
the next century.

7 History and Scholarship in the Seventeenth Century

This chapter refers to 'the seventeenth century'. This is somewhat misleading, since there will be occasion to look back to the sixteenth century, and on one or two occasions it will be necessary to cross the threshold of 1700. What can, I believe, be justified, is the rest of the title. At this time 'history' as commonly understood and enjoyed was drawing away from 'scholarship' as such or antiquarianism, if we can use the word without the pejorative connotation it has acquired in our own day.

History was now, by the time of the High Renaissance, a term which covered writing which appealed to a wide public. Literacy was universal among the middling groups in society as well as among the well-to-do and socially distinguished. The majority of the literate, we may guess from current experience, read only when they needed to for business or they read rubbish to idle away the time when the joys of hunting, bearbaiting, the table or the tavern were not available. But those who liked reading history liked books which either dealt with contemporary affairs, or else told in mellifluous style the story of the nation.

On the whole it has been the contemporary historians who have attracted most attention, and that for the simple reason that they are extremely useful to the modern historian of the late sixteenth and seventeenth centuries. At the time, writers like De Thou or Camden were admired both as Latin stylists and because their subject matter fell or almost fell within the recollection of many readers. Such works had the fascination exercised today by histories of Europe and its component countries from 1900 to 1945, a mixture of half knowledge and nostalgia. Likewise the 'memorialists' of time (for instance, Lord Clarendon in *The History of the Rebellion and Civil Wars*) might be compared to the Winston Churchill of *The World Crisis* (6 vols., 1923-31). Clarendon wrote better, was completing his work in detached exile; Churchill was an intriguing politician whose greatest hour was still a generation away. But both are prime 'sources' for the periods they cover.

This distinction between real or politic history and researches into antiquity was to grow stronger for a time; so far as England was concerned, it was firmly rooted in the Elizabethan period.[1] At the international level history (that is a background, geographical and political, to current affairs) was essential for the traveller, whether engaged on business or acquiring culture on the Grand Tour, which was becoming an obligatory part of a gentleman's education by the early seventeenth century. Such an interest threw up that new phenomenon, the guide book,[2] but it also encouraged publishers to issue works on various countries to be carried round by travellers who aspired to a polite acquaintance with the countries whose territories they were crossing or sojourning in, and who needed to be able to converse politely with the gentlemen whom they encountered. There were scores of such works,[3] perhaps the most famous being the set of small volumes, covering practically every country, published by the Leiden house of Elsevier.[4] The Elsevier volumes frequently consisted of reprinted texts of already existing volumes and in the end added up to thirty-five pocket-size volumes known as the 'Republics', the general adviser for the series being a Dutch businessman.

Much the most influential writer of contemporary history at this time also had connections with the Netherlands. This was Jacques-Auguste de Thou (Latinised as Thuanus) (1553-1617).[5] De Thou was a Gallican, a lawyer, a humanist bibliophile, and (in political affiliation) a *politique*, a man who desired peace in France at any reasonable cost. He had a fair amount of public experience, knew everyone worth knowing, wrote good Latin and tried to be independent of authority. The last proved beyond him. The price of peace was a strong monarchy and strong monarchy did not readily suffer criticism, even of the recent past, let alone the present. De Thou's *Historia sui temporis*, which began to come out in 1604,[6] attained so rapidly authority for the period it covered (1546 onwards) that he was under heavy constraint to revise and modify in successive editions and later volumes; he was in any case a perfectionist forever tinkering with his text. The result is a bibliographical nightmare of variants published and unpublished. He offended the Church and figured in the *Index* of prohibited books; he adopted in all good faith George Buchanan's version of the events leading to the fall and subsequent execution of Mary Queen of Scots, and this mightily offended Mary's son James, after 1603 King of England, who brought heavy pressure to bear on Camden to provide De Thou with a 'correct' account of the episode.[7] In his lifetime De Thou published various editions carrying the story down to 1584. The remaining sections of his work (down to 1607) were published by his executors through a German intermediary and appeared first at Geneva. The revisions and ameliorations of particular passages in response to the hostility of Rome, of sections of the French court, of foreign sovereigns like James VI and I, should not be overstressed. De Thou was a brave, conscientious and truthful man. He was also highly placed and only bent under the storm when it reached full force. Indeed the furore occasioned by his work is a measure of the public esteem in which he was held.

This esteem he held well into the eighteenth century, for the passions aroused by the Wars of Religion in France remained of lasting interest and his Polybian and Tacitean style were nicely combined with an old-fashioned teleological causation (God punishing his children) which admirably suited the cultivated gentry who read him. They, like De Thou, were Christians (however tepid) and humanist educated; the Bible and the Latin classics were the literary roots of their scheme of moral values. Yet the vastness of his Latin text meant that popularity was evidenced in synopses and translations. Since no adequate text of the original existed (or as yet exists) these summaries and vernacular versions give an even more dubious view of the man's main work, although they are the normal approach to it nowadays.[8]

It is perhaps this vastness which strikes one most of all. In
the Geneva edition, 'complete' so far as it could be, which
came out in 1620 there are four large folios, each consisting of
more than a thousand pages of Latin. While the first two
books provide a substantial backcloth taking events back to the
fifteenth century, sometimes even to the fourteenth century,
the bulk of the narrative is from the mid-sixth century.
Intended to be a world history, De Thou's *History* becomes
progressively móre concerned with the story of France. Yet
throughout, events from all over Europe are faithfully
introduced (which was why James I was so concerned that an
acceptable account of his mother should appear) and in a
more or less strict chronological order. De Thou's adherence to
chronology is an old-fashioned and limiting feature of his
work; and there is a conscious effort towards narrative within
the framework of the French kings' lives;[9] on the other hand,
compared with many writers the exactitude of his dates of day
and month deserves the highest commendation, even though
for a modern inexpert reader they are wrapped up in the
awkward Roman calendar. His work is not particularly
original in his inclusion of notes about famous men, and we
can see that his admiring remarks about Calvin[10] were not
exactly likely to endear him to Catholics in France or at Rome.
These *elogia* were later extracted and published separately
more than once, much as the speeches in Paulus Aemilius were
treated.[11] Further innovations deserving of remark are the
inclusion, in and after the edition of 1628, of epitomes for each
book and a list of the sources used, mainly other writers but
with a few legislative *acta* and legal proceedings. On the other
hand, there are no digressions, no analytical passages
regarding the social or constitutional problems of the day.

No author of comparable stature to De Thou appeared in
his own day or in the subsequent century. The nearest we come
to such writers are the English historians William Camden
(1551-1623) and Clarendon. Camden's real originality was as a
chorographer in his *Britannia*, which is mentioned later in this
chapter (below p.150). His *Annales rerum Anglicarum
regnante Elizebetha* were history in the sense that smart
gentlemen understood the term: elegant Latin, honest

chronology which added a tinge of spice because, despite his august prompter King James, this involved more than a tinge of honesty. He was first a schoolmaster, then a herald. Friendly with and patronised by Cecil and Sir Robert Cotton, he had access to first-rate material, though, like a good humanist, he restricted his use of this to enactments, legal proceedings and despatches. No hint of analysis here. But, unlike many humanists, he eschewed some of the meretricious devices of contemporary best-sellers. He was well aware that war and 'policy' were the things most proper to serious history, but felt obliged (as De Thou did) to include matters ecclesiastical.[12] His preface extols the Polybian programme for truth:

> *Why, how and to what end, and what hath been done, and whether the thing done hath succeded according to reason: and whatsoever is else, will together be an idle sport than a profitable instruction; and for the present it may delight, but for the future it cannot profit.* Mine own judgement I have not delivered by affection, whilst writing with an undis-tempered mind. I have rather sifted out the judgement of others, and scarcely have interposed mine in any place, no not *aliud agens*; whereas, notwithstanding it is a question, whether an historian may lawfully do it. Let every man for me, have his free liberty, to judge according to his cap-acity ...[13]

And he proceeds to disavow the traditional embellishments. There will be no set speeches, no sharp and contentious observations, no digressions, though he has not eschewed topography and genealogy, and as for chronology he has followed 'the chain and order of times as near as might be', and has begun the year, in the old chroniclers' way, with the first of January.

The annalistic framework for Camden was justified, as was much else, by the authority of Tacitus. But it was the practice also of the native chroniclers and much of their approach coloured his work. For example, he often gathers together brief accounts of celebrities at the end of the year in which they died, a trick which was medieval and certainly not classical. His aversion to digressions (i.e. discussion of matters other than wars, diplomacy, policy and — here he agreed with De

Thou — church matters) was indeed pronounced. In a work addressed primarily to a continental audience, not least to De Thou himself, there is far less help given over English institutions than Polydore Vergil provided a century earlier. For instance, his word for parliament is *ordines*, to be rendered, I suppose, by 'estates', which gives the foreign reader a totally erroneous impression of the bicameral English legislature. The intended continental audience is, incidentally, reflected in the typography. The Latin edition printed at London in 1615 is infinitely more graceful than the clumsy English print of early seventeenth-century versions.

De Thou had run into trouble with his account of the period after 1584. Camden likewise forebore to print his narrative for the years after 1588. Like De Thou he sought an executor whom he could trust to publish the remainder posthumously and found his man in one of those used by De Thou. The result was that the final volume appeared at Leiden in 1625 and a full text was not published in England until 1627, by which time both Camden and James I were dead.[14]

Camden and De Thou were men of some political prominence; indeed for a time De Thou was a considerable politician. Other politicians were also at work, men of even greater eminence in the field of public affairs, equally convinced that the function of the historian was not so much the inculcation of morality as preached, if not practised, from antiquity through the Middle Ages to the Renaissance, but political knowhow, political expertise acquired by reading — much as Bodin had advocated: this vicarious extension of experience was not productive always of significant history but it occasionally provoked a masterpiece. A piece of hack work may be instanced in Sir Francis Bacon's *Life of Henry VII*. Unlike his main source, Polydore Vergil (as transmitted by the English chroniclers), the work is full of invented speeches, sententious flattery of the 'English Soloman' who had arranged a marriage which had led in 1603 to a united Britain. It is hard to connect Bacon the statesman with such a perfunctory narrative, let alone Bacon the philosopher and essayist. He was, of course, trying to recover influence. But then so was Machiavelli when he wrote his *History of Florence*: the two books are scarcely comparable.

If Bacon out of office recalls Machiavelli, Clarendon out of office recalls Guicciardini. Edward Hyde, Lord Clarendon (1609-74), wrote a book with a compositional history almost as complicated as that of De Thou's great work. He completed his narrative of the *History of the Rebellions and Civil Wars* down to 1644 by the year 1648. In the late 1660s he then wrote his *Life*. The *History* in its final form was put together from those earlier works in 1671. The first published edition was not issued until 1702-4, when it appeared in London. By then the civil wars were all but over and Queen Anne was on the throne. Hyde's exalted influence with Charles I and Charles II, his access to memoirs and papers, his calm and cultivated detachment — all these factors were to make his writings a determinant in all subsequent interpretation of the seventeenth century. Fueter would add that Clarendon's greatness in part derived from his writing (again like Guicciardini) in a spirit where party rivalry encouraged a free treatment, even if a loaded treatment, of controversial issues. Both Guicciardini and Clarendon were thus emphatically not writing officially approved accounts of their own day; nor in any real sense were they 'humanists' although, like practically every other author from 1600 to 1900, they had had a 'humanist' education at school. 'A realistic and lively history could only emerge in England when historiography had stopped being a branch of literature'.[15] What Clarendon was precluded from putting into practice after 1600, his blend of reason, sensibility and idealism, was put into his writing, together with a providential view of the ultimate engineering of events.[16]

There were plenty of reasons for delaying publication — his outspoken criticism of the execution of Mary Queen of Scots, his blunt views of some of James I's actions, his criticism of the royalists during the Interregnum. But the fact remains that his book was not influential until a much later date. There are no continental contemporaries writing like Edward Hyde for the simple reason that by and large Europe lay under the control of autocratic princes, who did not tolerate the least criticism of themselves, their ancestors, the myths on which their *patrie* (as the word was now being applied to large nation states) felt itself to depend. (I have already mentioned the fate of the unfortunate scholar whom Louis XIV was constrained by one

of the man's enemies to condemn to the Bastille for query-
ing the historicity of Francus — p.67.) 'The School of
Guicciardini', of free and trenchant comment on current
events, involved a balance of factions, as in the Florence of the
period down to 1530. This existed in the seventeenth century
in England; it was not tolerated, it did not become the
accepted background of public and historical debate, until the
next century. On the contrary, the European pattern of history
at this time was official, censored, or self-censored: all in the
interests of the state.

This had, of course, begun long before the seventeenth
century, but mattered less then since few readers or writers
were affected. Venetian historians were state-appointed —
mediocrities at the beginning of the sixteenth century
(Sabellico, Bembo) and a brilliant exception at the end in the
remarkable friar of the Servite Order, Paolo Sarpi (1552-
1623), who was appointed by the republic as its official
apologist. His *History of the Council of Trent* was first
published in London (1619) and was a kind of Anglican
picture of the debates and decisions which defined so much
doctrine and did so little for reform.[17] But Sarpi, rather like
Clarendon, was to be grist to the mill of later historians and his
vivid and critical spirit had no echoes in the Italy of his day.
Popes, viceroys of Naples, grand dukes of Tuscany had no
desire for any writers save clients.

Censorship was practised everywhere, led by the list of
prohibited books issued by Paul IV in 1557 and frequently
brought up to date. Everywhere urban or princely authority
was applied to the printed book, partly to safeguard politics
and, to some small extent, morals, and partly to give authors a
modicum of protection against their works being pirated for
a time, at any rate in the territories of the magistrate issuing
the order. In England, for example, we have the royal
privilege and registration with the Stationers Company. This
repressive legislation (which, of course, had its roots in the
provisions of the Church for combatting heresy in the Middle
Ages) was, it may be assumed, a far less effective gag than the
desire of authors to avoid trouble by not offending. We have
encountered several examples of this. Polydore Vergil did not
publish his account of the years 1509-37 until 1555, when he

may well have considered that the old ecclesiastical order had been permanently restored and when in any case he was far away from England, in or on his way back to Urbino. De Thou and Camden each made elaborate arrangements to have the dangerous final portions of their books published both posthumously and in foreign cities.

Governments could, of course, dangle rewards in front of obedient writers as well as threats of imprisonment. And the official, accredited narrator makes his appearance in the sixteenth century nearly everywhere. Here again there were precedents — Italian towns commissioned eulogistic accounts, and so did Italian princely families. The Burgundian court had a Chronographer of the Golden Fleece: Georges Chastellain (above p.77) seems to have been the first. And, as we have seen, a monk of Saint Denis was latterly paid by the French crown for the task of keeping up the *Grandes Chroniques de France*. These were the predecessors of the court historiographer, or Historiographer Royal.

The Historiographer Royal was pioneered by the French, not surprisingly perhaps considering the bloody civil wars and reversals of policies the country experienced in the second half of the sixteenth century. From 1550 onwards the Historiographer Royal figures in the French court and (when he was lucky) in the household accounts, and his office was to be continued down to the Revolution.[18] The French placemen who carried the title were sometimes historians, and sometimes wrote history. But it was really a way of attracting a man of letters to support of the king, whoever the king may have been. It would be meaningless to transcribe the names of some of the mediocrities who bore the official title in France; one or two slightly more reputable figures will be identified in what follows. It is, however, of some small significance that there was no parallel appointment made in Britain until after the Restoration. Then, perhaps in simple emulation of French practice, or because sympathetic writers were needed around the king of a divided land, the situation changed. In 1661 James Howell was appointed the first Historiographer Royal for England; a few years later came Scotland's turn, when William Turner occupied the new post. That Howell is remembered as a writer on current affairs, as a compiler of dictionaries, is some confirmation of his feeling that diplomacy and history should go together. But in both Scotland and England nonentities — often priests — almost entirely monopolised the position until it died in England after the absurd appointment of the novelist G.P.R. James (d. 1860), while in Scotland it survived because Bute appointed to it in 1763 the Rev. William Robertson (below pp.179-81), the greatest historian of his age. And because Robertson was followed by other serious historians, the office survives in Scotland to this day.

This brief account of the sponsored hacks (as most of them were) in Britain has taken us far from the seventeenth century and it is important again to stress that what the public wanted was humanist history in the vernacular, effortless, easy narratives to while away dull hours in drawing room and library. It would be easy to multiply examples of the genre. Those that follow are drawn from France and England.

On the whole, oratorical history in what might be termed a humanist vernacular was perhaps more strongly established in France and perhaps lasted longer there than in England. The best of the French, and by a long margin, was François Eudes de Mézeray (1610-83), whose *Histoire de France* appeared in three folio volumes from 1643 to 1651; he later abbreviated it himself and the *Abrégé chronologique* (1618) was frequently reprinted and, in convenient salon size, had a long career. The original edition, illustrated with engraved portraits of kings, of medals and so forth (clearly of small scholarly worth), attracted some hostile governmental attention from Colbert, although Mézeray was Historiographer Royal and member of the Academy; and the various recensions of his work pose problems somewhat analogous to those of the texts of De Thou.[19] While emulating the humanist — in speeches, epigrams and a nice combination of polite superiority regarding certain expendable legends (e.g. the mythical ancestry of the Gauls) — Mézeray also took account not merely of the writing of Paulus Aemilius (on whom he greatly depended) but also on the *érudits* of the sixteenth century. His awareness of institutions is interesting and it is instructive to look at the admirable indexes in the later editions of the *Abrégé* under *Église, états généraux, parlement*; it was in fact the implication of his treatment of the origins of *Chambre des comptes* and *tailles* which incensed Colbert. But Mézeray, eccentric and latterly well-to-do, could afford a certain indifference. He was writing in the atmosphere of the Frondes. His liberty of speech was not to be trammelled as was that of his successors who lived and worked under Louis XIV. It is a comedown from Mézeray to Gabriel Daniel, S.J. (1649-1728), another Historiographer Royal, whose *Histoire de France* was innocuous, even although he was able to depend on a mass of erudition which had appeared in the interval. In so far as his aim was to supplant Mézeray he was not successful, despite his original three folios (1713), dedicated to *le roi soleil*, being, like his rival's, subsequently issued in more manageable quarto and duodecimo formats, and in abbreviated editions. Father Daniel's neglect of source material has been perhaps exaggerated, but it gave rise to damaging anecdotes which, despite his laborious life, nevertheless represent something of the truth. Likewise the Abbé René Aubert de Vertot (1655-1735), whose accounts of 'revolutions' in England, Sweden, Portugal and Rome (but not in France).[20] were immensely popular, but were composed with a careless dependence on other authors and a minimum of research even as contemporaries regarded it.

Something of the spirit of this popular history is well caught in the words of Paul Hazard:

> All the historians at this time wanted to be Livys, but even more eloquent, even more embellished ... They wrote splendid prefaces, indicating impartiality as their most earnest concern ...

The anecdotes which survive do not lack plausibility: when Vertot had finished his account of the siege of Malta (part of his history of the Knights of St. John) and he was shown some relevant documents, he replied that it was too late, his siege was complete. Father Daniel went to see the volumes in the Royal library, spent an hour among them and declared he was very satisfied. Happy man! He himself said the citing of manuscripts did great credit to a historian, that he had seen many, but that reading them was more of a labour than it was worth.[21]

While Frenchmen were taking pleasure in the writings of Mézeray, Daniel and Vertot (and many similar authors), what were the Englishmen reading of similar substance? Probably the most frequently perused volume was written by the bankrupt Sir Richard Baker (1568-1645) while in the Fleet prison. Among his large output, poetical, educational, religious, was his *Chronicle of the Kings of England from the time of the Roman Government unto the Death of King James*. First published in 1643, a later edition reported in his preface[22] Baker's modest affirmation 'that it was collected with so great care and diligence that if all other of our chronicles should be lost, this only would be sufficient for posterity of all passages memorable and worthy to be known'. 'Modest' is perhaps not ironic; the humanist historian did not expect his narrative to be redone and undone and scrapped by succeeding generations. Certainly Baker's sententiousness was to the taste of the public for which he was catering. Take this piece from his life of Edward II:

> And yet for all these advantages, there wanted not fear for him in the minds of many, who could not but remember what pranks he had played not long before ... and if he did such things being but Prince, what might not be feared of him being King. For seldom doth advancement in honour alter men to the better, to the worse often, and commonly then when it is joined with an authority which sets them above controlment.[23]

One can imagine a dreary pedant using such a sentence as an exercise for translation into Latin. Baker's narrative is, of course, worthless, though it would have been more so but for Polydore Vergil and the scholars to whom we shall shortly be turning. But he appealed not only to the grammar school boy; he included lists of noblemen, and listed the mayors and sheriffs of London. This work, in various forms, some with continuations, was printed at least a dozen times. Addison, in the *Spectator*, tells us that Sir Roger de Coverley frequently read it and that it lay always in his hall window.[24]

It became fashionable to decry Baker. A later work provides a conspectus of the vernacular humanist histories in vogue in seventeenth-century England. It is *The Compleat History of ngland*, three noble folios, enhanced with engraved portraits f sovereigns, organised by John Hughes (1677-1720), and ublished in 1706, with a second edition in 1719. These are the ontents:

Vol. I   From the earliest time to William the Conqueror. By Mr. John Milton. Lives of kings from William I to Henry VI. By Samuel Daniel Esq.

Edward IV. By John Habington Esq.

Edward V, Richard III. By Sir Thomas More, with continuations from Hall and Holinshed and George Buck Esq.

Henry VII. By the Rt. Hon. Francis, Lord Verulam, Viscount St. Albans.

Vol. II   Henry VIII. By the Rt. Hon. Lord Herbert of Cherbury.

Edward VI. By Sir John Hayward, Ktd., Doctor of Law.

Queen Mary. Translated from the Latin of Francis [Godwin] by John Hughes [i.e. the general organiser of the whole work].

Queen Elizabeth. By William Camden, translated by Mr. Davis.

Annals of James I. By William Camden, never before in English.

Vol. III   James I. By Arthur Wilson Esq.

Lives and reigns of Charles I, Charles II, James II, William and Mary, William III. All new writ by a learned and impartial hand [i.e. White Kennett].

Just before the publication of the revised edition White Kennett was appointed Bishop of Peterborough (1718), and so ubstantial was his contribution (in effect, nearly the whole of he seventeenth century) and so controversial did his views eem to Tories, that the whole three volumes are often referred o under his name.

Apart from Kennett, the interesting names in the *omnium atherum* (other than those which have occurred in earlier ages) are those of Daniel and Milton. Samuel Daniel 1562-1619) is usually described as a poet but his History was a retty substantial narrative and came out in two sections, first

in 1612 (as far as King Stephen) and, as a whole, in 1617. I
was frequently reprinted and continued, and though, like the
other literature I am discussing at this point, it is neglected i
not decried, the book has a certain sense of occasion, of perio
one might say. The opening lines, dealing with the
consequences of the Norman invasion, regard that event as a
turning point in quite an impressive and wide ranging
way.[25] Hughes, in his preface, is extremely complimentar
regarding Daniel's method and his style, he shows judgemen
in preventing his poetry 'from infecting his style' and i
achieving an English comparable to the 'purity and grace' o
the early eighteenth century.

On the other hand, 'Mr. Milton chose to write (if thi
expression be allowed) a hundred years backward' and thi
seems a fair comment not only on manner but to some degre
on matter.[26] Milton excused himself on poetical grounds fo
introducing matters which 'judicious antiquaries ... explod
for fiction'. After all, 'our English poets and rhetoricians ... b
their art will know how to use them judiciously'.[27] And so o
to Japhet, Albion, Brut and (a bit later) Arthur; one i
reminded somewhat of Winston Churchill insisting in hi
History of the English Speaking Peoples on introducing heroi
fables such as King Alfred burning the cakes. Milton's stylisti
preoccupations were classically based and fundamental to hi
work as a historian.[28] 'It was to the classics then an aspirin
young historian should turn for instruction in the art, not t
the revolutionary advances in historiography which had beer
made in the sixteenth and seventeenth centuries. To Milto
the ancient writers were still the best guides.'[29] History, s
turbulent in his own day,[30] was of its essence calm. 'I inten
not with controversies and quotations to delay or interrupt th
smooth course of history ... but shall endeavour ... with plai
and lightsome brevity to relate well and orderly things wortl
the noting, so as may best instruct and benefit them tha
read.'[31] This curiously old-fashioned book was first pub
lished in 1671, a few years before his death in 1674. It wa
reprinted in 1677 and 1695, and, as part of the *Works*, in 169
and later. Mediocre as history it may have been but peopl
read it, perhaps partly because of his reputation as a poet an
publicist.

It would be profitless to pursue the *Compleat History* much further. Herbert of Cherbury's *Henry VIII* (first published in 1649) is of interest for the contemporary documents he quotes and, indeed, it is fair to say that volume II does contain a good deal of newly published documentary material. Of White Kennett's massive vol. III we need only recall that it was in all essentials contemporary history, which (since he would have been accused of bias) he did not put his name to. He is nowadays dismissed as a 'party historian' (Sir George Clark). In another perspective he deserves consideration as one of the first Whig interpreters of the past.

Three further points need to be made. First, we must constantly remind ourselves that the readers of Milton, Samuel Daniel and the other contributors to the *Compleat History* in England, and those who read Mézeray, Gabriel Daniel and similar writers in France — not to speak of such works in other European countries — regarded them as the main historians of their day. One may hesitate to qualify them as best sellers — in the way (for instance) some of Erasmus' educational and satirical works were best sellers. But cumulatively the bulk of narrative history, of what Milton called the 'smooth' variety (permissibly interspersed when appropriate by 'revolutions', especially those occasioned by battle), must have been vast. Our old libraries are full of the fat volumes; they are still commonly the earliest volumes to be found in the libraries of old country houses. They constitute what educated people in the seventeenth century regarded as 'history'. Second, we must remember that these educated persons had all passed through a grammar school curriculum (some few grandees had tutors) which relied heavily on the Latin prose of Livy, Caesar, Tacitus and — for the clever boys — the Greek historians. When Milton urged Sallust as a model his readers knew what he meant. Third, the more popular works were translated during the seventeenth century from one European language into another. This is too vast a topic to engage on, save to say that, just as there was an accepted 'style' in the fine arts — painting, sculpture, architecture, and the minor decorative arts — so there was in literature, and not least in history.

In moving now to the innovations in historical scholarship
during the seventeenth century we must not, of course, give the
impression that there were no scholarly innovations earlier
than that, without which (to be fair) the historians with whom
we have been dealing would have been skimpier and more
derivative than in fact they were. Bodin has been mentioned,
but his contribution was rather of a philosophical and
pragmatic character than a contribution to erudition as such:
he proffered a technique in the *Methodus* and displayed it
there and in the *Republic*. What was urgently needed was the
provision of those raw materials Bodin demanded, and studies
based on records and other 'original' documents. A start on
this vast programme was made in the disturbed age of the
Reformation (but not on confessional lines). And at the same
time an impulse to justify the part one's own country played
led not only to popular accounts, such as those discussed
above, but to genuinely Gallican and Anglican approaches to
the antiquities of France and England. These have been much
studied of late and some high claims have been advanced
which may sometimes be a trifle exaggerated.[32]

I can see little point in cataloguing the medieval narrative
histories which were printed in the sixteenth century.[33] Some
were undoubtedly made available because they catered for a
traditional and not a new scholarly interest. This was surely
the case with Geoffrey of Monmouth's *Gesta Regum* (above
p.59), which was published at Paris in 1508,[34] as with
Einhard, Gregory of Tours, Paul the Deacon, Sigebert of
Gembloux and, of course, Bede, all printed at about this time
or earlier.[35] Where one should be alert is when one comes
upon the deliberate editing of a text in order to establish a
historical point, or else to make it available in a scholarly
edition. This was, as we have seen, the point made by Bodin
regarding the validation of historical evidence: more and
better texts. To restrict ourselves to English examples, a case of
the first impulse is the edition of Polydore Vergil of Gildas
(Amsterdam? 1525). Gildas was a British writer of the sixth
century and Vergil's aim in editing him was to prove that he
did not mention King Arthur; Vergil's treatment of the text
was cavalier, for he tampered with style and (in passages
critical of the clergy) with matter.[36] Much more impressive

nd sustained effort is to be associated with Matthew Parker
1504-75), who became Archbishop of Canterbury in 1559. He
ot only searched out and collected manuscripts, many of
hich had been in monastic libraries until the Dissolution, but
:cured publication of a large number, in this being helped by
thers and notably by his secretary, John Joscelyn. In this way
ditions appeared of the *Flores Historiarum* (1567, repr.
570), Matthew Paris' *Great Chronicle* (1571), Thomas of
Valsingham's *History* (1574) and an edition of Asser's *Life of
lfred* (also 1574).[37] These texts are poor by modern
:andards, even by the standards of the seventeenth century;
nd Parker's lasting contribution was undoubtedly his
ollection of books, which ended up in Cambridge University
.ibrary and the library of Corpus Christi College, Cam-
ridge.[38]

Parker and his friends were not isolated. They had
redecessors in an antiquarian like John Leland and the
emarkable bibliographer John Bale. Their contemporaries
nd successors formed the 'First Society of Antiquaries' and the
iolent reaction to Vergil's sceptical account of early British
istory led to a pouring forth of a mass of local patriotic
terature, not least from Wales (after all, the country was
uled by the Tudors, a Welsh dynasty). All of this has been
nuch and well discussed of late.[39] It is, perhaps, worth
nsisting on the ecclesiastical motives behind Parker's activ-
:ies:

> ... there can be little doubt that the driving force behind all
> this antiquarian activity was Parker's desire to present the
> history of the Church of England in a way that would justify
> the Elizabethan settlement. Hence, the emphasis laid on the
> earlier periods, before the full development of papal claims,
> and the preference for authors like Matthew Paris who were
> critical of the papacy.[40]

.s his secretary Joscelyn explained: 'he [Parker] thought [these
xamples] would be most profitable for the posterity to instruct
hem in the faith and religion of the elders'.[41] This concern
or a valid Church of England, with unimpeachable
ntecedents and orders which could not be impugned, was
trongly felt and continued to exercise influence on scholarly

activity. But the impulse, if somewhat different, is found no
just in protestant countries like England. In France and i
Spain the post-Reformation Church was also totally subser
vient to the State and so a desire to urge the ancient characte
of Gallicanism or the 'independence' of the Roman Churc
in Spain also influenced research.[42]

Far and away the most important figure in England befor
the seventeenth century was William Camden, the Camde
not of the *Annals* already mentioned (above pp.136-7), but o
Britannia. The ancestry of this book goes back throug
Leland to the chorography of Flavio Biondo, the *Itala
illustrata*, and his Italian successors working all over th
peninsula in the sixteenth century, collecting coins an
inscriptions, measuring ruins, identifying Roman plac
names. The immediate inspiration of Camden was th
cartographical and chorographic activities of Abraha
Ortelius (1527-98), a wealthy man, son of Germans who ha
settled in Amsterdam. The second half of the sixteent
century witnessed the birth of modern cartography, owing
improved surveying methods (for detailed maps) and bett
understanding of how to 'project' the spherical globe o
sheets of two-dimensional paper — a technique perfected b
Ortelius's friends and contemporary, the Fleming Gerar
Mercator (1512-94). These two Roman Catholics had a wid
circle of scholarly acquaintances and helpers — a hir
already of that republic of letters which was coming int
being. Ortelius's *Theatrum orbis terrarum* (Antwerp, 157
and very many revisions and reprints) was based on th
collaboration of some eighty or ninety scholars all ov
Europe.[43] From 1579 Ortelius began publishing maps
the ancient world (*Parergon*). He had earlier used the Englis
and Welsh maps of Humphrey Lloyd; for the map of Roma
Britain he finally turned to Camden.

From the start of the investigations which resulted i
Britannia (first ed. 1586), Camden's activities and intere
extended beyond merely tracing the Antonine Itineraries an
identifying Roman names with current sites. Roman remair
were recorded but — and this became truer of subseque
editions — so were names of families (with their genealogies
notes of interesting features of town and country, ar

publication of a certain amount of source material was
added. The work was based on his own journeys around the
country, on the libraries of his friends, on the communi-
cations received from friends and correspondents all over the
country. In encouraging so much interest in 'Britain'
Camden was also, perhaps unconsciously, encouraging a
political phenomenon: in 1603 James VI and I ruled a United
Kingdom, and proclaimed himself King of Great Britain in
1604. By that time there were five London editions of the
Latin text and one (Frankfurt, 1590) printed in Germany;
another was to follow at London in 1607 and Philemon
Holland's English version was published in 1610, and
reprinted in 1625. One suspects that in this way[44] Camden
did more to unite Britain in the long run than did King
James. He also undoubtedly encouraged a trend, already
influential, towards the composition of regional and
especially county histories: 'once the *Britannia* was available
a man could attend to his own bailiwick.'[45]

Camden's *Britannia* and its consequences lead one directly
to a review of English scholarship in the Stuart period. It can
be brief, since the subject has been attractively and
authoritatively dealt with in recent books and it will be
sufficient to make some general remarks.[46] First of all, it
was remarkably prolific, but this, as we shall see, is true of
seventeenth-century scholarship as a whole. Second, it
witnessed a quite new respect for record sources as opposed
to narratives, and an insistence (familiar enough in the
exacting field of classical scholarship) on precision of
reference to authorities, whether narrative or record. Third,
the publishing of source material gathered momentum and
became more scientific. Finally, investigation of institutions,
of particular social problems and their solutions, began to
emerge from the welter of local and more general
antiquarianism. In connection with this last point it is
obvious that historical precedents were frequently adduced
during the institutional upheavals of the seventeenth century
and that in turn this led men to investigate legal and
parliamentary origins.[47]

These general remarks can, with certain adjustments, be
applied to other European countries. Political and legal

debates are found in France and Italy; nearly everywhere
religious disputes led men to invoke medieval or patristic
authorities which had to be validated — and the most
interesting point to note in this connection is that we are
hardly dealing with the state polemics of 'protestantism'
and 'catholicism' *simpliciter*: we are dealing with the
agonising and acrimonious debates engendered inside these
broad confessional areas. The varieties of protestantism are
well enough known (in insular terms Presbyterians, Puritans,
Levellers, Anglicans of high and low degree, non-jurors)
but there were differences as pronounced between Jansenists
and Ultramontanes, between Gallicans (religiously regarded)
and more obedient scions of Trent. Even in Italy the Holy
Office found it difficult to keep the faithful toeing an
orthodox line. And needless to say, everywhere politic
became embroiled in religious divisions. This is a subject
extensively rehearsed in English scholarship for the last thirty
years, but it mingles in with *Frondisme* and decentralising
movements in seventeenth-century France: 'the Edict of
Nantes led irrevocably to the Revocation of the Edict'
politiques were prepared to sacrifice principles to ensure
peace. Elsewhere politics and orthodoxy in faith frequently
marched hand in hand. We have seen poor Baronio in
difficulties over his account of papal sovereignty in the
kingdom of Naples; we will encounter in the next chapter
Muratori, whose personal devoutness and regularity as a
parish priest did nothing to mitigate his pro-Este sympathies
so that he remained *persona non grata* in Rome.

Everywhere national origins and national institution
attracted patriotic attention and this, one may be sure, would
have occurred without the stimulus of dynastic or doctrinal
antipathies. If northern countries had no 'questione della
lingua' they have long had an interest in their medieval
literature, and this led to a study of their linguistic
antecedents quite different from the puerile etymological
guesswork of medieval writers. With patriotism on the grand
scale — of England, Scotland, Spain, France and so on —
went patriotism on a smaller scale; we should remember that
it was only in the mid-eighteenth century that the French
Academy accepted *pays* as signifying more than a locality

And so local history, of a new and accurate kind, is found nearly everywhere, varying in quantity but truly impressive in bulk, and covering English counties, French *provinces* and many of the greater towns. All of this was generally done within the framework of national history: it assembled the national story and, in a sense, exemplified it by detailed studies. Moreover, such local history was increasingly based on archive or 'record' material and by the end of the century there was born the conviction that 'official' records are sure to be purer than narratives reflecting the biases of their authors.

In a sense basic to all other developments, the seventeenth century witnessed a series of advances in what modern methodologists would call the 'ancillary' disciplines. Great strides were taken in sigillography (seals), numismatics (coins and medals); bibliography of areas, periods, subjects; library catalogues gradually appeared in print and more systematic indices and guides to archives were slowly compiled; philological aids in the form of grammars and dictionaries led the student through the pitfalls of old languages and foreign languages, and with these came works of encyclo- paedic intentions, enabling the puzzled reader to identify concepts or persons novel to him. The study of old documents both from a viewpoint of their structure (i.e. the fixed formulae used in documentary material, which was termed 'diplomatic' from *diploma* = a charter) and also the handwriting and materials used in writing them — the study of old writing of 'palaeography' — greatly improved accuracy in the interpretation of ancient texts. Virtually none of these aids to research, taken for granted from the eighteenth century onwards, were available to the sixteenth- century scholar. Erasmus, collating manuscripts for his edition of the Greek New Testament, had only the haziest idea regarding the relative ages of the codices he was using and hence of their relative antiquity and perhaps authority.

Works such as those by Professors Douglas and Pocock make it easy to illustrate these developments from England,[48] and since many of the English characters were unusual men the tale can be made very entertaining.

Publication of texts continued unabated, steadily achieving higher standards of accuracy. (One should recall in this connection the powerful influence in the same direction and at the same time of classical studies; several scholars were engaged in both types of research, for instance Thomas Gale, d. 1702, editor of ancient and medieval texts). Such publications covered charter material and narrative records and much of it, in view of religious issues, was aimed at a public concerned with Anglican antiquities, such as the *Anglia Sacra* of Henry Warton (1691) and the *Monasticon Anglicanum* of Sir William Dugdale and Roger Dodsworth (3 vols. 1655-73). The greatest single figure among editors, especially of narrative texts, was Thomas Hearne, non-juror, expelled from office in the Bodleian library, shabby and bad tempered, but meticulous and prolific; he edited Leland and in all issued some forty odd texts of various kinds dealing with British history.[49] Publication of 'record' sources was stimulated not only by the religious controversies, but by the English preoccupation with the English constitution — under the Stuarts, under the Commonwealth and after the Glorious Revolution of 1688. The political upheaval also drove men to their titles and the history of their locality: Dugdale's *Baronage* (1675-6) and his *Antiquities of Warwickshire* (1656) are admirable examples of genres found all over Europe.

Dugdale, and Camden before him, were heralds and this facilitated consultation of the official records by them — and their friends, for there was a freemasonry of scholarship which often took little account of political or religious differences. The records themselves were in a parlous condition,[50] and scattered in dozens of repositories. Their custodians sometimes knew the material in their charge but depended to some extent for their livelihood on levying search fees, so that working among the documents, unparalleled as they were for continuity and coverage (outside the Vatican) of the offices of the Crown of England could be painfully slow and painfully expensive. It was only in 1732 that the House of Commons attempted (without much success at the time) to promote indexes and calendars, and to concentrate the repositories. None of this was really to come about for century and meanwhile Henry Spelman, Dugdale and Humphrey Wanley and their friends had to scribble in ill-lit, rat infested, damp and largely uncatalogued collections in the Tower of London, the Palace of Westminster, Westminster Abbey and a score of other places, all in the charge of administrative personnel, not librarians or archivists. Only Chancery material was relatively well ordered. It is remarkable that out of this came a mass of historical publication, most of it illustrating local history or family descents (often treated as much the same thing), often subordinated to the solution of problems or the description of matters which nowadays would seem fairly peripheral, but cumulatively adding up to a massive publication programme of records which had been accumulated in administration and which had earlier seldom been treated as important historical evidence. The only works which were devoted to subjects which still retain value in the study of medieval history were by David Wilkins, Prussian by origin, who compiled, with the help from many others, the *Concilia* of the English Church (1737); and the pioneer, Thomas Madox, whose *History and Antiquities of the Exchequer* (1711) remains an astonishingly 'modern' work; of his *Formulare* I shall say a word below, for here he was following (to his credit) in the footsteps of an even greater scholar, Mabillon.

The greatest of the record searchers and publishers was the failed poet and dramatist, Thomas Rymer, whose great *Foedera* (1703-17) remains to this day an important work of reference. Here, too, a continental predecessor of greater eminence inspired the project, Gottfried Wilhelm von Leibnitz, who had unsuccessfully applied in 1714 for the post of Historiographer Royal in England[51] and who had published his *Codex juris gentium diplomaticus* at Hanover in 1693.[52] This was intended to supply statesmen with the current treaty structure and legists with a secure basis for their study of comparative institutions.[53] Rymer's royal commission 'to publish all records of alliances and other transactions in which England was concerned with foreign princes' was a scheme wider than Leibnitz's in that he began at 1101 and planned to continue until his own day, narrower in that he limited himself to the foreign relations of England.[54] Rymer died in 1713 and at that point fifteen great folios had appeared, taking the material down to 1586; two further volumes were issued by Robert Sanderson, Rymer's assistant, in 1715 and 1717. The whole work covered the period from Henry I to 1625.[55] Rymer had been Historiographer Royal with a stipend, sometimes honoured, of £200 p.a. He lived in poverty and died in poverty; his *Foedera* was, however, posthumous reward enough. Rymer's transcripts may not be faultless, for he and some of his amanuenses were often working hurriedly in unfavourable conditions. But the collection remains an astonishing one. It is by no means confined to treaties, but covers safe conducts, military contracts and scores of other documents which might otherwise have been overlooked; some indeed have perished or been lost since his day and the text in *Foedera* is the only copy we have.

Hearne and Rymer were the most productive publishers of unpublished material in England in the seventeenth and early eighteenth centuries, even if they were not the ablest or most critically minded of their brother scholars. And in England, as on the Continent, the ancillary disciplines were also pursued.

Clearly language and linguistic studies bulked large, since the understanding of English (or British) antiquity depended on two dead languages, Anglo-Saxon and Celtic, perhaps three if we allow for Norse and Icelandic literature. This was the province of Thomas Gale (above p.154), of George Hickes (1642-1715) whose *Thesaurus* of the 'northern languages' came out in 1703, and earlier of William Somner (1598-1669) and many others. Another area, again related to the Church, was the compilation of a remarkable reference work by John Le Neve, *Fasti Ecclesiae Anglicanae* (1716), which, unlike most earlier works in England and on the Contentent, did not merely list bishops for each diocese, but also deans, archdeacons and canons. Subsequently revised on a massive scale on two occasions, Le Neve remains a standard authority.

Another important field which was well cultivated was bibiography. In a sense Leland and John Bale (above p.118) were pioneers in this type of study, although their aim was only to provide a list of English authors. Subject bibliography came later; Bodin's *Methodus* ended up with just such lists and it is some indication of the rapid expansion of historical writing and research that within a couple of generations the historical bibliography had become a necessary and elaborate tool of the historian everywhere in Europe. In England John Pits is an early example; a Roman Catholic exile, confessor to the duchess of Cleves, he died in 1616 and his *De illustribus Angliae scriptoribus* was issued at Paris in 1619. Sir James Ware published in 1639 a sound account of Irish historians and in 1627 Thomas Dempster brought out a rather inferior *De scriptoribus Scotiae*. But these manuals were all superseded by two other works, which in some degree retain their value today. Bishop William Nicolson (d. 1727) published between 1696 and 1724 his *Historical Library*, which covered England, Scotland and Ireland, listing both printed and manuscript sources; consolidated editions appeared in 1714, 1731 and 1776. Nicolson was also indefatigable in forwarding other projects. The other compiler was also a bishop, but a quainter man and a non-juror. This was Richard Rawlinson (d. 1755), who translated, with extensive additions, the *Méthode pour étudier l'histoire* of the stormy but learned abbé, Nicolas Lenglet Dufresnoy, which was first published in 1713 and was frequently translated, reprinted and extended. Rawlinson, as prolific and as awkward a man as Lenglet Dufresnoy, first published his own *New Method* in 1728; in the second volume there are voluminous bibliographies by area and subject which may still usefully be consulted for a conspectus of historical learning in the first half of the eighteenth century, as may those in Nicolson.

Finally, we must note that in Britain, as abroad, the great libraries were progressing and increasingly opening their doors to scholars. The great English collectors are headed in time and perhaps in importance by Sir Robert Cotton (1571-1631), patron of Camden, Dugdale and scores of others. Robert Harley (Lord Oxford) is named next in Nicolson's Preface, and he then names the collections of the College of Heralds, the university libraries at Oxford, Cambridge and Dublin. The greatest library, the Royal Library, is not mentioned by Nicolson, but it was to be amalgamated in the end with the Harleian and Cottonian collections to become one of the greatest collections in the world — the British Museum Library, now to be entitled the British Library. Many of these

private collections had experienced librarians — as Harley
employed Humphrey Wanley. Catalogues, manuscript at first,
later to be printed, became available. In view of the chaotic
state of the public records (above p.155) it was helpful to
researchers that many 'state papers' had found their way into
private hands and so were accessible in these better-kept
collections.

The previous pages have resembled a catalogue, I fear,
because I have named so many English[56] scholars while
omitting the controversies, acrimonious and often futile, that
so often drove them on. And even so the catalogue is very far
from complete. But one final note must be made. There was
an immense amount of collaboration. Hence the productions
of Dugdale, 'the great plagiarist', and of men like Hearne, who
were often helped by persons who had little sympathy for
them. The correspondence of these men of letters is
formidable and fortunately much of it has survived. A symbol
of this collective effort was the establishment, firmly from
1717, of the Society of Antiquaries,[57] in which Harley's
friend and librarian Wanley played a large part; very
gradually the Royal Society (1662) ceased to interest itself in
the humanities. Nor was this spirit of collaboration limited to
British scholars writing to each other. Many of the greatest had
correspondents across Europe; even poor Rymer maintained
close contact with Leibnitz. But this leads us on to the scholars
in France and Italy, with which this chapter must conclude.

They must be treated much more cavalierly than those in
England, which is a great pity since many of them were great
men and only the very greatest will find a place in what
follows, many more deserve detailed discussion. Moreover,
as in the case of Madox's *Formulare*, already mentioned
(above p.155)), the scholars of this time on the Continent
were in general greater men. It is a very great pity that
we have no general surveys of the history of historical scholarship on the Continent, after at any rate the sixteenth century
when, in works already referred to, the scholarship especially
of France and Germany has been studied.[58] The best
brief surveys of some critical figures are in fact by the

English monk, Dom David Knowles, who has just died (1975) and who fortunately devoted his four inaugural lectures as president of the Royal Historical Society to some 'Great Historical Enterprises', two of which bear directly on developments in this period — the Bollandists and the Maurists.[59] Dom Knowles also reprinted a separate paper on Mabillon.[60] In what follows, therefore, continental examples will be given of developments which have been mentioned somewhat more fully, if hurriedly, for England.

It will have been noted in the account of English scholarship that a preponderance of scholars were clergymen. This was partly because higher education was a monopoly of the Church, partly because so much prompting towards historical enquiry was due to the violent ecclesiastical (and politico-ecclesiastical) controversies of the age. The majority of continental scholars were also clergy, and for much the same reason. Continental clergy, on the other hand, had a further reason for turning their pens to historical writing. Those who were members of religious Orders frequently had at hand superb collections of manuscript and printed books, consultation of which was sometimes facilitated by the continuance of the so-called 'congregational' systems of the later Middle Ages, by which groups of reformed houses accepted mutual support and control: the Benedictine congregation of St Maur is the most remarkable of such associations at this time. England, of course, had seen virtually no 'congregations' of this type before the Reformation, and at the Reformation monastic libraries had been scattered and many of their contents perished. But the existence of religious Orders had a further effect on scholarship. It continued to stimulate not only healthy rivalry but unhealthy competition and violent argument was now often sustained by monks and friars wielding historical facts or suppositions. In this way much heat was generated but also a good deal of light.

Our sample must, however, begin with the activities of a small group of men who were members of a relatively recent Order — the Jesuits, founded by Loyola in 1534-9 and particulary active in areas where protestantism was vulnerable to counter-attack, a corporation of 'regular priests' who were given in their seminaries (and in their schools provided) the best education of the sixteenth and seventeenth centuries. One small band, established at Utrecht, was gathered round Father Herbert Rosweyde. He conceived the notion of compiling, on strict critical principles, the authentic texts dealing with the lives of all the saints. It would be arranged on a calendar basis, so that it would deal *seriatim* with the *acta* of the saints of each month. We have already seen how important a group of sources are represented by saints' lives (above pp.36-7). But Rosweyde did not realise just how vast was the number of saints and the bulk of material to be sifted scientifically. When he died in 1629 nothing had been published of the projected *Acta Sanctorum* and Rosweyde's collections were passed to John Bollandus (d. 1665). Under Bollandus helpers were systematically collected and it is reasonable that the sub-group of Jesuits who to this day labour on the work should be named after him. The first two volumes appeared in 1643 and, though interrupted by nationalist persecution of the Jesuits which culminated in the suppression in 1773, it continued with steady regularity. Bollandus recruited Godefroid Henskens (d. 1681) and later Daniel van Papebroche (d. 1714). The 1643 volumes had covered January; the three volumes of 1658 covered the saints of February; March (3 vols) appeared in 1668 and April (also 3 vols) in 1675; but for May (1675-88) no fewer than seven volumes were needed and as time went on the scale of the enterprise was steadily enlarged. This was partly because of steadier support from superiors in the Order and from the popes, partly due to voluntary cooperation — scholars communicating their discoveries to the learned Jesuits of Antwerp and active investigation of continental libraries by visiting Bollandists.

Much of the work resulted in what we would call the debunking of popular and much-loved legends. This earned the compilers much dislike and criticism. Their systematic establishment of the truth, though sought with faith and sincerity, tended to ally them with the avowed sceptics of the late seventeenth century — men like Bayle and Fontenelle.[61] Papebroche's demonstration that there was no evidence that Elijah had established the Carmelite Order had a clamorous reception; the Maurists were irritated at the treatment of St Maur, patron of charcoal burners, whose name had been appropriated by the Congregation. And everywhere it seemed as though rigorous sifting of documents might endanger property rights by exposing hoary documents as hoary forgeries.[62]

The congregation of St Maur, centred at St Germain des Prés in Paris, had been established in 1621 but it was only in the 1670s that it began to turn out a stream of brilliant historians. (In the light of such scholarship one must feel that a quite undeserved importance has been attributed to the ramshackle if interesting *Recherches de la France* of Étienne Pasquier, mentioned above pp.131-2.) To list them in full would occupy far too much space; 105 scholars have been associated with the Congregation at this time.[63] The father of Maurist erudition was Luc d'Achéry (d. 1685). He published his *Spicilegium*, a vast thirteen-volume collection of unpublished medieval documents, from 1655-77 and began the *Acta Sanctorum Ordinis Sancti Benedicti*, which was ultimately completed in nine volumes (1668-1701), largely by the efforts of d'Achéry's most brilliant disciple, Jean Mabillon (d. 1707). It will be seen from any catalogue which lists Mabillon's works how prodigious was his output. Subsequently, it has been argued, the Maurists produced work of less high quality, although much of it (such as the *Art de vérifier les dates*) has only just lost its usefulness, and that partly because great folios are hard to shelve and to handle.

Mabillon's most remarkable achievement lay in producing the *De re diplomatica* (1681), which has already been alluded to in connection with Wanley's *Formulare* (above p.155). It began because the Bollandist Papenbroche had, on the basis of serious study, decided that certain early French Benedictine charters were spurious. In Dom Knowles' words:

> Mabillon saw that the authenticity of a whole class of documents was at stake, and resolved to extract from all the charters and diplomas of which he had knowledge their characteristics of writing, style, form, dating, signature, sealing and the rest, and to propound thence rules for the authentication of various types of record. In less than six years, and without abandoning his other commitments, he had done his work, and it is the measure of his learning

and his genius that the first major work on diplomatics
was definitive on its subject.[64]

Nor was diplomatic alone the beneficiary of his skill:
chronology, and above all palaeography,[65] were enormously
advanced. Ultimately Papebroche generously admitted
Mabillon's case and the two men became firm friends. It was
the composition of this book which inspired the description of
Mabillon as 'the Newton of history'.[66]

Team work characterised the Bollandists. In effect, many of
the enterprises of the Maurists — their editions of patristic
texts, their compilations like the *Gallia Christiana* and the
collection of texts known familiarly as Bouquet's *Recueil* —
while organised by one or two men, were the effort of several
scholars surrounded by friends and sympathisers: 'when once a
project had been approved and was under way ... a scholar
could draw upon his community, and even upon the whole
congregation, for assistance in copying manuscripts, reading
proofs, and the like ...'[67]

The examples of seventeenth-century erudition I have selected
from Italy are, on the contrary, characterised by individual
effort. This was partly due to the curious ecclesiastical state of
Italy from Trent to the advent of the French revolutionary
armies. Popes were autocrats, but weak and, however
enlightened themselves, were surrounded by members of curial
commissions (especially the Propaganda and the Inquisition)
who seldom allowed an adventurous idea. Possessed in the
Vatican of the finest collection of manuscripts in Christendom,
they entrusted it frequently to obscurantist and suspicious
custodians, for whom even another council was a lively fear, let
alone a reform of the curia itself.[68] There were frequent
wars and threats of war between the countries of the Peninsula
and often letters between scholars were held up for months or
had to be routed via distant but neutral countries; communi-
cations were infinitely easier and more certain in France and
England. Yet against these serious disadvantages, to which
must be added the relatively ignorant nature of the average
Italian prelate, let alone the parish clergy, there were great
compensations.

The world of fashion and learning now gravitated to Italy as if by routine. The intellectual *iter italicum* of scholars will occupy us briefly later (below p.167); the Grand Tour for nobles and gentry complemented the travels of the scholars by building up a favourable atmosphere of patronage in trans-Alpine Europe. Nor were the impediments raised by the Holy Office as difficult as might at first appear; there were ways round them, and if a book in the *Index librorum prohibitorum* was harder to get in Italy than in Protestant Germany or Britain (where such a condemnation was a kind of certificate of orthodoxy) it was by no means impossible. Indeed, the voracious Italian *lettore*, clerical or lay, also found the *Index* a useful guide to interesting books. If you were well-connected diplomatically it was not too impractical to acquire the works of the Enemy.[69] Nor did communication present difficulties beyond the physical ones already mentioned. Protestants of all kinds and Catholics of all kinds (and we sometimes forget how divided the undivided Church was) all went to *lycées, gymnasia,* grammar schools, academies (to use the favoured Scottish term), where the bedrock of instruction was commonly the Bible and the Latin classics (plus Greek for the handful of clever children). Historians, like mathematicians and physicists, corresponded in Latin.

This was the background of Ughelli and Muratori, chosen here to represent scores of other Italian *eruditi* whose works profoundly affected their contemporaries and continue to be used by later students. Ferdinand Ughelli (1596-1670) has been sadly neglected.[70] He was a Tuscan and a Cistercian, who at the end of the day became abbot of the Tre Fontane, south of Rome, and now a Trappist house.[71] He collaborated in revising Alfonso Chacon's lives of the popes and cardinals (Ciacconius, first ed. Rome, 1601) and composed various other books of his own. His monument, however, is the massive *Italia Sacra*, one of the most influential pieces of scholarship ever assembled.

It is not by any means the first book of its kind, though for a long time none was produced doing exactly the same thing or doing it so thoroughly. There was every reason why in protestant England efforts should be made to establish the validity of English orders by tracing the episcopal descent from as early a date as possible. The first significant work of this nature was Francis Godwin's *Catalogue of the Bishops of England*, published in English in 1601 and in a Latin translation in 1616. And this kind of inspiration was, as noted earlier (pp.149-50), responsible for much antiquarian activity in Elizabethan and Tudor England. But as a sophisticated exercise it is in Gallican France that we find three notable books which unquestionably were well known to the *literati* in Ughelli's Rome.[72] In 1621 Jean Chenu (d. 1627) published his *Archiepiscoporum et episcoporum Galliae chronologica historia*, and in 1626 it was followed by Claude Robert's (d. 1637) *Gallia Christiana*. Chenu was a Gallican lawyer and his interest in the 'liberties' of the French Church are self-evident. Robert was a priest and his book was revised and enlarged by two twin members of the Sainte-Marthe family, Scévole and Louis, in their own *Gallia Christiana*, 4 vols. 1656. All these handsome volumes must have been handled by Ughelli and we know from the preface to the Sainte-Marthe's work that he had actively helped the brothers, notably by consulting consistorial records, *libri provisionum* and various registers. The Sainte-Marthe's book, which is arranged by dioceses, has a skimpy account of each town mainly relating to classical sources but includes lists of senior dignitaries of cathedrals and abbots, generals of Orders and so on, besides full indices and an Easter Table (to 1699).

Despite these earlier models, Ughelli set himself a quite different task. There was no tradition of an 'Italic' church, as there had been for centuries Anglicanism and Gallicanism. And it was his aim not merely to list each bishop, diocese by diocese, but also to provide the reader with a concise description of the diocese itself — the size and number of towns, number and nature of convents — so that the resulting *Italia Sacra* provided in some sense not only a picture of the Church in Italy but of Italy itself. The magnitude of the task is obvious. There were almost as many dioceses in Italy as in the rest of pre-Reformation Christendom put together and Ughelli included also notices regarding dioceses that had perished.[73] There were various, often tendentious, works in print which Ughelli was sent, but, apart from recourse to Vatican archival material, his principal source was a voluminous correspondence with friends and officials all over the peninsula; many of them communicated charter material. Letters to him have survived in considerable quantities and, as the work progressed, it is clear that an earnest desire to figure in the monumental pages became widespread. The first volume came out in 1644; the ninth and final one in 1662. They were printed at Rome and are not very attractive to look at but from the side of scholarship there is not much to complain about: indices are admirably complete, annotation and references full, corrigenda to earlier parts are printed in later volumes. A revised edition, prepared by Nicolò Coleti, was printed (1723-33) at Venice in ten volumes.[74] This is the form in which it is normally consulted. It remains a quite indispensable tool for anyone working on the Italian Church, save for the earliest period, where much research has been devoted to elucidating the history of sees. The sense of Italy pervading it, and communicated by Ughelli to his correspondents, is a factor not to be ignored considering the steady if slow growth of a national, as opposed to a provincial, consciousness at that time.

Ughelli basked in papal approval. He had every encouragement from well-placed admirers like the Barberini and the Medici; he might, had he so chosen, have joined as a bishop his own *series episcoporum* and perhaps he might have become a cardinal. The other Italian scholar I wish to deal with is Ludovico-Antonio Muratori (1672-1750). He was a librarian to the dukes of Este and Modena. As a defender of their political privileges he was suspect at Rome, as we have seen, and the only thing he shared with Ughelli was that both men were clergy — Muratori becoming provost and parson of a small church in Modena.[75] Another difference between Muratori and Ughelli is that Muratori (who greatly admired Ughelli's *Italia Sacra*) concerned himself mainly with political events, which admittedly in Italy involved the Church very heavily indeed. Finally, Muratori had the advantage of being born a century later than Ughelli and thus could depend on the techniques and expertise of French and especially Maurist scholarship: his veneration for Mabillon was profound and he was able to apply the new higher criticism of documentary material on a scale which compares favourably with even the greatest of the company of St Germain des Prés. The volume of Muratori's published work is truly astonishing.

The greatest single effort was undoubtedly the *Rerum Italicarum Scriptores*, those twenty-five great folios (Milan, 1723-51) which still contain a mass of chronicle and other documentary material which has never been republished. Next I should place the six volumes of the *Antiquitates Italiae medii aevi* (Milan, 1738-42), in which the scholar discussed a series of constitutional, social and similar problems (I shall return to this work in my final chapter). Muratori himself digested this material into three volumes in Italian. Last of his major works is the Italian *Annali d'Italia*, twelve volumes, published in Milan from 1744 to 1749, in which the materials of Italian history, not least those he himself had so laboriously assembled, are collected in a chronological survey going down to 1749, somewhat along the lines of Mabillon's *Annals of the Benedictine Order*. They make tedious reading today, although for centuries they were reprinted and continued as the only accurate survey of *Italian* history — this work of continuing the *Annali* was still going on in the late nineteenth century.[76]

If Ughelli has been neglected by modern scholars the same cannot be said of Muratori, who has been celebrated in several conferences and half a dozen memorial volumes, besides more sustained studies.[77] If Ughelli does not deserve his neglect, Muratori does deserve his fame. In many ways he was, if not the father of modern historiography, then at least the grandfather.

These men — Ughelli and Muratori — were loners, so to speak, at any rate compared with the Bollandists and other scholars of the Congregation of St Maur. But it would be misleading to exaggerate their uniqueness or isolation. They each had a voluminous correspondence — letters and books crossing the Alps and, equally difficult at times, the war-tossed boundaries of contemporary Italy. Ughelli's *epistolario* is now at last attracting attention; Muratori's letters have been generously looked after.[78] These men had friends and helpers in virtually every important library in nearly every large city in Europe. Muratori and Mabillon were as familiar to English and Spanish scholars as to Germans and Poles. In a very real sense we have a *république des lettres* or rather, perhaps, a *république des hommes de science*.

This is very clearly revealed in the famous *voyages littéraires* of Mabillon and other Maurists, of Papebroche and other Bollandists. If the Italians did not travel so much it was because they had their riches at home, so to speak. Cooperative activities were also stimulated by learned societies. I am not thinking of the universities of Europe which, until the end of the eighteenth century and in Germany, were sluggish in promoting historical research. When George I established regius chairs at Oxford and Cambridge he did so as a prop to the diplomatic service. Modern history (in that polite and political sense which, as we have seen, gentlemen gave to the expression) went with a foreign language, especially French and Italian, and the new chairs went with teaching in those languages, to be paid for by the professors, who were thus aptly described as trainers of bear-leaders, 'English leaders of English bears'.[79] No wonder that the new professors were not distinguished as teachers of history. Learning had, in fact, largely deserted universities (and not just in the field of history) for lively non-academic societies, meeting in the larger towns. Some of the more famous were destined to last to our own day: The French Academy, the Académie des Inscriptions, the Royal Society, The Society of Antiquaries, the Lincei, the Accademia della Crusca and others. The scholars who attended bodies such as these rubbed shoulders with gentlemen, amateurs of learning and sometimes very learned themselves, just as the two groups mingled and conversed in the growing 'public' libraries. From this cross-fertilisation modern scholarship in the arts and sciences was to emerge.

Nor should the reader be left with the impression that the 'smooth' history of the seventeenth century and its practitioners ignored the antiquarian scholarship so prominently figuring in booksellers' shops and libraries. It was rather that they (and their readers) conceived of history as a subject which should be treated so as to yield entertainment, to instruct in political and moral virtues. History was not to lay bare the structure of dead societies or catch the atmosphere and evaluate the problems of the past.

In conclusion, it is chastening to the modern student to

remember that the writers discussed in this chapter (and the
remark will apply equally to those who come before us in the
last chapter) worked with pen and paper, and travelled
laboriously by creaking coach, by horse or on foot. That was
one reason why they corresponded so fully and kept their
correspondence. They had no typewriters, no photocopying
machines, no dictaphones. It is true they were not perpetually
disturbed by the telephone (but even to invite a near
neighbour in for a talk involved a letter). When these men
encountered a manuscript or a rare book which they needed
for their work they had to copy it by hand, and to copy it
carefully if they were not later to commit blunders for which
sharp critics would hold them up to ridicule. True,
amanuenses with considerable talents were, it appears, fairly
plentiful and fairly cheap; the hand that did the copying was
not always the hand of the scholar who digested the
transcript.[80] But the scholar had himself carefully perused
the original before spending money on a secretary or scribe.
This care should be compared with the temptations today to
glance at a manuscript or book and arrange for it to be
photographed for the scrutiny one has not immediate time for,
and perhaps will never have time for, so easy is it to
accumulate ever more material. Why transcribe now when it
can be done later? Why transcribe at all when you have a film
in a tube or box? The old masters of our subject, copying long
chronicles or charters, drawing seals and coins for the
engraver, exercised an intensity of observation and were
inspired by an impetus for discriminating reflection which
we are in danger of losing.[81]

8 Historians and Antiquaries in the Eighteenth Century: the Emergence of the Modern Method

This chapter can be short. It records the coming together of the historian and the antiquary and the development of history as something more serious than a mere narrative of fairly recent events, as an activity which involved 'research' and analysis. Of course it is not in the eighteenth century that we reach the end of the story. A further and most important step was to be taken with the elaborate academic teaching of all branches of history, largely through German inspiration and by means of the seminar, in the course of the nineteenth century.[1] And the techniques of the historian, the type of problem he is trying to elucidate, continue to evolve in our own day, as is proper in a living discipline; it would be a sad day if one could point to 'the end of the story' of the writing of history or any other learned activity. At the present time some professional historical journals carry reports of statistical and other sociological devices applied to the examination of periods and problems remote in time from our own day — indeed I am pretty confident that some recent adventures with novel methodologies and 'models' would have been totally incomprehensible to those masters of a century ago, Ranke and Stubbs; they would probably have defeated even giants like Maitland and Bloch, the two greatest historians of recent times.[2] In short, new ways of analysing the past are still being worked out and the history of historiography is far from being a closed book. But these developments, from what Sir Herbert Butterfield called the 'Göttingen school' onwards, need not detain us here, where I am concerned only to illustrate the emergence of conditions which favoured a mature approach to the history of earlier times.

One important precondition of a sound and scholarly investigation of remoter periods had been finally disposed of; the labours of the Bollandists, of Mabillon and other Maurists, and of scores of other painstaking scholars, had put paid to pyrrhonism.[3] Scepticism about the possibility of exact knowledge being attainable had a curious recrudescence at the end of the seventeenth century and the beginning of the eighteenth; Paul Hazard writes brilliantly about this episode in his *Crise de la conscience européene*.[4] I do not think any fundamentally fresh arguments were put forward to those advanced by pyrrhonists like Cornelius Agrippa of Nettesheim (1486-1535) or Francesco Patrizzi (1529-97), whose scepticism, as Julian H. Franklin has said, was not to be surpassed until the nineteenth century,[5] and whose views had found theoretical answers in the writings of Jean Bodin and some of his contemporaries, as we have seen.[6] By the end of the seventeenth century the cloud of witnesses had grown much greater and means to test their veracity had also multiplied. Even the writings of the ancients — of Herodotus, Livy and the other historians of antiquity, regarded by the humanists as sacrosanct — were now subject to criticism in the light of the scientific study of epigraphy, medals, coins, more controlled archaeological excavations and so on.[7] Even the Bible itself began to be the subject of acute philological study with Richard Simon (1638-1712), who thus inaugurated the critical analysis of the Old Testament, paying the price of expulsion from the Order of the Oratory though remaining a devout son of the Roman Church. If ancient and biblical history could now be written with an increasing conviction that one was getting at the truth, *a fortiori* this was possible for later periods, usually better furnished with source material of all kinds, and especially with the documentary (i.e. non-narrative) authorities — the public and private administrative records, inscriptions and so on, which were accorded higher estimation because it was assumed that they were of their very nature more unbiassed, less liable to be the vehicles of propaganda and brainwashing.[8]

The traditional picture of the development of historiography in the eighteenth century gives all the initial credit to Voltaire (François-Marie Arouet, 1694-1778), and notably to his *Essai sur l'histoire générale et sur les moeurs et l'esprit des nations*, 7 vols (1756).[9] All of this is treated by Fueter under the general rubric the 'Enlightenment', his title for book iv of his survey. He allows England a large role in the Enlightenment but argues that, since the settlement of 1688 more or less satisfied everyone, there was no incentive, as there was in France, to criticise the autocratic monopoly of power by Church and State in cooperation or collusion. This contains a germ of truth, although the violence of the arguments over Church and State in England, especially over the non-juror issue and the Hanoverian succession, were tense and continuous and often produced works which turned to history for explanations, causes and justifications; much as the crises of the seventeenth century had driven scholars to study 'the feudal law and the ancient constitution'.[10] Moreover, to the extent that commonsense was one of the Enlightenment historians' main weapons in evaluating the probability of what they encountered in the sources, the 'commonsense school' had certainly developed earlier and more securely in Britain than in France. Voltaire, it must be recalled, had spent formative years in England (1726-7).

There is no gainsaying that Voltaire displayed considerable originality both in his *Siècle de Louis XIV* and in the *Essai sur les moeurs*. Both works abandoned the traditional chronological treatment for discussion of topics, although in the *Louis XIV* the topics are sharply separated in vol. ii from the traditional narrative in vol. i. This was a very big change from the procedures of the other smart historians of the day; and Voltaire must also be numbered amongst the smart historians, for he was competing with them for the favours of the *grand public*; the learned admired him often, but often with reservations.[11] *Louis XIV* was at first remarkably free of nationalist sentiment or reforming zeal; later it was modified to imply criticism of the cultural defects of Louis XV. To deal with internal government, commerce, the Church, the arts as separate and distinguishable phenomena does give Voltaire's books a novel dimension compared to the histories of other popular writers. Yet it should be remembered that it was virtually contemporary history, in the humanist tradition, in the chronicling tradition and in the tradition of the ancient practitioners. Voltaire wrote his *Siècle de Louis XIV* as a cultivated man of the world. But in all essentials it was a world he knew at first hand.

Not so with the *Essai sur les moeurs*, which may fairly claim to be the first general or universal history of mankind. Here Voltaire's learning, which was extensive, was extensively concealed. He seldom revealed the gritty authorities from which he had often derived his matter. Instead he presents his 'quick-silver mind', delighting the reader with a striking parallel or metaphor. Quite why Voltaire was so reticent presents something of a puzzle. He was far from ignorant of the erudition of his own and the previous generation. But he hedged his bets, it seems. His little duodecimos did not compete with the heavy folios of Mabillon or Muratori: you could not read the *Acta Sanctorum* in bed without breaking a rib; you could not lay even one volume of Ughelli on your *escritoire* without causing severe damage. Voltaire, in short, represents the first and perhaps the best example of that genre of scholarship for which we have to use the French term *haute vulgarisation*. Wit, intelligence and an acidulated prose style naturally precluded laborious references to large Latin volumes, which might be in the library of a great gentleman's house but were certainly not to be found in his drawing room or his wife's boudoir. Besides, was not plain mother-wit just as reliable an 'authority' as tons of erudition in oak-boards? Later on Principal William Robertson was to complain about this, when he in his turn gave a survey of medieval Europe in his 'view of the progress of society in Europe', prefaced to his *Charles V* (1769):

> In all my enquiries and disquisitions ... I have not once mentioned M. de Voltaire, who, in his Essai sur l'histoire

générale, has reviewed the same period and treated of all these subjects. This does not proceed from inattention to the works of that extraordinary man, whose genius, no less enterprising than universal, has attempted almost every different species of literary composition ... But as he seldom imitates the example of modern historians, in citing the authors from whom they derived their information, I could not, with propriety, appeal to his authority in confirmation of any doubtful or unknown fact ... [12]

Robertson was in reality saying that, brilliant and stimulating though Voltaire was, as an historian he was old-fashioned.

To appreciate the force of Robertson's criticism we have to look at the *Essai* itself. Here is a very short passage, which attracted my attention many years ago as displaying (in part) Voltaire's attitude to the Renaissance in Italy:

For all these fine inventions we are indebted to the Tuscans only, who by mere strength of genius revived those arts, before the little remains of Greek learning, together with that language, removed from Constantinople into Italy, after the conquest of the Ottomans. Florence was at that time a second Athens; and it is remarkable, that among the orators who were deputed by most of the cities of Italy to harangue Boniface VIII upon his exaltation to the holy see, eighteen of them were natives of this city. By this it appears, that it is not to the refugees of Constantinople we are indebted for the restoration of letters: those men were capable of teaching the Italians nothing more than the Greek tongue.

It may appear somewhat remarkable, that so many great geniuses should have started up of a sudden in Italy, without protection, or any model to go by, in the midst of dissensions and domestic broils: but among the Romans Lucretius wrote his beautiful poem on nature, Vergil his Bucolics, and Cicero his philosophical works amidst the confusion of civil wars. When once a language is ascertained, it is a kind of instrument which eminent artists find ready to their hands, and which they make use of for their purposes, without troubling their heads about who governs, or who disturbs the earth ...[13]

It is fascinating to observe the steady penetration of
erudition into histories designed for a wide audience; it is
fascinating to see the authors of such books combining
narrative with social description and analysis, appropriating
the learned researches of specialists so that, embedded in a
framework where they could illuminate a situation or throw
light on a problem, they would in turn lead the historian to his
own research. The two authors who first moved decisively in
this direction were both Scots. This was not accidental.
Scottish universities and the coteries of cultivated men in the
bigger towns were lively intellectual centres at a time when
universities in Europe, and especially the two torpid seminaries
of Oxford and Cambridge, were in their doldrums. At
Edinburgh in particular, with its High Courts of Justice and a
well-educated bar, a good university with many able teachers,
three libraries which in some sense were 'public' and in all
senses were remarkably well furnished with books of scholarship, we have a centre of research facilities without its equal in
contemporary Europe.[14] David Hume (1711-76) and
William Robertson (1721-93) were both Edinburgh men.
Hume was for a short time librarian of the Advocates
Library,[15] and as we know from surviving borrowers'
registers Robertson drew steadily on the extensive holdings of
the University Library.

Hume nowadays is remembered best as a very great
philosopher. But for the greater part of his life he had a hard
time of it to lead a comfortable life, having a number of
precarious employments. Then he embarked on the series of
histories which were finally put together as *The History of
England*. The work has a complicated bibliography, having
been written and published in disparate sections, reminding
one of the way Michelet published his *History of France* a
century later. The section covering England under the Stuarts
came out first as *The History of Great Britain* (Edinburgh,
1754-7; for the title we have to remember that James VI and I
so decreed it in 1604 and that it became a reality of sorts in
1707). A Tudor portion next appeared as a *History of England*
(London, 1759). Finally came *The History of England from
the Invasion of Julius Caesar to the Accession of Henry VII*
(London, 1762). As a complete work from the Romans to 1688

t was first published in 1763; there were very many reprints
and Hume became a wealthy man. The first volume of the first
part was not an unqualified success, but in the end the
enterprise makes Hume the harbinger of the historical
best-sellers of our own day. And this despite his being — in
Principal Robertson's phrase — a 'modern' historian. Scholarship could return a dividend, a very handsome one.

Hume not only wrote well, he quoted his authorities in both
text and footnotes. Here, quite at random, are a few lines from
his account of the reign of Edward III:

> [... The battle of Sluys, 13 June, 1340] ... Two hundred
> French ships were taken; 30,000 Frenchmen were killed,
> with two of their admirals; the loss of the English was incon-
> siderable, compared with the greatness and importance of
> the victory [a footnote here refers to Froissart, Avesbury,
> Hemingburgh, each in a precise way]. None of Philip's cour-
> tiers, it is said, dared to inform him of the event, till his fool
> or jester gave him a hint, by which he discovered the loss he
> had sustained (Walsing., p.148).
>
> The lustre of this great success increased the king's
> authority among his allies, who assembled their forces with
> expedition. Edward marched to the frontiers of France at
> the head of above 100,000 men, consisting chiefly of
> foreigners, a more numerous army than, either before or
> since, has ever been commanded by any King of England
> (Rymer, vol. v, p.197) ...[16]

It was only in what earlier writers would have termed
'digressions' that he hesitated to mingle analysis and discussion
of society and its structure with the political narrative which he
regarded as history proper. Robertson is somewhat like Hume
in this respect, as we can see especially clearly in his 'View of
the progress of society in Europe', prefaced to his *Charles V*,
from which I have already quoted his observation regarding
Voltaire and his authorities. Robertson's long prefatory essay
was in itself an innovation, providing the reader with a
back-cloth, so to speak, against which to place the history of
Charles V which was to follow.[17]

Nevertheless we must be cautious in evaluating the
originality of Hume and Robertson, and this for two reasons:

they had a number of predecessors as examples or partial examples; and they had a number of reservations in integrating certain aspects of the new erudition with narrative history of countries or periods of time.

As for their predecessors, I have tried to explain above (p.161) why it seems to me exaggerated to regard a writer like Pasquier as taking a long step in the direction of a truly sophisticated historiography. But a century later I believe we have arrived at an awareness, so widely diffused as to be influential, of the need to examine historical situations from a variety of angles, rather than merely to tell a tale of public men in public arts, however elegantly, however well-founded. The *New Method of Studying History* by C. Rawlinson, mentioned already in connection with libraries and bibliographies, may give us some indication of what had happened in the world of historical scholarship by the early 1700s.[17] In vol. ii of this work (London, 1728) we find listed an enormous number of books. The index lists well over 3,500 authors, several with half-a-dozen or more works. The titles are assembled in a long series of chapters and subsections. Besides narratives devoted to regions and their towns or provinces, chapters deal with the history of the churches and of religious orders (some seventy works are listed from the sixteenth to the early eighteenth centuries dealing with the ecclesiastical history of Britain), and the work ends with bibliographies of Asia, African, America, Travels and Voyages, Heraldry and Genealogies, Festivals and Funeral Pomps, Treatises on Inscriptions, Dissertations on Medals.[18]

The most significant writer of history in the form of dissertations was unquestionably Muratori. Hitherto he has been considered only as one of the learned band who edited texts and as the compiler of the *Annali* (above pp.165-6). Now his most original work falls to be briefly discussed, the *Antiquitates Italicae medii aevi*, 6 vols (Milan, 1738-42). It is to Fueter's credit that he breaks his own rule to mention this remarkable work in a couple of lines: 'a complement to the annals, which brought together research on institutions, opinions, habits and customs in Italy from the fifth to the thirteenth century';[19] to Fueter's discredit he does not see what an impressive work Muratori had attempted, nor that in

a sense it constituted a history of Italy, conceived on novel
methods. Muratori saw it in some such way. 'My researches',
he wrote, 'offer various views of Italy and the Italian nation,
rather in the way one might describe a great city or an
imposing palace ... I have chosen to deal with a number of
important problems regarding medieval Italy.' Classical Rome
was well-served by existing books, he went on, but not so the
antiquities of the barbarian period', for which materials were
scarce and scattered. To penetrate such scholarship, which is
often rather unattractive, the archives are essential. Hence the
dissertations' digest not only narrative authors (which he had
assembled in his *Scriptores*), but a vast range of other material
— charters, coins, medals, seals and other 'fragments of the
past'. The *Antiquities* (he himself translated them into Italian,
a significant gesture, and this version in three volumes was
published posthumously, Milan 1751) can be summarised in
his own words. He aimed to produce studies of Italian
institutions: 'Kings, dukes, marquises, counts and other
magistracies, the various ceremonies of governments, and
private habits. Liberty and servitude, the judges, the army,
cities and finally religion'. So that it is fair to regard the
Antiquities as constituting in some sort a topical or analytical
survey of medieval Italy.

It would take up too much space adequately to illustrate
Muratori's achievement in this book. Yet some indication may
be derived from a list of the first dozen of his dissertations:

I   Concerning the barbarians who mastered Italy.
II   The kingdom of Italy and its frontiers.
III   The election of the Roman emperors and of the kings
        of Italy.
IV   The court officials of the former kings of Italy and of
        the emperors.
V   The dukes and former princes of Italy.
VI   The former marquises.
VII   The counts of the sacred palace.
VIII The counts or viscounts of the barbarian centuries.
IX   The royal legates (*missi*) or judges extraordinary.
X   Lesser judicial officials.
XI   Allodial property, vassals, benefices, fiefs, castellans.
XII   Notaries.

In all there were seventy-five dissertations, the last twenty or so
being devoted to various aspects of religion and the Church
and the last to what is in our own day the very fashionable
topic of lay confraternities and flagellants. Although aspects of
the ancient civilizations of Greece and Rome had been steadily
studied from Biondo onwards, nothing as elaborate as this
could really be attempted for antiquity, given the paucity of
the kind of documentation which Western scholars were now
disposing of and which Muratori put to such good use in the
Antichità, which must be read, properly to savour the mixture
of learning and good-temper.

Hume's dissertations are scattered in a series of appendices
through his work: for example the first, which follows his
chapters on Anglo-Saxon England, is on 'The Anglo-Saxon
government and manners'. These appendices are very heavily
documented compared with the narrative chapters, and
abound in references to the scholars discussed in the previous
chapter — Spelman, Wilkins, Lindenbrog, Brady *Or
Boroughs*, and so on.[20]. But the separation of them from the
body of the book reflects the continuing dichotomy, which we
have already noted, between learning and literature, between
the antiquary and the historian, which had developed in the
sixteenth century and reached its highest point in the
seventeenth. Then the works of the *eruditi*, Bollandists,
Maurists and the scores of other scholars, were doubtless
sometimes bought by the well-to-do to line the high library
shelves of *palazzo* or *chateau*, but, as I have said, the histories
that were currently read by ladies and gentlemen were the
smooth and undemanding narratives of Mézeray or Daniel.
And this continued into the eighteenth century.[21] When
reading histories of historiography, even as well-researched as
Fueter's, one all too readily comes away with the impression
that by the 1740s and 1750s everyone was reading Voltaire.
This was not the case. And in any event we have seen that for
Voltaire (and his readers) the parade of learning was not
polite. And for similar reasons Hume and Robertson made a
sharp distinction between their art prose and its scholarly
supports and props.

Of the two Scotsmen, there is no doubt that Robertson came
to understand what was required more than Hume did. There

a whiff of the professional about Robertson, of the gifted amateur about Hume. After all, Robertson was a reverend professor, principal of a great university. But beyond that Robertson was surely the abler historian of the two, more shrewd, better informed, an historian's historian. It is therefore hardly surprising that, all through the nineteenth century, Robertson was destined to have the profounder influence on historical learning. Hume was, of course, enormously important as a force in philosophical thought — indeed one has the impression that in our own day his reputation is higher than it has ever been. Doubtless he could have turned to history in as solid a way as Robertson had he so wished. In one or two of the *Essays* we occasionally encounter the digested materials of the past in a form strikingly similar to *dissertazione* by Muratori; I am thinking, for example, of the long essay 'Of the populousness of ancient nations'.[22]

In thus placing scholarship beside narration, moving towards a technique of narration in which the scholarship was essential, if subordinate, to the narration, Hume and Robertson — especially the latter — were taking a very important step towards the creation of a more penetrating, adaptable and scientific way of describing the past. The future was to see historians concentrating on the understanding of the 'knot of reality' (Marc Bloch's phrase), the tangled web of institutions, economies, cultural and religious forces. As I wrote twenty five years ago in connection with Polydore Vergil, the future of historiography was to lie precisely in the discursive treatment of particular issues rather than the chronological enumeration of events' — those matters which Vergil had apologetically inserted as 'digressions'.[23] Hume and Robertson in their learned and non-narrative passages are dealing with problems and not personalities. They perfected this, I believe, from a careful study of Muratori rather than in any other way. This is seen more clearly in Robertson than in Hume, not only because he was more concerned with European history in early periods to an extent that Hume was not, but also because he had a vivid sense of the importance for modern history of the centuries when the nations of Europe had been formed.

If we look at the annotation of the famous panorama of the

Middle Ages in Robertson's *Charles V*, we find that Muratori
name occurs more often than that of any other scholar. The
are all there — Ducange, Mabillon, the *Acta Sanctorum*
Dugdale, Spelman and the name most often quoted. A rapi
survey of the references shows that for every reference to hi
other works (*Scriptores, Antichità Estensi, Annali*) there ar
six or seven to the *Antiquitates*. It is no accident that in th
fine portrait of him by Raeburn, which hangs in the Universit
of Edinburgh Senate Hall, among the books he has chosen t
surround himself with we can see the *Antichità italiane*.[24
This is by no means to argue that Muratori is the only autho
to inspire Principal Robertson; even among the Italians h
drew much from Sarpi (above p.40) and even more, perhap
on account of his attitude to the Roman Church, fron
Giannone,[25] whose 'boldness and discernment' he expressl
comments;[26] it was from Giannone that both Hume an
Robertson derived their views on the rise and influence o
Roman law.

Robertson explained the function of his 'proofs an
illustrations':

> The chief intention of these notes was to bring at once unde
> the view of my readers, such facts and circumstances as ten
> to illustrate or confirm what is contained in that part of th
> history to which they refer. When these lay scattered amon
> many different authors, and were taken from books no
> generally know, or which many of my readers might find i
> disagreeable to consult, I thought it would be of advantag
> to collect them together.[27]

The very expressions Robertson uses recall Muratori's prefac
to the *Antichità*, and 'cotesta erudizione non sempre amena'
this 'not always attractive erudition'. It is true that they do nc
proceed to that exciting invitation Muratori extended to other
to improve on his work.[28] The notion that a history book o
any other scientific study, would go out of date, present to th
poor provost at Modena, had not, I guess, arrived ii
Edinburgh.

The reader of these pages must not assume that th
judgements just delivered are based on a profound study of th
technical scholarship of Voltaire, Muratori, Hume o

Robertson: this important work has, so far as I know, not been attempted by anyone. It must therefore remain an impression that Muratori was the most professionally competent of them all. Hume, one feels, frequently compiled references rather than digested them and too often the philosopher in him led him to Man in the abstract rather than to the messy public activities of men and women, contradictory creatures, which constitute the province of the historian. Many of Robertson's 'proofs and illustrations' are brief enough and only about thirteen of the first thirty (that is, those dealing with medieval European history) are comparable to the essays of Muratori, and while the analytical approach to problems was the route that nineteenth-century historians were to follow, it would be a long time before such an approach was to dominate academic history. Politics retained its primacy, for very good reasons; and chronological narrative remained the basic pattern of exposition.[29]

The third of the triumvirate of British historians on whom the new scholarship laid its imprint (particularly through Muratori) was Edward Gibbon, surely the greatest narrative historian of the last two hundred years. This reintroduces the influence of Muratori's *Annali*, but before considering this matter another deserves attention. National history was becoming the dominant form of exploration of the past; so it had almost always been with popular history — now it was to be the case with erudite works as well. We should not suppose that Muratori, gentle, liberal, humane and intellectually cosmopolitan as he was, displayed a strong sense of *Italianità* only in the *Annali*. The conception and execution of the *Scriptores* and of the *Antiquitates* equally reflect a profound love of Italy and a desire to illustrate its past: *patriotisme avant la patrie*, one might say. Looking at the erudition of Europe at his time Paul Hazard wrote: 'England [he means Britain] concerned itself more with Greek studies, Holland with Latin, France with hagiography and Italy with her own past'.[30] Of the numerous *eruditi* of Italy (Muratori names many of them in his prefaces, and they fill pages in the various 'methods' and bibliographies, such as that already mentioned by Laeglet du

Fresnoy[31]), the majority dealt with regional history, as was
to be expected of Italian scholars dwelling in a land divided up
into a number of small states (the case of Germany was
parallel). Muratori's work for the Este family illustrates this.
But he always had Italy in mind: witness the title of his
Antichità Estensi e Italiane, which came out in 1717. And the
design of and intentions behind the *Antiquitates* itself was the
scientific study of the Italian nation in the Middle Ages. In this
form, as has been noted already, the *Antiquitates* constituted a
topical or analytical review of the history of Italy down to the
thirteenth century.

But it was, of course, the *Annali* to which readers went who
sought the history of the peninsula. In the *Annali* (above,
p.166) Italy had unquestionably the most complete and
scientifically documented history of any European
country,[32] a fact all the more impressive considering the
absence of a central government and (compared to London,
Paris and Madrid) a capital city. As already mentioned,
Robertson used the *Annali* but it was, of course, Edward
Gibbon who gave the work its British *imprimatur*, if one may
put it that way. This was not only by using it, but by explicit
commendation. In the survey of medieval Rome given in
chapter LXIX Muratori was described as a basic authority.
Gibbon writes:

> The dates of years in the margin may, throughout this
> chapter, be understood as tacit references to the Annals of
> Muratori, my ordinary and excellent guide. He uses and
> indeed quotes, with the freedom of a master, his great Col-
> lection of the Italian Historians, in xxxviii volumes; and, as
> that treasure is in my library, I have thought it an amuse-
> ment, if not a duty, to consult the originals.[33]

(This is to treat the *Annali* as a sort of chronological index to
the *Scriptores*, which of course it is, although the latter work
did not go up to Muratori's own day, as the *Annali* did.) At the
end of chapter LXX Gibbon lists the authorities he has used in
dealing with Rome and the papacy in the later Middle Ages.
They are mostly 'in the Collections of Muratori, my guide and
master in the history of Italy'. After listing Muratori's main
works, Gibbon adds that: 'in all his works Muratori proves

himself a diligent and laborious writer, who aspires above the prejudices of a Catholic priest'.[34]

The paradox of Gibbon's admiration for Roman Catholic scholars has repeatedly (and in my view erroneously) engaged the interest of later critics.[35] Giorgio Falco wrote that he 'accepted and reconciled reason and revelation'. Christopher Dawson, himself a Roman Catholic, marvelled that the inheritor of the devout and self-effacing Tillemont should not have been some latter-day Bossuet 'but the infidel Gibbon ... who used the material which Tillemont had so laboriously collected, in order to explain away Christianity and to rationalise the history of the Church'.[36] Giuseppe Giarrizzo has rightly stressed the character of Muratori's disposition so far as religion and history are concerned: 'Moderate and discerning, Muratori preferred to justify than to condemn. Moreover, he understood the whole of history, both ecclesiastical and secular, as civil history, in which man and not God is at the centre of the picture.'[37] This 'moderatismo' was profound in Muratori and in Robertson and Hume; it obviously appealed to the cool and detached attitude which Gibbon attained, 'all passion spent', in the late 1760s. Giarrizzo has also pointed out how congenial to Gibbon was Muratori's attitude to the question of the Italian nation, which derived partly from the Englishman's desire to oppose an Italian consciousness as a bulwark against the temporal ambitions of the popes, and partly from the need to explain the reception of Italian cultural values outside Italy despite the all but universal repugnance inspired by the Roman Church at all times.[38] It is easy to see why Gibbon preferred Muratori to Count Scipio Maffei; his own explanation for this was typically enough wrapped up in pretty irrelevant social terms: Maffei wrote as a proud noble, Muratori as a plebeian.[39] It would be gratifying to be able to trace Gibbon's very theme to the Italian he admired and depended on so much, but it would not be true. He was fired to history by Hume; and he shared with, but did not derive, the idea of the *Decline and Fall* from Poggio, Biondo, Sigonio.[40]

I have indicated that it seems to me 'erroneous' to try to build spiritual bridges between the sceptical mentality of Gibbon and the unquestioning religious faith of Tillemont or

Muratori; after all, it is even more surprising to find Hume so
receptive of the scholarship of the great divines of the
seventeenth century, while Robertson was not only principal of
the University of Edinburgh but also a minister of the Kirk of
the Grey Friars and for many years moderator of the General
Assembly of the Church of Scotland. What brought these men
together (and a few others like them) was a common respect
for and enjoyment of both historical research and writing
history. And none felt this respect and enjoyment more than
Gibbon: let us recall the phrase quoted above (p.182) in which
he talks of consulting Muratori's work as an amusement and a
duty.

The argument I have tried to present in this final chapter is
that with Hume, Robertson and above all Gibbon the
erudition of the seventeenth and early eighteenth centuries was
to be welded to the exposition of the historian, so that the
discipline of historical research that we are familiar with in the
canonical works of the nineteenth century was established. I
shall rephrase the point in Professor Momigliano's words:
'Gibbon broke new ground not by his ideas on the fall of
Rome, but by offering the treasures of erudition to the
contemplation of the philosophical historian.'[41] Perhaps we
should not allow ourselves to be too distracted by that word
'philosophical', by which (I think) is meant surveying the past
in large swathes rather than by means of little tunnels.[42]
Gibbon stands out also because his popularity and value as a
historian has survived Hume's and Robertson's. Unlike their
works, *The Decline and Fall of the Roman Empire* has
remained (in J.B. Bury's edition) on the shelves of the student
today.

Hume said in one of his *Essays* that every cultivated person
should know the history of Greece and Rome, and of his own
native land.[43] This was sometimes an invitation to chauvinist
history, a chauvinism about the past from which Britain
perhaps suffered less, although 'the Roman and the Teuton'
was to bedevil some worthy men; a chauvinism regarding
origins violently distorted much German and French scholarship. At the end of the eighteenth century, however, the
historian could contemplate earlier times with a calmness and
a certainty, a sense that he was not merely 'scribbling', as

George III's brother described to his face Gibbon's work, just to amuse the *beau monde*. On the contrary, the meritorious historian could have the sense that he was enlightening his contemporaries with solid pictures of substantial if vanished worlds. The extraordinary sales of the new historians' work show that the public was ready for them.

Bede, taking leave of the world at Jarrow in 735, died in the beauty of holiness, and cannot be compared with Gibbon in 787, surveying the evening from the summer house of his villa at Lausanne, having just taken leave of the last words in his great work. But, so far as the history of history is concerned, they are linked. Bede, Janus-like, looking backwards at the ancient world and forward to the world of Christian conversion and of the new Christian chronology he did so much to refine and justify, was to lead on to the medieval chronicle, limited in readership until the Renaissance and the invention of printing. With the Renaissance there came, as we have seen, the deep division between historians and antiquaries which took long to be overcome. The next stage was the further development of the new history in the nineteenth century and the professionalism which has since overtaken the academic historian. But that is another story.

Notes

Preface

1 Our equivalent for the German and French books on medieval sources was (and in certain respects still is) the out-of-date work by C. Gross, *The Sources and Literature of English History to 1485* (first ed. 1896, second ed. 1900). This has now been largely replaced by Edgar B. Graves, *A Bibliography of English History to 1485* (Oxford, 1975), published under the auspices of the Royal Historical Society and the American Historical Association, learned bodies on both sides of the Atlantic; similar sponsors were likewise responsible earlier for bibliographies of Tudor, Stuart and eighteenth-century sources and related literature.

2 Antonia Gransden, *Historical Writing in England, c.550-c.1307* (London, 1974). My own essay had been written before this was available to me. I should also like to draw attention to Sir Richard Southern's four presidential addresses to the Royal Historical Society, printed in *Proceedings*, 5th Series, vols 20-23 (1970-73). I hope these will be reprinted and extended.

Chapter 1

1 Below pp.44ff and 78ff.

2 Trans. Arnold J. Toynbee, *Greek Historical Thought* (London, 1950), 23.

3 *Ab urbe condita*, trans. B.O. Foster, vol.i, Loeb Classical Library (London and Cambridge, Mass., 1967), 243-5.

4 *De Oratore*, trans. Southern and Rackham, Loeb Classical Library (London and Cambridge, Mass., 1917) 234-5

5 Trans. R. Livingstone, World's Classics (London, 1943), 91.

6 Or '28 March 58 B.C.', which is how we would put it.

7 Trans. Toynbee, 31.

8 P.G. Walsh, *Livy: His Historical Aims and Methods* (Cambridge, 1961), 222.

9 See *Ad Herennium*, ed. H. Caplan, Loeb Classical Library (London and Cambridge, Mass., 1954), 175-73, which supplies further elaboration.

10 *Ibid.*, analysed in the introduction, lvi-lvii.

11 Eric Auerbach, *Mimesis* (New York, 1957, Archon Books), 5-66 *passim*. These pages (which pay particular attention to Tacitus) are also basic to an understanding of historical narrative in both Old and New Testaments.

See below, pp.23-5.

12 A full text had in fact been discovered in France twenty years earlier by N. de Clémanges: R. Sabbadini, *Le scoperte de' codici latini e greci ... Nuove ricerche* (Florence, 1914), 84-5, 247-8. But it was Poggio's discoveries that mattered.

13 Cf. Robert A. Nisbet, *Social Change and History. Aspects of the Western Theory of Development* (New York, 1969), esp. 29-61.

14 *Ed.cit.*, 224.

Chapter 2

1 Quotations from the Bible in this chapter and elsewhere are from the Authorised Version.

2 The above summary of a very complicated subject is derived from H. Wheeler Robinson, ed., *The Bible in its Ancient and English Versions* (2nd ed. 1954, Oxford), 1-127; a more technical treatment will be found in G.W.H. Lampe, ed., *Cambridge History of the Bible*, vol.2: *The West from the Fathers to the Reformation* (Cambridge, 1969), 1-101.

3 R.A. Markus, *Saeculum: History and Society in the Theology of St Augustine* (Cambridge, 1970), 189. See also G.W.H. Lampe, 'The exposition and exegesis of scripture: to Gregory the Great', *Camb. Hist. of the Bible*, vol.2 (Cambridge, 1969), 155-83.

4 Lampe, 'Exposition and exegesis ...', 175.

5 Cf. Markus, 42-8. See below p.23.

6 Peter Brown, *Augustine of Hippo* (London, 1967), esp. 287-329.

7 Augustine's summary of history in the *De civitate dei* is in Book XVIII, ch.i.

8 Esp. XIX, chs v, xvi.

9 *The Political Aspects of St Augustine's 'City of God'* (London, 1921), 29.

10 Trans. Marcus Dodds (Edinburgh, 1872), ii, 326-8.

11 Cf. below pp.50-3.

12 Cf. A Momigliano, 'Pagan and Christian historiography in the fourth century A.D.', in *The Conflict between Paganism and Christianity in the Fourth Century* (Oxford, 1963), 89.

13 For the whole question of 'sermo humilis' see the chapter so entitled in Eric Auerbach, *Literary Language and its Public in Late Latin Antiquity and in the Middle Ages*, trans. R. Manheim (London, 1965), 27-66.

14 *Ibid.*, 52.

15 *Ibid.*, 51-2.

16 *Mimesis* (see Ch.1, n.11 above), 40 (the narrative from Mark 14: 54-72).

17 Above p.5.

18 What follows is mainly paraphrased from the admirable account in R.L. Poole, *Chronicles and Annals* (Oxford, 1926), 20-25.

19 Bede's *Ecclesiastical History* provides a very early example: Britain was visited by Julius Caesar 'in the year 693 after the building of Rome and 60 years before the Incarnation' (*ante ... incarnationis dominicae tempus*

anno LXmo), I: ii (ed. C. Plummer, i, 13, and again in the Summary, i, 352).

20 II Peter iii, 8 could be understood to mean that each of these epochs lasted one thousand years. This was to appeal to medieval prophets. See also below p.28.

21 Markus, 16-21; Brown, 318-20.

22 As far as the Old Testament is concerned, this is also the case with the *Antiquities of the Jews*, written by the Jew Josephus, c.A.D.94. Later on Christian writers took their account of the first five ages from compilations, such as that of Petrus Comestor. Cf. below, p.63.

23 Below p.64; cf. above, n.20 on 'one day is with the Lord as a thousand years', which brought apocalyptic possibilities also to the six ages.

24 Cf. Momigliano, 90-91.

25 See the useful appendices in the Penguin Classics ed., *The History of the Church*, ed. G.A. Williamson (Harmondsworth, 1965). This is somewhat abbreviated. The Loeb text and translation is by K. Lake (1912-13); the completest English version with commentary is ed. H.J. Lawlor and J.E.L. Oulton (London, 1927-8).

26 Rufinus's procedures are displayed very clearly in the edition of Eusebius' history edited by E. Schwartz and T. Mommsen (Leipzig, 1903-8) for the German 'Christlicher Schriftsteller der ersten Jahrhunderte'. The *Ecclesiastical History* is printed with Rufinus' translation on facing pages; his extension of the story is edited by Mommsen, ii, 960-1040. Extension is perhaps misleading. Rufinus filled in gaps in earlier parts in an interesting but disjointed 'book x' and then embarked on a short 'book xi'.

27 It was edited by W. Jacob and R. Hanslik as vol. lxxi of the *Corpus Scriptorum Ecclesiasticorum Latinorum* (Vienna, 1952). The Latin translations of Sozomen, Socrates and Theodoret, on which Cassiodorus based his accounts, were made by Epiphanius.

28 Eds: by S. Haverkamp, reprinted by Migne in the Patrologia Latina xxxi (Paris, 1846), by C. Zengemeister, in Corpus Scriptorum Ecclesiasticorum, v (1882).

29 Procopius, *History of the Wars* and *Anecdota* in Loeb Classical Library, ed. and trans. by H.B. Dewing (1914-35); *History* in vols i-v, *Anecdota* in vol.vi; an abridged one-volume trans. by A. Cameron (New York, 1967).

30 The *topos* is briefly discussed by E.R. Curtius, *European Literature and the Latin Middle Ages*, trans. Willard R. Trask (London, 1953), 83-5: 'Affected Modesty'.

31 Text ed. T. Mommsen, Monumenta Germaniae Historica, V, i (Berlin, 1882); Eng. trans. C.C. Mierow, *The Gothic History of Jordanes* (Princeton, N.J., 1915; repr. New York, 1966).

32 Auerbach, *Mimesis*, 77.

33 *Ibid.*, 73. The whole discussion, pp.67-83, is valuable; and cf. his *Literary Language*, 109-10.

34 J.M. Wallace-Hadrill, 'The work of Gregory of Tours in the light of modern research', *Trans. Roy. Hist. Soc.*, ser. 5, i (1951), 45.

35 There are several critical editions. That in the Monumenta Germaniae Historica, ed. B. Krusch (Berlin, 1937-42), is regarded as the best. There is a translation by O.M. Dalton (Oxford, 1927).

36 Above p.27; cf. below p.45.

37 Ed. C. Plummer (Oxford, 1896), 5, 8. There is another ed. with a good translation by B. Colgrave and R.A.B. Mynors (Oxford, 1969).

38 He must have been about sixty years old and died a few years after the *Ecclesiastical History* was completed.

39 Auerbach, *Literary Language*, 327.

40 Ed. Plummer, 112-13, 183-8. On Bede's knowledge of pagan classics cf. Plummer's introduction, lii-liii.

41 E.g. ed. Plummer, 110, 209.

42 *Ibid*, 112.

43 *Ibid*, 249-52. Matthew 26: 58-75, Acts 12: 6-10.

44 Auerbach, *Literary Language*, 113, quoting E. Norden, *Die antike Kunstprosa* (1915).

45 The preferred edition is by L. Halphen, with a French translation (Paris, 1947). The most accessible English translation is by S.E. Turner, ed. S. Painter (Ann Arbor, Mich., 1960). There is a vast literature, much of it contentious. For reference to recent work see D.A. Bullough,'*Europae Pater*: Charlemagne and his achievement in the light of recent scholarship', *Eng. Hist. Rev.*, lxxxv (1970), esp. 68-9.

46 But cf. below p.56.

47 A. Molinier, *Sources de l'histoire de france au moyen âge*, 6 vols (Paris, 1901-6), i, 107-65.

48 See below pp.53-4, and, for the *Acta Sanctorum*, below pp.159-60.

Chapter 3

1 P.G. Walsh, *Livy: His Historical Aims and Methods* (Cambridge, 1961).

2 Above p.27.

3 An admirable note by Charles W. Jones, in his edition of Bede's *Opera de temporibus* (Cambridge, Mass., 1943), 345, summarises the matter. For Isidore, see further below p.59.

4 R.L. Poole, *Medieval Reckonings of Time*, 'Helps for Students of History' (London, 1918), gives a brief and authoritative account of the start of official years; see p.43.

5 Above p.27. The fullest discussion of the computation of Easter and of related controversy is by Jones in his introduction to the book referred to in n.3 above.

6 For common and embolismal months see Jones, 32.

7 These details do not always follow the same order. For another illustration, this time for an eleventh-century manuscript which displays a different pattern, see *The Anglo-Saxon Chronicle*, ed. G.N. Garmonsway, Everyman's Library (London, 1953), xxiv-xxv.

8 Cf. Garmonsway's comments on the manuscript reproduced by Poole: *Anglo-Saxon Chronicle*, xxi.

9 Jones, 117; but cf. on p.16 a more cautious statement: 'we think ... of the Easter-Table as prognosis ... after the year has passed the prognosis becomes a historical record'.

10 *Op.cit.*, 119: 'Had Bede created *De temporum ratione* without a chronicle, his work would have been incomplete ...'

11 As Plummer points out (ii, 343): 'the very way in which Bede wrote his history, by subjects, rather than by order of time, rendered a chronological summary [the annalistic 'recapitulation' at the end] very necessary'.

12 The preface is translated in Dorothy Whitelock, *English Historical Documents c.500-1042* (London, 1955), 818-19.

13 See for what follows the ed. by Garmonsway, xxx-xliv; and the ed. by Miss Whitelock, 109-18; both of these give translations, that by Miss Whitelock only to 1042. The original texts are complicated. Reference is normally made to the editions by J. Earle (Oxford, 1864) and C. Plummer (Oxford, 1892).

14 Trans. Garmonsway, 26.

15 *Ibid.*, 58. I have not indicated the editor's corrections of wrong dates; e.g. Charlemagne died in 814.

16 Garmonsway, 5.

17 Jones, 201-2, 303; cf. 307-15, 345. Above p.27.

18 The fourth son of Noah is normally given as Sceaf. See Garmonsway, 66 and n.; and see also my *Europe: the Emergence of an Idea*, 2nd ed. (Edinburgh, 1968), p.47 and references.

19 Ed. by C.L. Bethmann, Mon. Germ. Hist., Scriptores V (1844), reprinted by J.P. Migne, *Patrologia Latina* 160 (Paris 1880), which is the ed. I have used. The Migne ed. contains Sigebert's other works.

20 On this complicated text see J.M. Wallace-Hadrill, *The Fourth Book of the Chronicle of Fredegar* (Edinburgh, 1960), where it is partly translated.

21 There are critical editions of Jordanes and Paulus Diaconus in the German Monumenta. There is an English version of Jordanes above ch. 2 n. 31. Paulus Diaconus has been translated by W.D. Foulke (New York, 1907).

22 See pp.52, 66.

23 Prolegomena, cols 26-8. For Martinus Polonus (of Troppau), see below p.64.

24 G.R.C. Davis, *Medieval Cartularies of Great Britain, A Short Catalogue* (London, 1958), pp.xiii, 3, 366-8.

25 Or 'Renascences' as Erwin Panofsky would say, to distinguish them from the later Italian movement: *Renaissance and Renascences in Western Art* (Stockholm, 1960; reprinted London, 1970).

26 Below p.56.

27 See above p.28.

28 *The Two Cities*, prologue to book i. The most recent critical edition is by A. Hofmeister, Scriptores ... in usum scholarum, (Hanover and Leipzig,

1912); I have used the ed. by R. Wilmans, Monumenta ... Scriptores, xx (Hanover, 1868). There is a good translation, with a valuable introduction by C.C. Mierow (New York, 1928), from which the above quotation is taken, p.96.

29 The *Historia Pontificalis*, ed. and trans. Marjorie Chibnall (Edinburgh, 1950). John regarded this account, mainly of his experiences of the papal court, as a universal chronicle continuing that of Sigebert. It covers the years 1148-52. The *topos* of history being a teacher, backed up with a line from Cato, on p.3.

30 Trans. Mierow, 93.

31 *Ibid.*, 95.

32 Cf. VII, 20 where the Emperor Lothar's death (1135) provokes the very un-Augustinian comment: 'Had he not been forestalled by death he might have been the man to restore, by his ability and energy, the imperial crown to its ancient dignity' (Mierow, 428).

33 Of whom three were only *beati*.

34 For an admirable discussion of patterns of sanctity see H. Delehaye, S.J., *Les légendes hagiographiques* (Brussels, 1905); Father Delehaye was a Bollandist; see below p.170. It is important to remember the ambiguity of 'legend' in connection with saints' lives, where it means 'to be read (*legenda*) on the saint's day'. The pattern of martyrdom instanced above was, of course, only one type of sanctity. I have learned much about medieval sanctity from my colleague, Dr M.G. Dickson.

35 The best critical ed. is by L. Duchesne (Paris, 1886-92); to Gregory I, English trans. by Louise R. Loomis (New York, 1916).

36 Guibert, *De vita sua sive monodiarum suarum libri tres:* ed. with a French version by G. Bourgin (Paris, 1907); trans. C.C.S. Bland (London, 1925); revised ed. by J.F. Benton, *Self and Society in Medieval France* (New York, 1970). *The Chronicle of Jocelyn of Brakelond*: ed. with a trans. by H.E. Butler (Edinburgh, 1949); there are several other English translations — that by Ernest Clarke (London, 1903) is still more useful than Butler's. Thomas Carlyle helped to make this work famous with a long essay in *Past and Present* (1843).

37 A convenient ed. with French trans. by H. Waquet, in Classiques de l'histoire de France au moyen âge (Paris, 1929). Suger also wrote an autobiographical work, considerable portions of which are translated by E. Panofsky, *Abbot Suger on the abbey church of Saint-Denis* (Princeton, N.J., 1946).

38 Waquet, 3-5.

39 *Ibid.*, 287.

40 *Ibid.*, 36-7.

41 *Ibid.*, 172-9.

42 'Quo facto, nostrorum modernitate nec multorum temporum antiquitate, nichil clarius Francia fecit ...' *Ibid.*, 230.

43 Below p.66.

44 Ed. by William Stubbs, Rolls Series, 2 vols (London, 1887-9); trans.

J.A. Giles, Bohn Antiquarian Library (London, 1847); *Historia novella*, ed. and trans. K.R. Potter and R.A.B. Mynors (Edinburgh, 1955). In what follows discussion is limited to the *Gesta Regum*.

45 See also Marie Schütt, 'The literary form of William of Malmesbury's *Gesta Regum*', *Eng. Hist. Rev.*, xlvi (1931), 255-60.

46 V.H. Galbraith, *Historical Research in Medieval England* (Creighton Lecture for 1949; London, 1951), 15-19.

47 Giles, 113.

48 Giles, 258.

49 Poole, 7-8; Galbraith, *Historical Research*, 2. Gervase died early in the thirteenth century.

50 Isidore, *Etymologiae*, I; xliv, ed. W.M. Lindsay, 2 vols (Oxford, 1911). For Isidore's views on the purpose of history see above p. 59. It should also be noted that Isidore discussed *Chronica* in a quite different section — that on Time. *Chronica*, he says (V;xxviii), means 'a series of times', and he gives as an example the Eusebius-Jerome *Chronicle*.

51   For references see my *Europe — the Emergence of an Idea*, 42-51

52 The best ed. of the *Historia Regum* is by E. Faral, *La Légende Arthurienne*, 3 vols (Paris, 1911-29); Eng. trans. by Sebastian Evans, Everyman Library 1912, revised by Charles W. Dunn (New York, 1958). See also Robert W. Hanning, *The Vision of History in Early Britain* (New York and London, 1966). For *The Brut* see below p. 72.

53 The extensive and controversial literature on the sagas, many of which are available in a number of translations, is too extensive to be dealt with by a non-expert; but see W.P. Ker, *Epic and Romance* (London, 1897) and Stefan Einarsson, *A History of Icelandic Literature* (New York, 1957), where many of the arguments of scholars are briefly assessed, pp.14-68, 106-56.

54 'Nus contes rimés n'est verais. Tot est menssongie ço qu'il en dient quar il non seivent riens fors par oirdire', Brian Woledge and H.P. Clive, *Répertoire des plus anciens textes en prose francaise depuis 842 jusqu-aux premières années du XIIIe siècle* (Geneva, 1964), 127. Professor Woledge kindly drew my attention to this paragraph.

55 *Ibid.*, 32.

Chapter 4

1 It is reprinted (from a late seventeenth-century edition) in Migne, *Patrologia Latina*, cxcviii (Paris, 1855). A continuation took the *Historia* to the end of Acts. See Beryl Smalley, *The Study of the Bible in the Middle Ages* (Oxford, 1952; rept Notre Dame, 1964).

2 It was first printed in 1473; the Douai edition of 1624 is said to be defective although it is that most commonly found (repr. 1965). See B.L. Ullman in *Speculum*, viii (1933), 312-26.

3 Ed. L. Weiland in Mon. Germ. Hist., Scriptores xxii (Hanover, 1872). Also called 'Martinus Strepus'. Cf. the French version, the *Chronique martinienne* (Paris, 1503?).

4 Above p.54. For a brief account see A. Molinier, *Sources de l'histoire de France au moyen âge* (Paris, 1901-6) v, paras 160-5, and his entries for the various authors, esp. nos. 2530 and 3099. See also the Edinburgh Ph.D. thesis of Sarah Farley (1969), and references therein to articles and books by Charles Samaran, important for the later centuries. There are two modern editions of the French: by Paulin Paris (to 1380), 6 vols (Paris, 1836-8) and by J. Viard, Société de l'histoire de France, 9 vols (Paris, 1920-37). For the Latin texts see Molinier's *Sources*.

5 There are editions of the *Chronica majora* of M. Paris by H.R. Luard; of part of the *Flores Historiarum* of Wendover by H.G. Hewlett; minor writers, and of much of Walsingham, by H.T. Riley — all in the Rolls Series; V.H. Galbraith edited Walsingham's last section, *The St. Albans Chronicle 1406-1420* (Oxford, 1937). There are translations of Wendover (omitting matter before A.D.447) and Paris (1235-59) by J.A. Giles (London, 1848 and 1852-4). For discussion of the St. Albans writers see Galbraith's long introduction and another valuable study by Richard Vaughan, *Matthew Paris*, (Cambridge, 1958).

6 Some forty to fifty volumes of twelfth-century date (not, of course, all historical) are noted as being of St Albans provenance by N.R. Ker (ed.), *Medieval Libraries of Great Britain* (London, 1964), 165-8.

7 Trans. Giles, i, 1-2.

8 *Ibid.*, 1, 3.

9 Cf. V.H. Galbraith, *Roger Wendover and Matthew Paris* (Glasgow, 1944), 20: 'Henceforth for two centuries the St. Albans history is as it were, an *apologia pro baronibus*'; and Richard Vaughan, 139-43, who is sceptical of this view as applied to Paris.

10 On Paris's abridgements see Vaughan, 110-17. The yearly summaries and the fifty-year summary at the end of the annal for 1250, when Paris intended to finish, are to be associated with the process of simplifying and vulgarising the narrative.

11 For the extremely tangled tale of the 'descent of the St. Albans Chronicle 1259-1422' and for editions of such of the works as are in print, see Galbraith, *St. Albans Chronicle*, xxvi-lxxi.

12 Ed. Waquet, (see above, ch.3, n.37), 220.

13 Wendover, ed. Luard, i, 11-16; although he sometimes wrote in both Anglo-Norman and French (as indeed M. Paris did). See M. Dominica Legge, *Anglo-Norman Literature and its Background* (Oxford, 1963), 276-310.

14 The best ed. is by F.W.D. Brie, 2 vols, Early English Text Society (London, 1906-8); Brie's analysis of the work is in a Marburg dissertation: *Geschichte und quellen der Mittelenglischen Prosachronik The Brute of england oder The Chronicles of England* (1905). For French sources see Professor Legge's work and the useful pages in John Taylor, *The Universal Chronicle of Ranulf Higden* (Oxford, 1966), 13-32. The prologue (Brie, i, 1-4) recounts the unhappy fate of the thirty-three daughters of King Dioclician who finally reached Albion. There Albine and the others bred giants by the devil.

15 Edited by L. Bréhier, *Classiques de l'histoire de France au moyen âge* (Paris, 1924). There is an ed. with English trans. by Rosalind Hill (Oxford, 1962).

16 The Latin text, ed. A. Beugnot and A. Le Prévost, *Recueil des historiens des croisades* (Paris, 1844); trans. and ed. by E.A. Babcock and A.C. Krey, Columbia Records of Civilization, 2 vols (New York, 1944). A sympathetic recent study by R.H.C. Davis in *Relations between East and West in the Middle Ages*, ed. D. Baker (Edinburgh, 1973), 64-76.

17 Ed. E. Faral, *Classiques de l'histoire de France au moyen âge*, 2 vol (Paris, 1961) and many other eds in French; many English translations of which the most accessible is by M.R.B. Shaw, *Joinville and Ville hardouin: Chronicles of the Crusades* (Harmondsworth, 1963).

18 Ed. by N. de Wailly (Paris, 1874). For English version, see previous note.

19 It is best read in J. Viard and E. Deprez, eds, *Chronique de Jean Le Bel*, Société de l'histoire de France, 2 vols (Paris, 1904-5). There is no English version.

20 Of the many printed versions of the whole work the best are by J.A.C. Buchon, 3 vols (Paris, 1840) and the complete works, ed. Kervyn de Lettenhove, 25 vols (Brussels, 1867-77). A brilliant new edition by S. Luce and others began to appear in the Société de l'histoire de France (Paris, 1869ff) but has so far, with volume 14 (1966), reached the year 1388. It was translated by Lord Berners (London, 1523-5), reprinted ed. W.F. Ker (London, 1901-3); and by T. Johnes, 5 vols (Hafod, 1803-5). Selections in English: G.C. Macaulay from Berners trans. (London, 1895); trans. and ed. G. Brereton (Harmondsworth, 1968).

21 But note the interesting reference to prowess (*l'estat de proèce*) in antiquity: Joshua, David, Judas Maccabaeus; Cyrus, Ahasuerus, Xerxes; the Trojan heroes etc. Luce, i, 5-6 (not quite the conventional 'neuf preux').

22 For editions, none of them adequate, see Molinier, (see n.4 above), iv, nos 3946, 3955, 3957, 3961, 4154; and R. Bossuat, *Manuel bibliographique* (Melun, 1951), 499-503. Thomas Johnes translated Monstrelet, 2 vols (London, 1810); the Rolls Series, ed. by W. Hardy of Wavrin, 5 vols (London, 1864-91), contains an English version.

23 Again no decent edition. Reprinted Cambridge-Paris, 1927.

24 For scraps of heralds' narratives in England see J. Leland, *Collectanea*, ed. T. Hearne, 6 vols (London, 1770), iv, 185-333; C.L. Kingsford, *Engl. Hist. Lit. in the xvth Century*, (Oxford, 1913), 178-9, 379-88. Cf. Sydney Anglo, *Spectacle, Pageantry and Early Tudor Policy* (Oxford, 1969).

25 J. Huizinga, *Waning of the Middle Ages* (London, 1937), 50.

26 For Italian material see P.J. Jones, 'Florentine families and Florentine diaries in the fourteenth century', *Papers of Brit. school at Rome*, xxiv (1956), 183-205; Gene Brucker, intro. to *Two Memoirs of Renaissance Florence* (New York, 1967), pp.9-18; in this volume an attractive Eng. trans. by Julia Martines of the diaries of B. Pitti and G. Dati. *The Journal d'un Bourgeois*, ed. A. Tuetey (Paris, 1881) and trans. Janet Shirley, *A Parisian Journal* (Oxford, 1968).

27 Ralph Flenley, *Six Town Chronicles of England* (Oxford, 1911), 36-7.

28 The first editor was Karl Hegel. Published at Leipzig and then Stuttgart, 1862-1917. Reprinted Göttingen, 1961-8. There are, of course, other German civic chronicles published elsewhere.

29 There is no modern critical edition; I use the ed. by A. Racheli, 2 vols (Trieste, 1857-8) but there are many others, complete and partial. An attractive English version of Giovanni's chronicle down to 1321, giving all chapter headings, but a text only to illustrate Dante's works, is trans. Rose E. Selfe and ed. Philip H. Wickstead, *Villani's Chronicle* (London, 1906).

30 Selfe and Wickstead, 1-2.

31 Ed. Racheli, i; 392, 401-2. Note the use of 'oltremare' for 'foreign'.

32 *Ibid.*, ii, 416.

33 *Ibid.*, ii, 418-20.

34 For what follows I draw, by kind permission of the Director of the Institute, on my article in the *Bulletin of the Institute of Historical Research*, xxxv (1962), 111-27, 'History and historians in France and England during the fifteenth centuries'.

35 John Taylor, *The Universal Chronicle of Ranulf Higden* (Oxford, 1966).

36 *Id.*, 'The French Brut and the reign of Edward II', *Eng. Hist. Rev.*,lvii (1957), 423-37 and references.

37 Froissart, ix, 258-9. These difficulties became much more pronounced in the fifteenth century: Rymer (for whom see below, pp.155-6) ix, 656-9; T. Walsingham, *Historia brevis* (1574), 412-3, quoted by L. Douet-d'Arcq in his ed. of E. de Monstrelet, *La Chronique*, 6 vols, Soc. de l'histoire de France (Paris, 1857-62), i, 81; *Letters and Papers Illustrative of the Wars of the English in France*, Rolls Series, 2 vols (London, 1861-4), ii, 676-7.

38 An epitome translated from Sleidan's Latin version was published in London in 1608 and again in 1611.

39 Mr Goodman has pointed out to me that Berners' preface acknowledges the prompting of Henry VIII, perhaps in aid of his aggression against France.

40 Leland, *Collectanea*, iv, 185-300, v, 352-81; Kingsford, 178-9.

41 See above, p.77.

42 Flenley, *Six Town Chronicles*, 12.

43 Flenley, 29; Kingsford, 111.

44 For references to these see Molinier, v, 189 (p.cxxxii); iv, 34, 37, 38 (nos 3145-6, 3159, 3161). The Bordeaux 'chronicle' resembles a commonplace book. See G. Lefèvre-Pontalis in *Bulletin de l'Ecole de Chartres*, xlvii (1886), 53-70.

45 So I am informed by my colleague Professor Kenneth Fowler.

46 P. Dollinger, *Revue historique*, ccxvi (1956), 35-44.

47 *Chronicles of London*, ed. C.L. Kingsford (Oxford, 1905), intro. p.viii.

48 The luxurious volume in the series 'Histoire générale de Paris' edited by A.J.V. Le Roux de Lincy and L.M. Tisserand, *Paris et ses historiens au XIVe et XVe siècle* (Paris, 1867), is most misleadingly named: there are

no historians in it. The so-called *Journal d'un Bourgeois* is a private
diary: see above n. 26.

Chapter 5

1 For all facets of this development see Wallace K. Ferguson, *The Renaissance in Historical Thought* (Cambridge, Mass., 1948).

2 Paul Oskar Kristeller, *The Classics in Renaissance Thought* (Cambridge,
Mass., 1955), 10; reprinted as *Renaissance Thought* (New York, 1961).

3 The second edition was a French translation by E. Jeanmaire (Paris,
1914) which Fueter himself revised. The German edition of 1925 is a
mere reprint of the 1911 *editio princeps*. But in the third German edition
(Munich, 1936) a few notes were included of a bibliographical kind
which had been kept by Fueter down to his death in 1928 as well as a few
other references to later material. The Italian translation of A. Spinelli
(Naples, 1943), despite its claims, adds no references later than the mid-
1930s; this has been reprinted (Milan, 1970).

4 I summarise the French edition, pp.10-19.

5 Above pp.27-8.

6 For what follows see Ferguson, 1-28, 59-77 and refs, esp. G.S. Gordon,
Medium Aevum and the Middle Ages, Society for Pure English, Tract
XIX (London, 1925).

7 Below p.104.

8 *The Gothic Image*, trans. D. Nussey (London, 1961), 155n.

9 Roberto Weiss, *The Renaissance Discovery of Classical Antiquity*
(Oxford, 1969), 3. And see below p.92.

10 The above is based on E. Panofsky's essay on 'The first page of Giorgio
Vasari's "Libro"', *Meaning of the Visual Arts* (Garden City, N.Y., 1955),
169-225, much the best account of the development of a sense of anachronism known to me.

11 *Ibid.*, 212-3.

12 The best text of the donation is ed. Horst Fuhrmann, *Constitutum
Constantine*, Mon. Germ. Hist., in usum scholarum, *Fontes Iuris Germ.
Antiqui* x (Hanover, 1968); Valla's *Declamation*, ed. Schwann (Leipzig,
1928); and with that portion of the Donation which Valla used (from the
Decretum), ed. and trns. C.B. Coleman (New Haven, Conn., 1922). See
also F. Gaeta, *Lorenzo Valla: Filologia e storia nell' umanesimo italiano*
(Naples, 1955), 129-66.

13 *Storia de Firenze*, in *Opere*, ed. M. Bonfantini (Milan, 1954), 774.

14 Leonardi Aretini, *Historiarum Florentini populi libri xii*, ed. E. Santini,
XIX, 3 (Città di Castello, 1914-26), 3-4.

15 For some examples see F. Gilbert, *Machiavelli and Guicciardini:
Politics and History in Sixteenth-Century Florence* (Princeton, N.J.,
1965), 216-7. The whole chapter, pp.203-35, is useful. Gilbert's bibliographical note, pp.332-5, is also valuable.

16 W.H. Woodward, *Vittorino da Feltre and other Humanist Educators*
(Cambridge, 1897), 106-7; Woodward's own synoptic review of humanist
attitudes to history, pp.215-19.

17 Gaeta, 179, 185-6. By 'Moses' Valla meant the Pentateuch. Valla also

argued that the 'universal truths' of poetry were exemplified in history too, in those speeches inserted by the writers which distilled precepts of general applicability.

18 E.g. *De Oratore*, I, xi, 48; xii, 50; II, i, 5.

19 *Ibid.*, II, xv, 64.

20 Adapted from the literal translation of J.S. Watson (London, 1895), ii, 253.

21 Best ed. above n. 14. The official translation by D. Acciaiuoli was printed at Florence (1861). The basic studies are by E. Santini, 'Leonardo Bruni Aretino e i suoi "Historiarum Florentine populi libri xii",' *Annali della R. Scuola Normale di Pisa*, xxii (1910), and Hans Baron, *Leonardo Bruni Aretino, Humanistisch-philosophische Schriften mit einer Chronologie seiner Werke und Briefe* (Leipzig-Berlin, 1928), see also B.L. Ullman, 'Leonardo Bruni and humanistic historiography', now reprinted in *Studies in the Italian Renaissance*, 2nd ed. (Rome, 1973), 321-43.

22 The sequence of the years is readily identified in the 'indice cronologico' in Santini's ed. 377-401.

23 Cf. Santini's essay, 84-8, 96.

24 Ed. Santini, 48-9, 78-80.

25 Machiavelli, *Opere cit.*, 567; for the Ordinances and related events, pp.634-8.

26 Ed. Santini, 223: '... intestinae ... discordiae subsecutae quantum nunquam antea civitatem turbarunt'. This from the first sentence in book ix.

27 *Ibid.*, 194.

28 His writings were, of course, much more various than just the *History*. See Hans Baron, *The Crisis of the Early Italian Renaissance*, rev. 2nd ed. (Princeton, N.J., 1966).

29 1473 ed. at Venice and subsequent Venetian editions of the translation at Venice in 1476, 1485, 1492, 1561. There was an edition of both texts at Florence 1856-60.

30 Fueter, 61.

31 'Ses dons de feuilletoniste ...', *Ibid.*, 141.

32 *Memoirs of a Renaissance Pope*, trans. and ed. F.A. Gragg and L.C. Gabel (London, 1962); this is a slightly abbreviated translation of the unabridged manuscript, of which printed Latin texts were doctored from the start. The full translation first came out in Smith College Studies in History (Northampton, Mass., 1937-57). It is poorly edited.

33 See below p.150.

34 Above p.91.

35 For what follows see my lecture in *Proc. Brit. Acad.*, xlv (1959), 105-9, where documentation will be found. The edition of the *Decades* I used in this lecture was Basle, 1531.

36 Platina began an account of Sixtus IV, to whom the work was dedicated. The best edition is by G. Gaida, Rev. Ital. Script., III, i (Città di Castello). The first of the continuators was O. Panvinio (1529-68). There is an English version, not very reliable, by Sir Paul Rycaut, which was first published in 1685 and reprinted in 1688 and ed. Benham, 2 vols, n.d. (1888).

37 Note also that, although he does not mention the Constance assertion of
    conciliar supremacy, he does rehearse the provisions of the decree
    Frequens; ed. Gaida, 305.
38 Ed. Gaida, 388.
39 There is an admirable discussion of Platina's sources in the introduction
    by Gaida, xxxv-lxxxiv. This practical dependence of writers like Bruni,
    Biondo and Platina on medieval writers should be remembered when we
    read contemptuous humanist criticism, e.g. that quoted by Charles
    Trinkaus, 'A humanist's image of humanism: the inaugural orations of
    Bartolomeo della Fonte', *Studies in the Renaissance*, vii (1970), 102.
40 Ed. Gaida, 291.
41 Constantine: ed. Gaida, 53-8. For Papal States cf. account of Gil
    Albornoz, 277.
42 Ed. Gaida, 229.
43 See the Ph.D. thesis of Peter Spring (Edinburgh University, 1973).
44 On this down to 1527 see in general Weiss, *Renaissance Discovery of
    Classical Antiquity* (above n.9).
45 Cf. my short essay, 'The Italian view of Renaissance Italy', in *Florilegium
    Historiale*, essays presented to Wallace K. Ferguson, ed. by J.G. Rowe
    and W.H. Stockdale (Toronto, 1971), 3-17; Ugo Tucci, 'Credenze
    geografiche e cartografia', in Giulio Einaudi, *Storia d'Italia*, vol.5*
    (Turin, 1973), 48-85; and the Edinburgh Ph.D. thesis of Christine
    Rosemary Hill (Edinburgh, 1974) on the *Descrittione di tutta Italia* of
    Leandro Alberti.

Chapter 6

 1 Machiavelli's *Prince* and *Discourses on the First Decade of Livy* are
    essential to an understanding of his attitude to politics and to his view
    that one can learn from the past lessons which can be applied to the
    future. But they are not, in any ordinary sense, historical compositions.
    Guicciardini wrote for his own private use two accounts of Florentine
    history (1508-9 and 1527-30), both in effect dealing mainly with the
    fourteenth and fifteenth centuries. The earlier work was first published
    in 1859; the second, perhaps planned as a work for publication, was not
    printed until 1945. Both are valuable as illustrations of Guicciardini's
    slow journey 'from politics to history', to quote the title of the important
    study by V. De Caprariis (Bari, 1950). There are well-documented lives
    of both Machiavelli and Guicciardini by Roberto Ridolfi, which have
    been translated by C. Grayson: *Machiavelli* (London, 1963), *Guic-
    ciardini* (London, 1967). The literature about both writers is vast, but
    F. Gilbert's analysis (in *Machiavelli and Guicciardini; Politics and
    History in Sixteenth-century Florence*, Princeton, N.J., 1965) offers a
    very dependable guide and is the best single work on both men. Even
    when I disagree with Gilbert I have found his work most stimulating.
 2 Machiavelli's *Istorie fiorentine* was first published at Florence in 1532.
    There are many modern editions, of which I have used that in *Opere*, ed.
    M. Bonfantini, La letteratura italiana: storia e testi (Milan, 1954).
    There is a convenient translation, to which I refer, in Everyman Library,

by W.K. Marriott (London, 1908). Guicciardini's *Storia d'Italia* came out piecemeal at Florence, 1561, and Venice, 1567 (the last four books): as a unit from 1568. The canonical edition is by A. Gherardi (Florence, 1919), but the most accessible is by C. Panigada, 5 vols (Bari, 1929); of this there is a recent reprint with notes ed. Silvana Seidel Menchi, 3 vols (Turin, 1971), which I have used (it contains an introduction by Felix Gilbert). The first English version by G. Fenton was published at London in 1579. There is no modern translation of the whole book but selections by J. Hale, trans. C. Grayson (London 1964), and the rather fuller selections ed. and trans. S. Alexander (New York, 1969); I quote if necessary from this last.

3 One should not exaggerate this prudence, for Machiavelli has many remarks favourable to Cosimo and Lorenzo, as was essential in a work dedicated to their descendant the pope: cf. *Opere*, 771-2, 885, 904; trans. 181, 281, 297.

4 *Opere*, 618; trans. 44. Cf. the famous ending of his set piece on the battle of Anghiari: *Opere*, 820-1; trans. 225.

5 Somewhat of a misnomer and not his own title. See Gilbert, 294n.

6 *Opere* 569-70; trans. 3.

7 '... piu alto e maggiore spirito', *Opere*, 563; trans. xv.

8 Although Machiavelli (but not Guicciardini) felt that ancient history could inspire to virtue and valour.

9 *Opere*, 774; trans. 184.

10 *Storia d'Italia*, VIII, i (ed. Menchi, ii, 721); trans. 191.

11 Gilbert, 287.

12 Best ed. J. Calmette in Classiques de l'histoire de France, 3 vols (Paris, 1924-5). The 2 vols trans. by Isabella Cazeaux are introduced and edited by Samuel Kinser (Columbia, S. Carolina, 1969-73); this supersedes other English versions and Professor Kinser's introduction is useful.

13 Kinser, 38.

14 I regretfully leave on one side the Latin works of Thomas Basin, bishop of Lisieux (1447-74), now available in a modern edition by C. Samaran and his collaborators in the Classiques de l'histoire de France au moyen âge, 6 vols (Paris, 1933-74). They constitute a biased but lively history of the reigns of Charles VII and Louis XI, together with a remarkable 'Apologia'. These works were not published fully until the edition by J. Quicherat (Paris, 1855-7).

15 Fueter, 99-109 (F. Vettori, P. Nerli, B. Segni, J. Nardi, B. Varchi), 151-7 (G.-B. Adriani, P. Paruta, A.C. Davila, G. Bentivoglio), 182-90 (Commynes and other French memorialists).

16 See below pp.129-30.

17 F.J. Levy, *Tudor Historical Thought* (San Marino, Ca., 1967), entirely supersedes other accounts.

18 Levy, 217.

19 For edition and translation see my *Polydore Vergil* (Oxford, 1952); also the important revisions regarding the MS by Dr C.B. Clough in *Eng. Hist. Rev.*, lxxxii (1967), 772-83, the treatment of the subject in Levy's book.

20 I find no evidence that Vergil served in the chancery or Camera
    Apostolica although Castellesi climbed to riches by that route. Archivio
    Segreto, *Introitus et exitus*, vol. 352, fo.70 (1.9.1501).
21 The Yale Complete Works, vol. 2, ed. Richard Sylvester (New Haven,
    Conn., 1963).
22 There is not much on Aemilius in print, but see L. Thuasne's intro-
    duction to *R. Gaguini epistole et orationes*, 2 vols (Paris, 1903-4), and
    C.A.J. Armstrong's introduction to *The Usurpation of Richard III* by
    D. Mancini, (Oxford, 1936; rev. ed. 1969). And cf. Ph.D. thesis
    (Edinburgh, 1954) by Katharine Davies.
23 Robert Gaguin's *Compendium* (first ed. Paris, 1497) is a poor thing. See
    L. Thuasne as above and Dr Davies' thesis.
24 A passage added to the MS of 1511 in the *editio princeps* of 1534. Cf. my
    ed., Camden Series, vol. lxxiv (1950), 145 collation.
25 Cf. Fueter, book II, D; P. Joachimsen, *Geschichtsauffassung und
    Geschichtsschreibung in Deutschland unter dem Einfluss des Human-
    ismus* (Berlin, 1910). Two recent and interesting American books came
    out in 1963 at Cambridge, Mass.: Lewis W. Spitz, *The Religious
    Renaissance of the German Humanists*, and Gerald Strauss, *Historian in
    an Age of Crisis ... Aventinus*.
26 Fueter, book II, F.
27 Cf. H.R. Trevor-Roper, *George Buchanan and the Ancient Scottish
    Constitution*, Supplement 3 to *Eng. Hist. Rev.* (London, 1966) and
    references to earlier works.
28 *Ecclesiastica historia congesta per aliquot viros in urbe Magdeburgica ...
    13 centuriae* (Basle, 1561-74).
29 Fueter, 311.
30 Cf. above p.97.
31 I pick at random on lib. i, cap. x.
32 Fueter, 312; the whole discussion is useful, 309-14.
33 There is an interesting recent account, with good bibliography by A.
    Pincherle, in *Dizionario biografico degli italiani*, 6, 469-78.
34 I have used the Cologne edition of 1609, given to the University of
    Edinburgh Library by a minister of the town.
35 Donald R. Kelley, *Foundations of Modern Historical Scholarship* (New
    York, 1970), 305. For what follows see also the admirable work by
    Julian H. Franklin, *Jean Bodin and the Sixteenth-century Revolution in
    the Methodology of Law and History* (New York, 1963).
36 I quote from the text in the Everyman Library, *Prelude to Poetry*
    (London, 1927), where the *Apologie* is reprinted on 9-60.
37 Franklin, 102-54; for Baudoin and Bodin see also Kelley, 116-48,
    esp. 129ff.
38 Kelley, pp.132-3.
39 Conveniently, with other works, including Baudoin's ed. J. Wolf, *Artis
    historicae penus*, 2 vols (Basle, 1579), i, 1-396; Baudoin, i, 599-742.
    There is a trans. of Bodin's *Methodus* by Beatrice Reynolds (New York,
    1945, repr. 1966).
40 Franklin, 151.

41 The two texts differ significantly; there is a seventeenth-century translation of a conflated version reprinted with a helpful introduction by Kenneth D. McRae (Cambridge, Mass., 1962).

42 I use the Paris ed. of 1633. D.R. Kelley's book discusses Pasquier at some length, esp. 271-300, giving full refs. to the recent literature. Pasquier also published a large collection of his own correspondence, interesting both for antiquarian and political material.

43 On the other hand, there are lengthy extracts from documents regarding the University in book IX which are carefully printed; and his use throughout of literary sources, quite apart from their express treatment in books VII and VIII, is impressive.

Chapter 7

1 See the admirable chapter in F.J. Levy, *Tudor Historical Thought*, (San Marino, Ca., 1967), 237-85.

2 Cf. E.S. de Beer, 'The development of the guide book until the early nineteenth century', *Journal of the British Architectural Association*, 3rd ser., xv (1952).

3 Cf. Levy, pp.209-10.

4 There are several bibliographies in which the 'Republics' are listed, e.g. E.M. Goldsmid, *A Complete Catalogue of the Elsevier Presses*, 3 vols (Edinburgh, 1885-8).

5 The basic recent book is by Samuel Kinser, *The works of J.-A. de Thou* (The Hague, 1966).

6 In fact late 1603, Kinser, 7.

7 Kinser, 24; there is an entertaining lecture on this by H.R. Trevor-Roper, *Queen Elizabeth's First Historian, William Camden, and the Beginning of English Civil History* (London, Neale Lecture, 1971).

8 Another tangled tale unravelled by Kinser, 256-314.

9 Cf. Kinser, 31-2.

10 Geneva 1620, book xxxvii, 287.

11 *Elogia*: Kinser, 301-8; speeches from De Thou were also twice published separately, *ibid.*, 304. For Aemilius, above p.120.

12 Fueter (p.249) argues that the first writer to mingle politics and ecclesiastical affairs in a single narration was the German, Johann Philippson, called Sleidanus from his birthplace Schleiden, South of Cologne (1506-56), in his *Commentarii de Statu Religionis et rei publicae Carolo V Caesare* (1555) and *De Quatuor Summis imperiis* (1556). Relatively impartial, Sleidan's well-written works were frequently reprinted and translated, especially for the documents they contained.

13 *Annals*, trans. R.N., 3rd ed. (London, 1635), sig.c3vo. I have modernised the spelling.

14 Cf. above n.7.

15 Fueter, 214. And in general, including a discussion of Clarendon, 213-19. Note, too, the similarity with Guicciardini in Clarendon's picture of an idyllic pre-revolutionary England.

16 B.H.G. Wormald, *Clarendon: Politics, Historiography and Religion 1640-1660* (Cambridge, 1964), 238-9. For a general appraisal see the

centenary lecture by H.R. Trevor-Roper, *Times Literary Supplement*, 10 January 1975.

17 A necessary orientation now provided by Gaetano and Luisa Conti (eds.), P. Sarpi, *Opere* (La litteratura italiana, 35, t.i. Milan, 1969); see pp.728-9. There were many editions and translations, the first English version being published at London in 1620.

18 I can unfortunately refer to no other account of this office than my own short paper 'The Historiographer Royal in England and Scotland', *Scottish Historical Review*, xxx (1951), 16-29. There are some inferior works on the office of poet laureate in England.

19 The most convenient editions are the *Abrégé* in fourteen vols., (Amsterdam 1755) and other similar reprints.

20 On the contrary, Vertot argued that Britanny had always been part of France and it was he who was responsible for securing the disgrace and imprisonment of Fréret (above p.67).

21 Paul Hazard, *La crise de la conscience européene*, 3 vols (Paris, 1935), i, 41-3. The *Biographie Universelle*, 52 vols (Paris, 1811-28), is a valuable reference book for this period, both for biographies and bibliographies: e.g. Daniel; x, 511-12; Mézeray, xxlviii, 506-11; Vertot, xlviii, 293-8.

22 I quote from the edition of London, 1679.

23 *Ibid.*, 105a; modernised spelling.

24 The mildewed copy I possess must have had similar treatment. There is a useful account of Baker by Sidney Lee himself in *Dict. Nat. Biog.*, *s.n.* The continuations, probably beginning with that in the edition of 1660, were by John Milton's nephew Edward Phillips.

25 *Compleat History* (1719), i, 199. It seems probable that for the period from Richard II to Edward IV the continuation used was not that by John Trussel (1636), but was composed by Hughes 'after Mr. Daniel's method' (i, preface).

26 The best ed. of Milton's *History* is now by French Fogle, Yale Complete Works, V, pt i (New Haven, Conn., and London, 1971).

27 *Compleat History*, i, 1-2; ed. Fogle, 3.

28 Fogle, liii-xlix.

29 Fogle, xlvi.

30 Milton was at work on his history for many years, especially in 1645-7, in the 1650s and after the Restoration.

31 *Compleat History*, i, 2; Fogle, xlvii, 4.

32 In restricting my observations to England and France I proclaim partly my ignorance but, I suspect, partly the weight of current research. For England: Thomas Kendrick, *British Antiquity* (London, 1950); May McKisack, *Medieval History in the Tudor Age* (Oxford, 1971); and cf. the excellent book by Levy, *Tudor Historical Thought*. For France, apart from Donald R. Kelley, *Foundations of Modern Historical Scholarship* (New York, 1970), see George Huppert, *The Idea of Perfect History* (Urbana, Ill., 1970).

33 A useful list in W. Wattenbach, *Deutschlands Geschichtsquellen*, i, 1-20 for Germany, and in T. Duffus Hardy, intro. to *Monumenta Historica Britanniae*, ed. Petrie (London, 1848).

34 E.P. Goldschmidt, *Medieval Texts and their First Appearance in Print* (Bibliographical Society, London, 1943), 75-7.

35 *Ibid.*, 73-4. Most of this interesting little book is devoted to literary texts.

36 Cf. my *Polydore Vergil* (Oxford, 1952), 30-31.

37 May McKisack, *op.cit.*, 26-49.

38 On 'Parker and his circle' see May McKisack, 26-49 and refs.

39 See May McKisack, F. Levy and also F. Smith Fussner, *The Historical Revolution: English Historical Writing and Thought, 1580-1640* (London, 1962).

40 McKisack, 39.

41 *Ibid.*, spelling modernised.

42 Cf. below p.159.

43 For an admirable short account see G.R. Crone, *Maps and their Makers* second ed. (London, 1962), 110-27; for Camden's *Britannia*, see Levy, 144-59.

44 Cf. below n. 56.

45 Levy, 159.

46 D.C. Douglas, *English Scholars* (London, 1939); Levi Fox, ed., *English Historical Scholarship in the Sixteenth and Seventeenth Centuries* (London, 1956).

47 Cf. J.G.A. Pocock, *The Ancient Constitution and the Feudal Law* (Cambridge, 1957; the New York ed. of 1967 has a useful additional bibliography), which is really a study in the history of historiography; and see also Douglas, ch. vi: 'The Norman Conquest and Dr Brady'. The critical reader may observe that I have left out of what goes before, and can offer no accommodation in what remains, for any discussion of Sir Walter Raleigh's peculiar *History of the World*. Raleigh (d. 1618) completed only one vast volume, which reached 200 B.C., of the three he contemplated (London, 1611; 5 reprints by 1634). It is a curious combination of up-to-date philology and blinkered chronicle — leading nowhere, though enjoying a distinct popularity with Puritans. It was, of course, a work written in prison.

48 See n.47 above.

49 In Thomas Duffus Hardy's Appendix to the *Materials relating to the History of Great Britain and Ireland* published in the Rolls Series in 1862, the author lists (pp.807-10) forty-three of Hearne's editions, some in several volumes.

50 R.B. Wernham, 'The public records in the sixteenth and seventeenth centuries', in Levi Fox, ed., 11-30.

51 R. Klibanski, 'Leibnitz's unknown correspondence', *Medieval and Renaissance Studies*, i (1941-3), 142, 148-9.

52 Although Leibnitz is known chiefly as a philosopher he was responsible

204 *Annalists and Historians*

for publishing many narrative texts: *Scriptores rerum germanicorum*, 2 vols (Hanover, 1968-1700); *Scriptores rerum Brunswicensium*, 3 vols (Hanover, 1707-11).

53 Douglas, *English Scholars*, 290.

54 Sir Thomas Duffus Hardy's 'Summary' in his great *Syllabus in English of the Documents in Rymer's Foedera*, 3 vols (London, 1869-85), xxx.

55 Sanderson produced an eighteenth volume in 1731; see T.D. Hardy, *Syllabus*, lxxxviii.

56 While the bulk of substantive scholarship was English, we should not forget some very impressive figures elsewhere in Britain. James Ussher (1581-1656), one of the earliest products of Trinity College Dublin and archbishop of Armagh in 1624, was a massive if controversial scholar; and eighteenth-century Scotland was graced by Thomas Ruddiman (1674-1757), graduate of Aberdeen, Librarian at the Advocates Library at Edinburgh (permanently from 1711) which he helped to make one of the great libraries of Europe (below p.174), and whose first printed *Catalogue* he brought out in 1742. His learned works included a canonical edition of *George Buchanan's Works*.

57 The short-lived 'Elizabethan Society' (c. 1586-1608) was never very influential. See McKisack, *op. cit.* ch. vii.

58 See above pp.121-5 and notes.

59 These four essays are in *Trans Roy. Hist. Soc.*, 5th series, vols 8-11 (1958-61). The essays were published separately as *Great Historical Enterprises*, each essay containing a succinct but up-to-date bibliography (London, n.d. = 1963). Those not touched on in my pages were devoted to the German Monumenta and the English Rolls Series.

60 *The Historian and Character* (Cambridge, 1963), originally in *Journ. Eccl. Hist.*, x (1959).

61 See Knowles, *Great Hist. Enterprises*, 15.

62 See below, p.161.

63 Although at any one time the scholars formed a tiny minority of the whole Congregation. See *Great Hist. Enterprises*, 41 n.

64 *Ibid.*, 47.

65 The actual word palaeography derives from the *Palaeographia graeca* of another Maurist, Dom B. de Montfaucon, published in 1708.

66 I have failed to trace the source of this epigram.

67 Knowles, *Great Hist. Enterprises*, 41. See also his essay in *The Historian and Character* (Cambridge, 1963), 213-39. The spiritual affinity between these two monks, separated by two and a half centuries, is very moving.

68 It is amusing to see, in a late eighteenth-century hand, one of Alexander VI's reform commission (1496) volumes endorsed with a librarian's warning that it was only to be lent 'con molta cautela'! Vat. Lat. 3883.

69 See my paper '1500-1700: the bibliographical problem. A continental S.T.C.', and references therein, in R.R. Bolgar, ed., *Classical Influences on European Culture* (Cambridge, 1976), 33-9.

70 I plan to deal with the broad achievement of Ughelli in a separate paper.

71 One is reminded of Mabillon's encounter with A.J. de Rancé, abbot of La Trappe. See Knowles, *Historian and Character*, 224-7.

72 As its purpose was somewhat different I do not here include Antonius Monchiacenus Demochares, doctor Sorbonicus, *Christianas religionis, institutionesque d. n. Jesu Christi, ... adversus misso liturgorum blasphemias* ... (Paris, 1582), although in any full account it would figure, as from fo. 19vo French provinces with suffragans are listed.

73 In all, Ughelli deals with over 270 sees (not including those in Sicily, Corsica and Sardinia).

74 The tenth is really a collection of the longer unpublished pieces scattered about in the *editio princeps*.

75 For some unaccountable reason, Fueter writes as though Muratori had been a layman, *op.cit.*, 396.

76 See Fueter. Fueter does not mention the *Rerum Italicarum Scriptores* since it is not narrative history; he similarly ignores other aspects of technical scholarship save, exceptionally, Mabillon.

77 See below p.176.

78 For Ughelli, we look forward to the outcome of the labours of Dr. G. Morelli and his collaborators. For Muratori see the *Elenco dei corrispondenti*, ed. by N. Càmpori (Modena, 1898), who edited them in 13 vols (Modena, 1901-15).

79 C.H. Firth, 'Modern History at Oxford, 1724-1841', *Eng. Hist. Rev.*, xxxii (1917), 1-21; the phrase quoted comes from F.W. Maitland. See also D.B. Horn, *The British Diplomatic Service, 1689-1789* (Oxford, 1961), 130-2.

80 The late Dom David Knowles told me once that he was sure that in the seventeenth century there was a distinct 'over-production' of clergy in Catholic seminaries; and Professor Gordon Donaldson tells me that he has the same impression of protestant Scotland, full of 'stickit ministers'.

81 In this connection I often recall the effects of photography on art historians. Burckhardt at first made drawings on his Italian visits; later he bought photographs. Even those of us with no professional interest in the arts have stopped contemplating in exchange for a rapidly taken snap or a rapidly purchased print.

Chapter 8

1 An admirable introduction to the next phase in Herbert Butterfield, *Man on his Past* (Cambridge, 1955).

2 Leopold von Ranke (1795-1886), William Stubbs (1859-1901), F.W. Maitland (1850-1906), Marc Bloch (1886-1944).

3 There are, needless to say, still those who hold that 'History is bunk'.

4 Above, ch.7, n.21; see also the interesting essay by A. Momigliano, 'Ancient history and the antiquarian', reprinted in *Studies in Historiography* (London, 1966), 1-39, where the emphasis is mainly on the treatment of ancient (Greek and Roman) history; see esp. pp.10-13. My account of the new scholarship does not cover advances in prehistory: two entertaining books dealing with aspects of this subject are by Glyn

Daniel: *The Idea of Prehistory* (London, 1962) and *Megaliths in History* (London, 1972); for a British pioneer, William Stukeley (1687-1765), see the study by Stuart Piggott, *William Stukeley* (Oxford, 1950).

5 *Op.cit.* (ch.6, n.34 above), 101.

6 Above pp.129-30.

7 This is the theme of Professor Momigliano's essay, just referred to.

8 Recent work on ancient coins (e.g. by Michael Grant) has shown how potent designs on them were in conveying a desired message to the ends of the earth. No one who has worked in the archives of a modern government will believe all he reads in the official records of any period or administration.

9 This first appears as *Abrégé de l'histoire universelle depuis Charlemagne jusqu'a Charles Quint*, 2 vols (The Hague, 1753). The full version of 1756 included the *Siècle de Louis XIV*, 2 vols (Berlin, 1751), a work he had begun about 1735.

10 Above p.151 and n.47.

11 Below p.173.

12 5th ed. (London, 1809), i, 574.

13 From the translation of Thomas Nugent, 4 vols (London, 1759-61), here quoted from my *Renaissance Debate* (New York, 1965), where other extracts are given, pp.13-16.

14 For what follows I draw heavily on my article 'Muratori and British Historians', *L.A. Muratori Storiografo* (Florence, 1975); I do not repeat the annotation there given. The three libraries were (and are) the University, the Advocates (now the National Library of Scotland), and the Signet.

15 The greatest of the eighteenth-century librarians at Edinburgh was Thomas Ruddiman (1674-1757), at the Advocates from 1702 and chief Librarian from 1730. See above ch. 7 n.56.

16 From vol.i, ch.xv.

17 Robertson's other historical works are his *History of Scotland* (London, 1769), and his *History of America* (London, 1777 and, greatly extended, London, 1794). These works were frequently reprinted.

18 Based on Lenglet du Fresnoy's work (see above p.157), but adapted from the Italian version of C. Coleti (1716). In vol.i, 323-60 is included Scipio Maffei's comparison of the use of inscriptions and medals. Maffei (1675-1755) is chiefly known for his *Istoria diplomatica* (1727), an important step in the advance of scientific palaeography, and for his history of Verona (1731-2).

19 p.395.

20 Two names, Lindenbrog and Brady, occur here who might well have been discussed in ch.7. E. Lindenbrog (1543-1647), a Dane who was son and brother of other distinguished scholars, among other works published a valuable collection of the laws of the Visigoths and other barbarians (1613), a work which became essential in studying early Germanic society. Robert Brady (1643-1700) almost merits a place in the present chapter as one who aggressively merged narrative and erudition

(especially from record sources) in his main works: *History of England* (1685-1700), *Historical Treatise concerning Cities and Boroughs* (1690); cf. discussion of him in the works of Douglas and Pocock, above ch.7 n.47.

21 Hazard, i, 40-4.

22 *Essays*, ed. T.H. Green and T.H. Grose (London, 1882), i, 381-443.

23 *Polydore Vergil* (Oxford, 1952), 100.

24 The other authors whose books are shown in the portrait are: Robertson's own *History of Scotland*, Tacitus, Zurita and St Jerome.

25 Pietro Giannone (1676-1748). The main work published in his lifetime was the anticlerical *Storia civile del regno di Napoli*, 4 vols (1723), in which as a lawyer he emphasised institutional history.

26 *Charles V*, i, 513.

27 *Ibid.*, i, 518.

28 'Tra quegli argomenti che ho preso a trattare, ve ne sono molti, che a un uomo erudito porger potrebbero materia, onde farne un competente volume': *Antichità*, pref., sig. b3vo.

29 Compare the structure of Bishop Stubbs' *Constitutional History* (first ed. 1873-8), especially the remarkable social history tucked away in the final chapter.

30 *Op.cit.*, i, 65.

31 Above p.157.

32 F. Venturi, *Settecento riformatore* (Turin, 1969), 716; the same author also demonstrates how valuable the *Annali* are as an influence in Muratori's own day, p.66.

33 *Decline and Fall*, ed. J.B. Bury, 7 vols (London, 1897-1902), vii; 216n. The original edition was published in London from 1776-88; there were immediate reprints, and it was in constant demand throughout the nineteenth century. Since this volume has gone to press there has appeared (Summer 1976) *Daedalus*, Proceedings of the American Academy of Arts and Sciences, vol.105, no.3, issued to celebrate the bicentenary of vol.i of the *Decline and Fall*; it contains a number of admirable articles with many up-to-date references.

34 *Ibid.*, vii, 299-300; cf. 263n.

35 G. Giarrizzo, *Edward Gibbon e la cultura europea del settecento* (Naples, 1954); C. Dawson, 'Edward Gibbon', *Proc. Brit. Acad.*, xx (1934); Giorgio Falco, *La polemica sul medio evo* (Turin, 1933).

36 Dawson, 167. Sebastien le Nain de Tillemont (1637-98) was a man of profound religious convictions, much attracted to Jansenism and Port-Royal, for which attitude he was obliged to leave the Order of the the Oratory. He was the author of several learned works on early church history, notably the *Histoire des empereurs ... durant les six premiers siècles* (1690-1738) and *Mémoires pour servir a l'histoire ecclésiastique des six premiers siècles* (1693-1712).

37 G. Giarrizzo, 459.

38 *Ibid.*, 461-2.

39 *Decline and Fall*, iv, 194; cf. Giarrizzo, 450n.

Annalists and Historians

40 Professor H.R. Trevor-Roper has kindly pointed out to me that there is other evidence of Gibbon's admiration for Muratori (e.g. *Misc. Works*, 1814, ii, 571: 'we knew not where to seek our English Muratori'!) He also feels that Montesquieu and Giannone were more important influences on Gibbon than Hume.

41 'Gibbon's contribution to historical method', *Studies* (*cit.* above n.4) 51.

42 The allusion is to J.H. Hexter's essay in *Reappraisals in History* (London, 1961).

43 *Ed.cit.*, ii, 390.

Index

Historical events as such are not normally included nor are references in the Notes save where they amplify the text.

214   *Annalists and Historians*

Robert, Claude, 164
Robertson, Rev. Principal William, 142, 172-82
Roger of Wendover, 68-72
Rolls Series, v
Roman historians, 1-11
Rome, role in patristic literature, 20-3
Ronsard, P. de, 59
Rosweyde, Herbert, 160
Rudinus, 30-2
Ruddiman, Thomas, ch. 7 n. 56
Rymer, Thomas, 155-6, 158

Sabbath, Age of the Eternal, *see* Seventh Age
Sabellico (Marcantonio Coccio), 99, 124, 140
Sagas, 37, 60-1
St. Alban's monastery, history at, 65, 67-71
Saint-Denis abbey, history at, 54, 65-7, 71, 83, 141; *see Grandes Chroniques*
St. Germain des Près, *see* Maur, St.
Saint Maur, *see* Maur, St.
Sainte-Marthe, Louis, 164
_____, Scévole, 164
Saints' Lives, 36, 53-4; *see Acta Sanctorum*
Sallust, 2, 7, 94, 120, 147
Sarpi, Paolo, 140, 180
Scala, Bartolomeo della, 99
Schedel, Hartmann, 79-80
Scholarship and history, 167-85; *see* Antiquarianism
Scott, Sir Walter, 61
Segni, B., ch. 6 n. 15
Seventh Age, 28
Shakespeare, William, 61, 118
Shotwell, J.T., v
Sidney, Sir Philip, 128
Sigebert of Gembloux, 46-9, 52, 66, 148
Sigillography, 153
Sigonio, Carlo, 183
Simon, Richard, 170
Simonetta, Giovanni, 99-100

Six Ages, 28, 38, 45
Sleidan (J. Philippson), ch. 4 n. 38, ch. 7 n. 12
Somner, William, 156
Speeches in histories, 3, 8-9
Spelman, Henry, 155, 178
Spenser, Edmund, 60
Stendhal (M.H. Beyle), 86
Stubbs, William, bishop, 169
Stukeley, William, ch. 8 n. 4
Sturluson, Snorri, 61
Suetonius, 2, 7, 36, 56, 120
Suger, 54-6, 58, 61, 65, 71

Tacitus, 2, 7, 11, 120, 137, 147
Theiner, Augustin, 127
Thompson, J.W., v
Thuanus, *see* De Thou
Thucydides, 2-3, 5-6, 32, 38, 130
Tillemont, Louis-Sébastien le Nain de, 183, ch. 8 n. 36
Tolomeo of Lucca, 105, 107
Trevisa, John, 72, 83
Trojan origins, 59-60, 67, 71-2
Turner, William, 141
Turpin, Pseudo-, 61-2
Twelfth Century Renaissance, 50-2
Typology, biblical, 18-20

Ughelli, Ferdinand, 163-6, 172
Ussher, James, archbishop, ch. 7 n. 50

Valla, Lorenzo, 92-3, 95, 124-5
Varchi, N., ch. 6 n. 15
Vasari, Giorgio, 90
Venice, historians at, 118, 140
Vergerio, P.-P., 94-5
Vergil, Polydore, 84, 119-21, 138, 140, 144, 148-9, 179
Vertot, René Aubert de, 143-4
Verulam, *see*, Bacon
Vettori, F., ch. 6 n. 15
Victorius of Aquitaine, 27
Villani, Filippo, 80
_____ Giovanni, 80-2, 88, 97-9, 105
_____ Matteo, 80
Villehardouin, Geoffrey of, 73-4